To DAD —
I'm sure GRANDMA MELVILLE
WOULD HAVE APPRECIATED THIS —
I HOPE IT's INTERESTING!

James
+
CHRISTMAS '82

'The Great Lover'

By the same author

Theater Biography
'The Great Lover': The Life and Art of Herbert Beerbohm Tree
   1979
Henry Irving and the Victorian Theatre   1978
Masks and Façades: Sir John Vanbrugh, the Man in His Setting
   1974
Sheridan: The Track of a Comet   1972

History and Historical Biography
Scotland under Mary Stuart   1971
Mary Queen of Scots   1969

Autobiography
Peers and Plebs: Two Families in a Changing World   1975
Cheapest in the End   1963

'The Great Lover'

The Life and Art of
Herbert Beerbohm Tree

Madeleine Bingham

'I would rather play a man who died for love than
for ambition.'

HERBERT BEERBOHM TREE

Atheneum
New York
1979

Library of Congress Cataloging in Publication Data

Bingham, Madeleine, Baroness Clanmorris.
    The great lover.

    Bibliography: p.
    Includes index.
    1. Tree, Herbert Beerbohm, Sir, 1853–1917.   2. Actors—
England—Biography.   I. Title.
PN2598.T7B5   1979   792′.028′0924 [B]   78–65197
ISBN 0–689–10950–4

Contents

Illustrations

between pages 118 *and* 119

between pages 150 *and* 151

Illustration 2a by kind permission of the Theatre Museum, Victoria and Albert Museum, London; illustrations 6b, 7, 12a, 12b, 13b, 14a and 14b are reproduced by kind permission of the Beerbohm Tree Collection, University of Bristol Theatre Collection; and 10a and 10b by kind permission of the Mansell Collection.

Acknowledgements

This book has been written and researched with the aid of Sir Herbert Tree's unpublished diaries and notebooks For family reasons connected with the late Lady Cory-Wright, I was not able to quote directly from these, or from other published family works. I have tried in all cases to preserve the flavour of the writings of Tree himself, and of Maud and Viola Tree. Tree's own published works have been quoted.

Mr. Paul Ridley-Tree, Sir Herbert's youngest son, kindly wrote to me giving me details of his mother's career.

Mr. Glen Byam Shaw helped me with word of mouth descriptions of his family and their connexions with Constance Collier. He also lent me invaluable albums of theatre cuttings and photographs.

Miss Brooke Barnett, Keeper of the Theatre Collection at the University of Bristol, aided me in the mining of the rich seams of contemporary criticisms, evocative photographs and dress designs, and all the details which bring the theatre of the past to life, contained in the Beerbohm Tree Collection at Bristol.

I have also to thank Miss Jennifer Aylmer and Miss Jean Scott Rogers, of the Theatre Museum at the Victoria and Albert, for their help.

I am grateful to the Society of Authors on behalf of the Bernard Shaw Estate for granting me permission to quote from Bernard Shaw's writings; to Curtis Brown Ltd. on behalf of the Estate of Constance Collier for permission to quote from *Harlequinade* (John Lane, 1929); to Frederick Warne Ltd. for permission to quote from *The Journal of Beatrix Potter* (1966); and to Mrs. Eva Reichmann for permission to quote from the chapter by Max Beerbohm in *Herbert Beerbohm Tree: Some Memories of him and his Art* (Hutchinson, *c.* 1920).

Every effort has been made to trace the copyright holders of the material quoted in this volume. Should there be any omissions in this respect, we apologise and shall be pleased to make the appropriate acknowledgement in future editions.

Chapter 1

A Tree and its Branches

A faint smile can cross the faces of the theatrical establishment at the mention of the words 'Beerbohm Tree'. The stage is immediately peopled with expensively toga-ed Romans, or nibbling rabbits. The Doric pillars of Greece, the sinister charm and cherry blossom of old Japan, the rich interiors of ducal Grosvenor Square, no setting was too rich to be plundered or displayed for the delectation of his Edwardian audience.

Tree was a pillar of his contemporary establishment. He joined it, exploited it, and enjoyed it. But there was another side of Tree, more complicated than the absent-minded *flâneur*, the part he had invented as his public mask.

Contemporary gossip refers to Tree's 'love affairs' as if he indulged in a little light flirtation on the casting couch. It was not entirely the truth. Tree had two families—by Maud Holt, his wife, he had three daughters who all married well, and were accepted in Society. By Beatrice May Pinney, who took the name Reed by deed-poll, he had five sons and a daughter. Miss Pinney's children included the famous cinema director Sir Carol Reed, and his other descendant to make a name in the cinema is Oliver Reed, son of Peter Reed, Miss Pinney's youngest son.

In the year Herbert Tree died, at the age of sixty-four, he had his last and tenth child, a son, Paul, by an English actress and dancer called Muriel Ridley. Paul was born in America, where he lived, grew up, and prospers.

The complications of Tree's families make the unravelling of his life an Edwardian mystery. But the astonishing variety and richness of talent amongst his descendants make a good argument for Tree's maxim that man was born to reproduce himself. It was a maxim which he lived and enjoyed.

If Irving was the manifestation of the Victorian ethic of self-help, hard work and simple living, Tree represented the expansiveness of the rich sybaritic Edwardians. It was an age dominated by German culture, German bankers and a half-German King. Tree understood his age because he was half German himself.

The Edwardians lived in a world of transition, of understated immorality and overstated decoration, represented by pretty women in tea-gowns in pseudo Louis Quinze drawing-rooms, a faint lingering odour of cigar smoke, and a burst of laughter from the gun room. Underneath the ice of Puritan morality the fashionable fish swam free, yet when they went to the theatre, they wished to see vice punished and virtue rewarded. Problems could be touched on, cupboard doors could be half opened, but the skeletons must be quickly buried with full regimental honours. It was not an easy public to please but Tree conquered it, and he managed it with panache, style and a great zest for living while fathering ten children. It was an astonishing achievement. What was the background of this man?

*

In 1928 Dora, the half-sister of Herbert Tree and sister of Max Beerbohm, compiled a loving chronicle of the history of her family. The Beerbohm arms was five poplar trees surmounted by three stars and the crest a helmet with crown and jester's cap.

Dora, an Anglican nun, prefaced her chronicle by a little poem:

The Poplar Trees

Five poplar trees erect and slim
Three little stars that shine,
What mean they on the silver shield
That shelters me and mine?
The trees tho' rooted in the earth
Point up to Heaven above,
The stars so pure and far away
Shed down their light in love.
The trees then teach of lofty aims,
The stars of lowly love,
And there's a meaning in the helm
Upon the shield above.
The helm is sign of battles fought,
The crown of battles won,
The Jester's cap of childish mirth,
Fine wit and kindly fun.

> Then all who claim to bear this shield
> Should ask to learn from it
> High aims, love too, that clearly shines
> Courage and kindly wit.

Herbert's feet were firmly rooted in the ground, his aims were high rather than lofty, he had courage and a kindly wit, and he certainly believed in love though perhaps hardly in the way his half-sister, the nun, meant. One thing he did take from his family coat of arms was the name Tree.

The Beerbohm family came from Lithuania, and seem to have been part of the ruling German establishment, for the three Baltic States of Latvia, Estonia and Lithuania were occupied by German knights who settled there and became the landowning aristocrats ruling the local population. The ruling families spoke German, French and Russian, but they did not encourage the speaking of the local languages by the people they ruled over. The name Beerbohm could be a corruption for Birnbaum (pear tree). A German saying has it 'der Apfel faelt nicht weit vom Birnbaum'—a vague translation could be 'like father, like son'. And fathers did follow sons in the Beerbohm family for many hundreds of years. They married into the fringes of the German aristocracy and they enriched their families by trading in timber from the Baltic ports.

Some time during the eighteenth century the Beerbohm family helped Frederick the Great with a little ready cash for a small war, and were rewarded with the gift of an estate called Bernsteinbruch. From then on the Beerbohm family were well regarded by the Royal family of Prussia. One of the Beerbohm girls—Tree's Aunt Mathilde—spent many years at the Prussian Court, and married General Baron von Unruh—a very appropriate name for a German general. Uncle General von Unruh was appointed military Governor to the Crown Prince, afterwards the Emperor Frederick, who had married the Princess Royal, eldest daughter of Queen Victoria. So, the Beerbohm family, though not aristocratically quartered with noble families, had aristocratic connexions, and were not entirely in the timber trade although that supported their way of life. Tree's grandfather Ernst Beerbohm married Amalie Henrietta Radke, who had Russian or Lithuanian blood, and he lived happily with his wife, fathering twelve children, of whom Julius, Tree's father, was the youngest.

The increasing prosperity of Britain in the nineteenth century attracted many foreign traders to seek their fortune in London. Julius Beerbohm, perhaps because he was the youngest of a large family, was one of them. He left his native Lithuania for France where he studied commerce and was nicknamed 'Monsieur Superbe-Homme', a reference to his elegant clothes and mien. From Paris he migrated to London where he seems to have arrived about 1830 and, keeping to the family trading tradition, set up in business as a corn merchant in the City. It was at the height of the Forsyteian expansion of trade when to be 'something in the City' was already acquiring a glossy aura. About the age of forty Julius married an Englishwoman, Constantia Draper. By Constantia he had four children, Ernest, Herbert, Constance and Julius.

Herbert Beerbohm was born in London at 2 Pembridge Villas, Kensington, on 28th January 1852. For most of his life he was thought to have been born in 1853, although his birth certificate was carefully amended by Somerset House to make it clear that 1852 was the correct year of his birth. They did well to correct it, as the mistake was made by them in the first place.

Transplanted to England the Beerbohm family were to produce in Herbert Tree its most astonishing 'sport'.

Although Julius, Herbert's father, was a man of wide interests with a great love of literature and a knowledge of six languages, he showed no originality of thought. He did however show originality of action. His wife died at the early age of thirty-two leaving him with four children. Eliza, Constantia's sister, had for some time been keeping house for the family, for Constantia was a woman little attracted to the domestic arts which she preferred to leave to her more practical sister. Victorian life seems to have been thick with useful sisters and aunts prepared to take on the duties of their less capable married sisters. But Eliza was luckier than most of these helpful spinsters, for on the death of her sister, Julius determined to marry her. As marriage with a deceased wife's sister was forbidden under English law, Julius ignored this Puritan eccentricity. He took Eliza to Switzerland where he married her quite legally and returned to Kensington to father another family of five children, the youngest of whom was Max Beerbohm.

Herbert once remarked that he was born old, and grew younger and younger. He does not seem to have been very interested in his childhood, like many people who enjoy living in the present and the future, the past had none of the bitter-sweet savour which can attract those who live in the imagination of the heart. Few anecdotes survive of his childhood. In his chaotic diaries he noted that his nurse had said to him, 'Master Herbert—what we want is deeds not actions.' He solemnly noted that the nurse had preferred the Anglo-Saxon to the Latin word, but it is tempting to feel that perhaps the nurse had said 'What we want is deeds not acting, Master Herbert.'

When Herbert was a very small boy, his father Julius, because of his family's intimate connexions with the Prussian Royal family, was invited to the wedding at St. James's Palace of the Crown Prince of Prussia and the Princess Royal. He was taken down to see his father in all the splendour of Court Dress, with knee-breeches, buckled shoes and sword. But on seeing the sword Herbert burst into tears, thinking that the sword meant that his father was going to the wars. He does not seem to have inherited the appetite for battle of his Teutonic ancestors.

Like most intelligent children Herbert did not relish being taken for a fool, even at the age of five. One of his father's business friends addressed him as 'My little tiddleywink'. The little tiddleywink looked solemnly at the visitor and replied loudly and firmly: '*You're* a tiddleywink—and a rascal too.'

Herbert's schooling in England indicates a constant changing of plans on the part of Julius for his sons. Herbert was at Dr. Stone's School in Bristol, at a prep school near Tunbridge Wells, and at the Westbourne Collegiate School in Westbourne Grove near his home. Eventually the three boys of the first marriage were sent to school in Germany at Schnepfeuthal, the school where their father had been educated.

It is possible that Julius Beerbohm remembered his own school-days with affection. He had been an exile in England for many years, and exiles so often remember with affection things which never existed. Or maybe, like the Prince Consort, he felt that a German education, where scholarship was taken seriously, would benefit his sons. Unlike the Prince Consort Julius was not a hard disciplinarian, he loved his sons, but possibly the exigencies of a second marriage and a new family growing up pushed the father towards this decision.

Like many foreign schools of the period, the schooling was hard and the masters far from understanding. Although Herbert learned

German and French, his German schooling, which his father had
hoped might enlarge his mind and give him a discipline and an
aptitude for learning, had the opposite effect. The harsh nature of
the regime and the cold cruelty of the masters left Herbert with a
lifelong hatred of any form of education. He professed to feel that
instinct and understanding could replace any form of learning.
Education, Herbert concluded, was a waste of time. Life was for
living.

To be sent to a German school at the height of the Prussian
domination of the German soul was an experience which could
have maimed a less resilient character, but Herbert in his insouciant
way seems to have put all his painful experiences behind him. He
was determined not to let a pack of schoolmasters alter his attitude
to life. It may be that his vagueness on which many people constantly remarked was developed when he was at school. To be
vague, and seemingly stupid, was a way to avoid trouble and to
float on the surface of school life without becoming too involved.

On leaving school all three of Julius's sons were in the usual
Victorian way expected to join the family corn business and
become highly respected members of the Baltic Exchange. But the
City had little attraction for any of them. The eldest brother
Ernest soon left England and finally settled down in Cape Colony
where he was alleged to have married a coloured lady. Julius, the
youngest brother, seems to have convinced his father that his
future lay in exploring and he set sail for Patagonia, and then
immediately sailed home again and wrote a book about it. His
subsequent career lay more in exploring possibilities nearer home,
and he had a wonderful capacity for raising money and losing it.
His only successful venture was to marry a rich young woman
whose fortune he successfully dissipated.

The elder and younger brothers having left the family business,
Herbert was the only son left to carry on the Beerbohm tradition
of trading. At the age of seventeen he already had a penchant for
acting and spent all his spare time with the amateur dramatic clubs
which proliferated at the time. They rejoiced in splendidly
Bohemian names, the Erratics, the Irrationals, the Bettertons, the
Philothespians. Among the Philothespians were two other clerks
chained to business desks, later to become actor-managers George
Alexander and Lewis Waller.

The stage was achieving respectability, and the audiences were demanding that the gentlemen in the gentlemanly plays should be played by gentlemen. At this time Wilson Barrett, the author of *The Sign of the Cross,* answered an advertisement which read: 'Wanted: A young actor with a good stage presence. Must provide own props and dress like a gentleman on and off the stage. Salary: One guinea weekly.'

Tree came in on the wave of gentlemen joining the profession. But he had many disadvantages. Owing to his background and schooling, his air and bearing had a slightly exotic and foreign feeling. He was tall and slim with pale carroty hair and pale turquoise eyes, shading to green. The day of the gentleman actor also demanded him to be dark and good-looking, with a clear cut profile tending to nobility. Tree did not fit into any of these categories.

An additional disadvantage to his starting a stage career was that his father was adamantly attached to the idea that at least one of his sons should carry the burden of the Corn Merchant's business. For eight years Herbert played at being a corn merchant, while seriously practising what he saw as his true profession in his spare time, often specialising in parodying leading actors, Irving; the comedian J. L. Toole; and the flamboyant Italian Salvini.

Harry Furniss, who was one of Tree's earliest friends, remembered his imitations at smoking concerts and Bohemian clubs. It was here he achieved his first successes. Furniss wrote, 'He was a brilliant, spry young amateur and very popular at Studio Smokes which flourished in those days. At one of these Irving appeared just as Tree was called upon for his famous imitations. Strange to say he was excellent as Toole and Wyndham, James, and Thorn (all contemporary celebrities), but his Irving was not a success, and in the presence of the original his imitation was even worse. Before giving it Tree asked Irving if he objected. "Certainly not, go ahead."

'Tree gave his imitation of Irving first and when he had finished his "turn" he approached Irving, who remarked: "Cap-i-tal, Cap-i-tal! I like the first one best, eh? When you were yourself." '

Tree's passion for acting led him to get into debt and he was forced into taking these reciting engagements at smoking concerts for the few guineas they earned him. But it was not the kind of work which attracted him. Some actors do not mind what kind of work they do, but for Tree acting needed the splendid setting of a theatre. Much later, when he was already a professional actor, and needed the money to support a wife and child, he had not conquered his distaste for reciting. He had been engaged as an 'after the theatre' entertainment by some people called Samuelson with a grand house in Lowndes Square. He was unhappy about carrying out the engagement, being acutely aware that he considered such recitations undignified. There was no wall between actor and audience. People were free to walk about, talk, or drink, ignoring both the performer and the performance. Whether he needed the money or not, reciting at private houses was a thing to be avoided in future.

From the beginning of his career, he already had his eyes on owning and governing his own theatre. He did not see himself as an actor who eked out slender talents in any theatrical field which needed to be tilled. He saw himself as a theatrical landowner, not a day labourer. Beerbohms did not work for others, others worked for them.

By the early seventies the old ranting days of the act-tor were numbered. Settings had become realistic and the 'new wave' of the day was represented by the productions of the Bancrofts at the Prince of Wales Theatre in Charlotte Street off the Tottenham Court Road. Here a mirror was held up to life, and ladies and gentlemen behaved in a socially acceptable way in rooms with real fireplaces and real furniture, the age of the ragged painted cloth had set.

At the Prince of Wales Theatre, Tree saw Ellen Terry for the first time when she was playing Portia. He was then only twenty-two, but already showed a keen critical eye for an actor or a production which was to stand him in good stead. He remarked that he had never seen a pit so empty as it was at the Prince of Wales. The criticisms, which had been damning, had hardly helped the production, but Tree felt they were justified. Coghlan as Shylock struck him as inoffensive, a character defect which hardly improved the play. But Ellen Terry's enchantment added that sparkle to the comedy which the other actors lacked.

Watching her he was amazed at her easy grace and gestures, she could have been one of Leighton's queenlike women. How could she smile with such naturalness? In the trial scene she astonished him by lounging against one of the pillars like a young barrister in court. He was pleased to see that the public warmed to her. Archer was adequate as Antonio, but perhaps a little too much of a gentleman, a gentleman who could never have spat at Shylock. Tree, though still an amateur, was forming his ideas of how things should be done, and thinking the part from within rather than from without.

His debts made the earning of money from his hobby a necessity, and Herbert began to take more professional engagements. From the beginning of his career he was always aware of the value of publicity. It was not only necessary to act well, but to inform others that one had acted well. The influencing of public opinion was the way to the top. So Herbert had a small pamphlet printed in which he quoted *The Era* ('never seen a better bit of amateur acting than Mr. Beerbohm as Achille Dufard'). The *Surrey Comet* dubbed him inimitable, and the *Figaro* found his performances full of artistic touches. But the first recognition by a critic with any influence was the *Sporting and Dramatic News,* which said that he showed originality and fertile humour adding that he had a line in grotesque eccentricity 'which is particularly his'.

The printing of this self-laudatory booklet was dated a year before Herbert went on to the stage and the name on the cover was H. Beerbohm Tree. He had already not only decided on his career but his name. He knew that his chance was to come and he would be ready for it.

Meanwhile, tired out from nights of acting, he still toiled in the furrow of the corn business. But his determination was gradually wearing down his father's opposition to his becoming an actor. At first Julius Beerbohm had taken the classic stand that acting was only acceptable if one was at the top of the tree. Herbert is said to have replied that the top of the tree was where he was going and with that idea in view he was taking the name of 'Tree'. But it is much more likely that a certain family pride in his lineage and his family's past made him choose the name of Tree. Possibly Herbert's lack of aptitude for business, total boredom with figures of any kind, and infinite capacity for taking no pains at all with the corn business, were additional reasons for his father being in the end willing to let him go. By this time Julius had other sons and possibly they would be drawn to the City.

Herbert's chance came in 1878 when he played Grimaldi in *The Life of an Actress* at a charity performance at the Globe Theatre. He was asked to join the Bijou Theatre Company for a tour which began at Folkestone Town Hall on Monday 20th May 1878. The Company proudly announced that 'Besides the well known members of this Company, the management have much pleasure in announcing that they have secured the services of Mr. H. Beerbohm Tree who will appear during the week in various pieces and on Wednesday and Friday will give (by special desire) his inimitable Dramatic and Mimictic Recitals. Stalls (price three shillings) are to be obtained at Goulden's Library, Folkestone.'

The first performances of Tree as a professional actor do not seem to have been financially successful. But the local paper commended the performers as educated ladies and gentlemen, graceful and natural. They did not drop their h's but behaved in the drawing room scenes as those accustomed to good society. The day of the gentleman actor had reached the provinces.

By the beginning of 1880 Tree was becoming an actor hardened to provincial touring. On 24th January he had arrived at Scanins Hotel, York. Already he was beginning to enjoy the cheerful raffishness of his chosen profession. The evening was convivial.

Two days later he was at Scarborough, and his salary had been increased to an astonishing fourteen guineas. His managers, Synge and Hurt, wanted him to sign for six months, but he turned down their offer, giving as his reason that if he were to die before the end of the contract, he would feel that he had not fulfilled his work on earth. A ghostly Herbert haunting the manager's office worrying about an unfulfilled contract leaves a pleasant, if unlikely, picture, in the mind.

Whether the management took this noble statement seriously is open to doubt. He was as critical of his own performances at this time as he was of the acting of others. He had acted badly after dining late and admonished himself sternly on the folly of late dinners. He was playing in *Madame Favart,* taking the part of the Count Pontsablé. In his beginning as an actor he was constantly cast as foreigners, counts, princes—and charlatans. His actual observations aided him to bring these exotic personalities to life. He had a pale skin, it was described as the colour of sand, much later he remarked that his face was like a canvas on which he could paint his own design.

But in the winter of 1880 he was a beginner, but a shrewd beginner. He was studying a book called *Various Expressions of the*

Emotions which had been published by John Murray in 1872. He carefully wrote down the passages which had struck him.

> Persons suffering from excessive grief often seek relief by violent, almost frantic emotion . . . but when their suffering is somewhat mitigated, they no longer wish for emotion but remain motionless and passive, or may occasionally rock themselves to and fro. The circulation becomes languid, the face pale, muscles flaccid, the eyelids droop, the lips shake and the lower jaw all sink downwards from their weight. Hence all the features are lengthened, the corners of the mouth always turn down in this condition.

Tree then drew the full face and profile of a man suffering from grief. He added a further note to the effect that the author had some excellent tips on playing a mad person. He must keep the book in mind when playing a maniac. He copied down endless passages on the expressions of life, decision, rage and hatred, adding 'See Bell (*Anatomy of Expressions* page 95) has some excellent remarks on the expression of rage.' Tree also noted that Herbert Spencer in his essay on misery had some equally excellent things to say about the character of the human voice under the influence of various emotions.

Mr. Bell also had something to say about short-sighted people. They were, said Mr. Bell, forced to reduce the aperture of their eyes and consequently wear a grinning expression 'as simultaneously with the contraction of the muscles round the eyes the upper lip is raised'. This would seem to be an impossible physical feat, perhaps Tree achieved it.

Apart from studying physical ways to express the various emotions Herbert did a little practical publicity for himself. He engaged a photographer to carry out studies of him dressed as Pontsablé 'in various positions'. No doubt for presentation to local newspapers.

When Miss Newton who had been playing the principal part left the cast Herbert found her replacement Cornelie d'Anka far from satisfactory. She did not know her lines, and neither did the Hector (Strathmore). Tree noted tartly that he had had to prompt both of them. No doubt the newcomers felt quite as tartly about Herbert's prompting. The houses were bad owing, he shrewdly suspected, to the bad performances. But a week later he had found a great deal of good in Cornelie d'Anka. Possibly she had been finding a great deal of good in Herbert Tree.

Female complications were already cluttering his life, for on 9th February, he had found a letter. Another illusion had crashed, and presumably the reputation of the lady who had written the letter had also crumbled to dust. He told himself sternly to be firm. But firmness with women was something which Herbert was never to achieve.

The trials and tribulations of the touring actor come vividly to life in Tree's laconic memories. The bill for a hotel was an astronomical £2 15s. so he decided to change to nice clean lodgings. He was afraid to call on Constance Ambler. Could she have developed a provincial attitude towards actors? His pride would have resented that, but when he did call on her she received him most kindly, he was, after all, very hard to resist.

The following week the company found to their consternation that the Huddersfield Theatre had burned to the ground, and they set off for Hull instead. They were somewhat cheered when they asked a comedian named Connolly whether they had missed anything, was there any money in Huddersfield? 'Yes, if you take it there!' Tree had already seen Connolly at a music hall in Dublin when he had come on and mimed a pawnbroker taking in a man's coat. He had looked it all over very doubtfully, and finally handed over the money reluctantly. It showed the value of attending to details when adding 'business' to a character. He was learning and noting how to achieve an effect.

A month after starting his tour they arrived at Huddersfield where a temporary stage had been rigged up in Armoury Hall. The audience, though thin, was encouraging and had cheered them. The notices were splendid. But the town was wretched, and the journey had been unpleasant. Good cheer and good company led to dissipation. It also led to thoughts of comfort. He had changed his mind about economising. If the town was a wretched place, the White Hart was equally wretched. What a mistake to put up there! He told himself that he must always put up at the best hotels. There are constant references to a girl called Rose with whom he dined and drove out. Finally a cryptic entry that Rose had had news that C.N. had returned to England. Was C.N. a rival or a manager?

On 9th March when he had only been touring for a few

weeks he noted an offer to go to the Prince of Wales Theatre.

On 13th March he went to London with Rose, and put up at the Euston Hotel; he was taking his own advice about the inadvisability of second-rate lodgings. There is no clue as to whether Rose shared both the journey and the hotel, but Herbert was hardly a man to appreciate *chambres séparées*. The following morning he went straight round to his family. It was unthinkable that he should arrive in London without seeing his father, for whom he had always cherished a deep love and admiration. Only five days before on March 9th he had sent his father a message on his birthday, which had as Herbert fondly noted greatly surprised and pleased him. It is not every son in hot pursuit of fame and fortune who can remember so trivial a thing as a father's birthday. Filial affection satisfied, Herbert then felt free to concentrate on his career, and went straight round to see Genevieve Ward about his engagement at the Prince of Wales Theatre. His first impression was that she was a most agreeable woman. This was not a view which was to last, but aspiring young actors are apt to find leading actress-managers agreeable.

Genevieve Ward was an American actress of international reputation. She had sung in opera under the unlikely name of Madame Guerrabella, but when on tour in Cuba had lost her singing voice following an attack of diphtheria. She had become an outstanding dramatic actress and at the time she approached Tree was already in management for herself.

The offer from so exalted a source left Tree full of doubts. Hamilton Synge, his manager, was promising to have a play written for Tree, either on the subject of Don Quixote, or Don Zacharias of Jules Verne, both subjects, Herbert happily noted, had been chosen by himself.

But was the offer of a London engagement firm, supposing it fell through? He was terribly worried. He did not want to part company with Synge on bad terms, but the fear in the back of his mind was that he might become a one-part actor. His imagination quailed at the prospect of playing the same part over and over again for long months. He was always to become easily bored with a part once he had created it. But finally the boredom overcame the fears and he told Hamilton Synge that he was at last convinced that he must leave the company. There was a time for touring, and a time for seizing an opportunity however slight. His mind was made up and he was on his way to the top of the tree as he had predicted. On 17th April he played Pontsablé for the last time, and two days later he was playing Prince Maleotti in *Forget Me Not*. He had rehearsed the part with Miss Ward at her house. At this point Miss Ward saw only the pleasure of encouraging the rising young actor. He had already drawn a picture of his idea of the prince complete with curling moustaches, 'imperial' beard, carefully arranged thinning hair and eye-glass. Tree had a facility for drawing, and much of his careful make-up stemmed from his observant eye and ability to reproduce what he had seen.

He was not complacent about his performance but was cheered by the fact his make-up was good, and had been generally praised. But he lacked the confidence of the professional and sometimes was overtaken by surprise at his own success. At the dress rehearsal he had been very nervous, and like many artists he never felt that he had achieved the best effect. At the end of a scene he was overtaken by a sense of failure, and then, just as suddenly, realised that he had made an impression. Although he made a mental note that this would be of great value to him professionally, he was never able to reproduce his effects. His performances to the end of his career were to remain as variable as a spring day both in shape and texture. A set performance was not his aim. He liked to rely on the inspiration of the moment.

On 10th May he played before the Prince of Wales for the first time. This was a charity performance and he was not being paid. But Genevieve Ward gave him a silver cigarette case and match box with a note: 'May the accompanying little souvenir remind you of the strides you made in your profession as Monte Prades and accept my thanks for your zeal in this enterprise.'

As a result of his successes with Miss Ward, Tree was offered a two year contract. But he was disinclined to tie himself down for so long. He had made a good beginning and noted that he felt it best to temporise. For now he was back in London and away from the setting of lodgings, landladies, and burned out theatres, he was meeting useful and influential people—Clement Scott, the famous critic of the *Daily Telegraph,* at Mrs. Tennant's he met Coquelin, the outstanding comédien of his age, and Madame Modjeska who recited in Polish, and he was introduced to Hamilton Aïdé the playwright. Here two pages were torn from Tree's diary and only the word 'Rose' remains. Had Rose also been the cause of disillusion?

Miss Ward was finding him helpful, and they seem to have given special performances of a play called *La Pluie et le beau Temps* at various private houses, including that of Hamilton Aïdé. Tree appeared to have overcome his distaste for acting in private houses. It was perhaps difficult to turn down an offer to act for the Prince of Wales, who seemed highly pleased with his entertainment. At supper the Prince sat between his reigning favourite, Mrs. Langtry, and Madame Modjeska, a Polish actress of some fame. Tree was astonished that the Polish lady outraged the conventions by smoking a cigarette.

At the end of July, when the London season finished, the theatre closed. Tree with his knowledge of French and German and quick capacity for sketching in foreign characters had been a useful asset. But when he rejoined her in October she seems to have changed her mind about him. Perhaps he was becoming too successful professionally and socially for her comfort.

The rift with Miss Ward grew wider. They had had repeated differences for some time. But the insults which Tree had suffered during the rehearsals of *Anne Mie* caused the final break. Miss Ward was a lady experienced in putting obstacles in the way of aspiring young actors. Sometimes Tree was so upset by her conduct that he could hardly go on with the rehearsal. He thanked God that he had not been goaded into replying to her insults. The company had complimented him on his patience and good humour under great provocation. But Tree managed to keep his temper cool and his public image bright. Rumours could ruin a reputation and he was not going to be set down as a difficult and temperamental actor. So he prudently wrote to the leading critic Clement Scott on the subject, and even more prudently kept a copy of his letter.

Having settled that small storm to the best of his ability, Herbert turned his mind to his acting. He had been told that when wearing costume he was inclined to drop his hands uncertainly. It was a mannerism to be avoided, one must be at ease in costume as if one wore it every day. Another tip he had been given was that when shrieking the breath must be drawn in, a normal shout could ruin the effect.

There is no diary for the year 1881—the year Herbert met Maud

Holt. She was eighteen and Herbert was already twenty-nine. They met at a fancy dress party, not the kind of entertainment to attract Herbert, but in her romantic way Maud felt that there must have been some conspiracy that they should meet. It may well be that the conspiracy was Maud's. Herbert was already becoming well-known and Maud was stage struck. She was a highly intelligent, not to say highbrow, girl who was teaching and studying Greek, Latin, Mathematics and Science at Queen's College in Harley Street. She had already appeared in amateur performances of Shakespeare as Ophelia and Beatrice and suddenly she came face to face with a real actor who attracted her. She refused to believe that he could be the old man who acted in *Forget Me Not*. To these flattering words, the tall, pale young man replied in a voice which was to fascinate and attract Maud all her life.

Tree seems to have had an appeal to women of all ages and the highbrow Maud was instantly drawn to him. With all the simplicity of a girl in the first grip of an attraction for a man, she took to haunting Garrick Street in the hopes of a chance encounter with Herbert, coming out of the Garrick Club, for she was convinced he must spend his time there.

When not haunting Garrick Street, she lived in the hopes that some friend, or the hand of friendly fate, helped perhaps by herself, would bring her once more into the aura of a man whose character seemed to her to be at once dominating and gentle.

But fate—and friends—failed Maud. She also failed to achieve a chance encounter in Garrick Street and decided to give the hand of fate a push in her direction. She wrote to Herbert to ask his professional advice. Should she leave her academic career and take a chance as a professional actress?

Herbert's reply was long delayed and laconic and gave much the same advice as Mr. Coward gave to Mrs. Worthington.

Dear Miss Holt should not go on the stage unless she felt she must. He asked her how she was and added that they would meet in the autumn. His few laconic words hardly struck a note of the instant attraction she had felt for him.

But Maud Holt was pretty and intelligent and Herbert could resist anything but temptation. When the winter came and the theatre season opened again he went to see the stage-struck Miss Holt. She was living in excellent large rooms over a shop in Orchard Street. Herbert dropped in more and more often to see

Maud in her excellent rooms. As the days got darker, Maud's heart became lighter. Herbert read poetry to Maud and she sang to Herbert, not very well, although he made the best of it and assured her that she *mimed* the songs so very well.

By the beginning of February 1882 he startled her by a passionate advance; Maud drew back. Herbert was hurt, he felt that he had nothing brilliant to say to her and in any case she did not seem to want him to declare his passion. But Maud's hesitation was temporary. Perhaps it was a strategic withdrawal—a girl must be careful of her reputation, especially if she were living in excellent rooms with the chaperoning eye of Mrs. Newman (bless her!) on the proceedings.

On 7th February he wrote to his dear Maud hoping she did not mind him calling her by her Christian name. Her kindness had made him light-headed. He had been forgiven for his hasty display of affection. He had laughed too much on the stage, was it because of the oysters he had eaten or his happiness at the idea of seeing her again? On 12th February Maud's strategy was rewarded and she had become an officially engaged girl. Herbert was ecstatic, everything was bright, radiant and all was tinged with the idea of Maud.

How wonderful it would be if their whole life together were to be like that day—all bright sunshine with sowing and reaping, all laughter and no tears. There was to be plenty of sowing and reaping in Herbert's life but unluckily for Maud not all the sowing and reaping were to be done by her.

Herbert's romantic illusions were not to endure, but in the first enthusiasm of being an engaged man it was as well for Maud, as well as for himself that he believed it. As an engaged man he knew, he said, how much her happiness depended upon his seriousness. He stressed how good she was to him. 'Good' being a current euphemism for physically affectionate.

Maud wore on her hand the diamond ring which Herbert had found in Kensington Gardens when he was a child and given to his mother. On her death she left it to Herbert to be given to his future wife. With Herbert's fervent sentiments ringing in her ears, and Herbert's sentimental gift from the past as a token of a happy future—Maud's cup of happiness was brimming. But there were speedily indications that it was not only brimming, but had sprung leaks.

Maud's acting ambitions which had drawn her to Herbert, did not draw him to her. When they acted in a one-act play at his parents' house, he began to treat her like an actress rather than a fiancée. He wrote an immediate apology, he was sorry that she should have seen him in a fit of brutal temper. Although he apologised he still saw her as an amateur. He was full of doubts about her becoming an actress. Perhaps he wished to keep her out of his working life. Husband and wife teams on the stage are a charming idea for the audience, but backstage they lead to tensions between highly strung performers. Herbert had got on very well, even brilliantly so far, without the aid of a loving wife, perhaps he viewed with suspicion an intelligent woman who was determined to 'help'. But women of Maud's generation were persistent. They gave the outward appearance of being fluffy little things. The clothes of the period with their feathers and furbelows, the curls and the frills enhanced this feeling. The photographs of leading actresses show sweet simpering little faces of ladies whose only wish was to be cared for and cherished. It was the effect they wished to create. Their men were to be 'managed' and woman-handled into carrying out their wishes. Tears, temper and temperament or the withholding of sexual favours, were the weapons which they used to achieve their ends, and while they smiled their sweet sentimental smiles, they were steelily determined to get their own way.

The difficulties during the engagement of Maud and Herbert were that Maud probably saw her role as the sweetly managing lady, but in Herbert she had picked a man who would never be managed. He had his own view of himself and his destiny. Their engagement was a stormy one broken by Maud's jealousies and uncertainties. Women were naturally attracted to Herbert. He had a way of making them feel more alive, and a caressing voice which was said to 'make the English language sound as beautiful as it is'.

Herbert had given Myra Holme, his leading lady, later the wife of Pinero, a lovely silk scarf from Liberty's. Injudiciously he asked Maud to admire it. Maud replied sharply that it was a little too lovely for Myra Holme. Herbert does not seem to have noticed Maud's tone of voice because he happily sat down and, using Maud's flamboyant writing paper with 'M' on it, proceeded to draw a wreath of flowers round the 'M' and changed Maud to Myra.

Herbert, though attractive, was hardly tactful and if Maud wanted a quietly adoring husband she had made the wrong choice.

The spring passed in quarrels and reconciliations. Family and friends joined in. Maud's eldest brother Willie after having lunched with Herbert, regaled Maud with his opinion of her intended. No one in respectable Richmond could dream of lunching out with frayed shirt cuffs, a man who committed such a social solecism was no husband for Maud. Helpful friends and acquaintances of Maud's joined in counselling prudence and delay, alternatively recommending long sea voyages or celibacy.

Maud sent Herbert back his ring. Herbert wrote desperate notes full of bitter blots and savage dashes. Maud showed a little complacency about this separation. She was revelling in Herbert's frustrated passion and taking a maidenly pride in his sadness at their separation.

But in June when the fields in Hampstead were filled with buttercups, Herbert sent a hansom cab with a final beseeching note. Maud capitulated. She did not reply by letter, but got into the hansom and drove from Orchard Street to Herbert's lodgings on the Heath and a sweet reconciliation took place. How she remembered that morning—the buttercup fields filled with sunshine, the smell of the hawthorn hedges and the warmth and love of that reunion with Herbert.

He had pursued his courtship of Maud with the enthusiasm he afterwards gave to his theatres, his productions and—to other women. There is nothing so attractive to a young and inexperienced woman as to feel her sexual power over a man. Here was an attractive man of the world, ten years older than she, grateful for any crumb of affection she could throw him. Maud remembered that summer as a golden time when she and Herbert walked hand-in-hand, dreaming of a future when they would always be together. Always is a word which comes readily to lovers before the consummation of their love.

Suddenly the dream ended in Maud's being summoned to look after her eldest sister who was ill at Aix-les-Bains.

This did not please Herbert. He felt that he should have taken first place in her thoughts. His tone became a little acid. He had put up with a great deal from Maud and now at the first call of her family duty she left him. Her sister obviously had claims on her—

greater claims than a mere fiancé. He quite understood that she must go and she mustn't trouble her head about *him*, he wrote.

He ended his letter by hoping that she was not dreaming of being married to a beautiful fairy-like being with no human failings, and signed himself her disappointing Herbert.

But while Herbert was away Maud's kind friends had returned to the attack with stories of Herbert's past. He learned from his step-mother and Maud's sister that Maud was wavering again. She was making him very unhappy. He found it very difficult to reconcile all this wavering and uncertainties with the love she had shown him. If the few miles between them were going to make all this difference what did Maud's love mean? What had he done to deserve this disappointment? He admitted that he had been foolish and possibly weak but not vicious or dishonourable. After all he had never pretended to be totally unworldly, he had told her of his peccadilloes, repented and been forgiven. Besides, there was no claim upon him, and he had made sure that even the remote possi-bility of any shadow on their future should be removed.

Who was the lady who had no claims upon him? Rose who had spent the night at the Euston Hotel?

Herbert was indignant, and with some reason. He had been patient both under Maud's accusations and the censure of her friends. He asked himself—and Maud—to whom was her loyalty due, to her friends and relations, or as he saw them, his calumnia-tors, or to himself, her future husband? If Maud thought that he was to be governed by the ideas of others she was wrong. He was not going to enter into competition with them for her favours. He would not contemplate her despising him, as she would begin to do, if her faith were not total. Their love was not to be controlled by family and friends.

Herbert was not a descendant of a long line of Beerbohms for nothing, and he was not putting up with any more 'manières'.

But before he had time to post his letter Maud, realising perhaps that she was pushing him too far and being aware of her genuine love for him, relented and wired to him to come to her at once.

He stuck to his point of view. He agreed to come at once but in order to make his position clear he enclosed the unposted letter. He felt it correct to send it, she might think his sentiments harsh but he was in no mood to keep them to himself. He looked forward to seeing her soon and signed himself her loving Herbert.

When Maud later wrote of Herbert's passionate wooing she left out her jealousies and hesitations. In retrospect all must be beautiful, with Maud as the goddess, and Herbert as the eternally pursuing lover. She gave the impression that unknown to her Herbert had suddenly arrived in Aix and that her hesitations were on the score of the impropriety of his arrival and her doubts as to whether her sick sister would view Herbert with friendliness. It was not in the spirit of the period for a lady to admit to having sent for her man. Ladies were pursued and not pursuing.

When Herbert arrived at Aix he put up at the Grand Hotel. He was already living up to his maxim that life was too short for second rate hotels. He immediately sent round a note to Maud. He was delighted with Aix, he had already had a sulphur bath and he longed to see her.

Having sent for him, Maud was now having second thoughts. She did not reply to his urgent note. So he wrote a longer letter— he had no intention of inflicting himself upon her, or of troubling her in any way. Indeed he was quite prepared to take the first train home. He would not blame her: it was obviously sad, very sad. She must think her decision over carefully. Should she come to the conclusion that parting was the best thing it was better if they did not see one another again. All he wanted was a word of decision one way or the other. It was an ultimatum.

Maud, like the poet Miss Barrett, was driven and drawn. She saw him, and they spent a happy fortnight walking in the woods, quoting poetry by running streams and planning a happy future. Herbert, secure in the knowledge that he was forgiven, possibly felt that Maud would never have the necessity to reproach him again. Maud, secure in the revelation of his deep love and reverence for her, was certain that he could deny her nothing in the future. They were both to be proved wrong.

Chapter 2

Riding into the Sunset?

'Il y a de bons mariages mais il n'y
en a point de délicieux.'
                    LA ROCHEFOUCAULD

Maud put Herbert's ring back on her finger and wedding bells
were firmly decided upon. Like most engaged couples they could
see nothing but a charming future in front of them. Herbert would
have his own theatre, Maud would become a famous actress.
Nothing was going to mar their continuing success and happiness.

Max, Herbert's half-brother, younger by nearly twenty years,
had a sharp eye for the past. He drew Herbert as he saw him at this
time. Lunching and dining with important and well-known
people, leaping out of hansom cabs and overpaying the driver, his
tie awry, his red hair disordered from running his fingers through
it, his top hat needing an iron, talking fast, walking fast, always in
a hurry, dismissing his hansom and then whistling frantically for
another one to take him to the theatre.

But there was a grandeur about Herbert which impressed Max
from an early age. He knew so many people and to amuse his step-
mother and Max, he would draw the people he met. 'This is
Whistler, the painter. This E. W. Godwin. Oscar Wilde the poet.'
Herbert was going out to dinner on a Sunday and Irving was to be
there. When Max was about nine he was invited by Herbert to
spend the day with him. Herbert was sharing rooms with A. K.
Moore who wrote for the *Morning Post*. Max, though impressed
with the idea that Moore wrote for a newspaper, was far from
impressed by the fact that Moore kept on roaring with laughter at
the idea of Herbert having a brother under ten. Herbert himself
was writing an article. As soon as it was finished he was to take
Max (and the article) round to the *Punch* offices in Bouverie Street.
And then the crowning event of the day—lunch at Herbert's club
where Max was presented to E. W. Godwin, father of Ellen

Terry's children, though the latter fact would not have been mentioned in polite circles at the time. It was a time when artists looked like artists with black cloaks and large black hats. Max thought Mr. Godwin had the air of a conspirator in a play.

Then Herbert became engaged. Miss Maud Holt in the full beauty of her twenty years was brought round to meet the family. She and Herbert came round to Clanricarde Gardens in Kensington every Sunday. She was received with open arms by the family. Intelligent, witty, well-read and amusing, she was everything which a family could desire. She sang and played the piano to further enchant them while Herbert hung over the piano, wrapt in devotion. Max voted her a goddess.

She was in looks the goddess of the period, slim and blonde with a curly fringe, and always elegantly dressed. A photograph of her wheeling a bicycle gives the impression of an early Shaw heroine. Though she never played in Shaw when she was young, she would have been type cast as Ann Whitfield, or Gloria Clandon. She played Mrs. Clandon but not till 1920.

Spring blossomed into summer and Herbert's family had taken an Elizabethan manor-house near Maidstone in Kent, and when Herbert returned from Aix happy in the knowledge that he and Maud were to be married he went to stay there to await the opening of the autumn theatre season.

Thurnham Court had literary and amatory connexions—Byron had leased it to be near Lady Oxford, one of the more elderly of his mistresses. From Kent Herbert wrote to Maud who was still in Aix nursing her sister. Away from her, he seems to have taken on her romantic attitudes. The glow of a love affair always gives the lovers the impression that they have everything in common, and when it came to illusions Herbert was no exception. He had been re-reading her sweet letter and his dearest wish was that she should be always beside him.

He had been wandering by a field of waving corn with the sun just setting, and had sat down under an old withered fir tree where he had thought long and earnestly of his dear one. His thoughts were romantic, if hardly original. It was hard that they should be separated when they could be so happy together. In the springtime of their love one felt, wrote Herbert, inclined to snatch at happiness. He would come down to the station to meet her and they would have a long four-mile drive—taking the hills slowly so as not to tire the horse. The house was old-fashioned with lots of rooms and a tennis court on which he was going to play, how he wished that Maud was going to be playing with him. He had not been to church, he had decided on *thinking* church. It is possible that he confounded his amorous thoughts of delicious moments with Maud as a substitute for church. He had been sketching, and reading Thackeray's *Newcomes*.

A few days later she wrote saying that she could not leave her sister. This plunged Herbert once more into despair. Everything was hopeless, all this waiting. He wanted her in his arms now, at this second. His heart was void and aching, only she could drive the shadows away.

Then her sister was better and Herbert was cheerful again. They could be married from Thurnham Court, he was arranging about the banns. The church was close to the house, and all was so peaceful.

On 27th August he was moved again to lyricism—the sun was setting in the west, lighting up the little clouds with bright gold and crimson, the ploughed fields were purple, the corn gold and the landscape lighted here and there with the sun's last rays, and above a glimpse of the last blue sky. He asked her to come as soon as she could so that he could ride with his dearest into the sunset.

A glimpse of blue sky was all Herbert was going to get for the time being. For Maud had heard that Herbert, in order to make some extra money for his coming status as a married man, had a hand in the Costume Society. And the head of that society was E. W. Godwin, Ellen Terry's ex-lover. To begin with Maud objected to something which was going to occupy him the greater part of the day. But her main objection was to Mr. Godwin. Herbert had promised to have nothing to do with Mr. Godwin but how could he work with him without being thrown into almost hourly companionship? Her sister Emmie had asked her about Mr. Godwin and, when she discovered it was Godwin *the architect*, she was utterly *disgusted* at the idea that Maud should know such a man. Emmie knew something about him, after all she *had* said that she would as soon have dinner with a snake, as with Godwin.

Maud trusted Emmie's knowledge and feelings for suspected immorality and felt thoroughly justified in her attitude towards Godwin. She felt absolutely in the *right*, she had guessed at the turpitude of Godwin's character and his total unsuitability as a friend for her dear Herbert. Emphasising this, she wrote in large letters that she was right, repeating the word three times. Women who vote themselves right are usually wrong. Herbert wanted a soft young lady straying under the stars with him and this was not at all the reply he wished after his lyrical descriptions of sunsets and withered fir trees.

To emphasise her points and the fact that she was determined at all costs to keep her Herbert from undesirable company, she announced that after they were married she would continue teaching three or four mornings a week and indeed she was arranging, by the same post, her plans for keeping her work.

She ended by saying that she was thinking of her heart's darling every hour of the day.

Back at the Criterion Theatre her heart's darling, away from the softening effect of sunsets, wrote in a less romantic strain. He had received her note. Not only was he surprised at the tone of her letter but he absolutely forbade her to take up her college work again and what was more he was not deceived as to her motives. Her threat was unbecoming. He had taken up other work to make Maud's life easier. He was quite prepared to give up the Costume Society but he would not have her speaking to him in this manner. It was not right, or becoming. It was not like her own dear self.

In the last sentiment Herbert was wrong. It was exactly like her own dear self. Underneath all the curls Maud was as determined as Herbert.

Herbert wrote his letter during rehearsal, slept the night at the Charing Cross Hotel and then sent it enclosed in another letter. He had re-read his letter and come to the conclusion that he thoroughly agreed with himself. The College scheme was utterly out of the question. Possibly she had written her letter when in a temper and said more than she meant. But he was not to be moved in this way. Nothing of this trivial kind must allow their bird of love to lose a feather in its flight. He thought he knew the source of the tales about Godwin, but in any case he had always been a good friend and he had no intention of cutting him heartlessly. Maud must realise that *he* was to be the breadwinner. There was in Herbert's mind no idea of Maud being a 'new woman'. She was to be his wife. His work was not her worry, and if once she got it into her head that she was allowed to interfere with it there was no knowing where her whims would lead her. Maud must understand that she could not act alone without his agreement. As far as he was concerned the whole matter must be dropped.

Maud complied. The plans for their wedding went ahead. Herbert was happy and pleased that he had won the battle. Maud was biding her time.

On 2nd September Maud came home at last and hurried plans were made for their wedding.

How happy they were going to be, always together. Maud had no need to worry about her debts, he had a large balance in the bank, from now on all the responsibilities were his.

Having settled Maud's yearnings for independence, he was able to give his mind to charming contemplation of their romantic future. There were only four more days before she would be entirely his with no chaperone to spoil the crowning of their love. He was struck with awe at the thought that this would be the last letter he would write to her as 'Miss Holt'. What a holy step they were about to take. He had perhaps not always seen it in that light, but as the day approached nearer the solemnity of the occasion overcame him.

The play was going well, there had even been shouts of 'Bravo Tree' at the fall of the curtain and he hoped that the Gods would shout 'Bravo Tree' when the curtain fell on their domestic drama.

Maud had decided on her sister's birthday for her wedding day. On 16th September 1882 Maud was married from Thurnham Court. The lovely old church seemed to Maud to have been planted there on purpose for her wedding to Herbert.

Maud had gone down to stay the day before the wedding with the Beerbohm family. Herbert had arrived on the wedding day itself. At this point Maud was more engrossed in her clothes for the ceremony; Herbert much to his chagrin had become more part of the day's proceedings than the passionate lover about to be joined to his beloved at last.

Maud remembered later the strong difference in their moods on that sunny wedding morning. Her head was full of her clothes, the preparations at the church, the bridesmaids' dresses—all the frills and furbelows of the great occasion. Looking back she felt that their wedding day had perhaps laid bare her own light temperament in contrast to the strange depths in Herbert's character. Julius, Herbert's brother, had disappeared to Spain on one of his unexpected journeys, and Max Beerbohm (aged ten) was to act as best man. He took his status seriously and awaited Herbert's arrival with some trepidation. For Max, always sartorially over-conscious, was worried about Herbert's careless appearance—surely he would have made a special effort on this day of days?

The preparations went ahead. There were triumphal arches of flowers described by the under-gardener as 'rustic' to Max's indignation. Max's sisters, Agnes and Dora, had decorated the bride's and bridegroom's chairs with flowers. The romantic church was flower-filled. All awaited the coming of the bridegroom.

The ten-year-old best man waited under the arches of flowers for Herbert. When he arrived his hat had the right gloss for Max's taste, and his suit was impeccable, but his expression was pale and anxious, and his eyes excited. Max, taking his duties as best man very seriously, said, 'Have you lost the ring?' But Herbert's excitement and pallor were merely due to the knowledge of the great step he was taking.

Someone had once described Herbert at the age of twenty-seven as acting as if he were fifteen, and now at the age of thirty, he was like a boy of eighteen getting married, full of hopes, fears and expectations, while Maud fussed about her clothes.

At this great moment Herbert was determined that marriage with Maud was the greatest step he was to take in his life. In some senses it was. But the men of the late Victorian period were marrying new women who saw their roles as helpmeets to their men. They were already alive with the new ideas which were being preached. Maud was clever and educated, Herbert was ten years her senior, but when it came to ideas Maud was in advance. Herbert saw her as his charming bride. She would settle down to bear his children and admire him. This was not Maud's view of her role.

The marriage service was touching in its simplicity. Maud promised to obey Herbert, while reserving her ideas of the part she intended to play in his life. But she remembered, as she listened to the wistful cadences of his voice as he called her his wife, the strong, warm feeling which stole into her heart. It was a protective love, a passionate wish to keep him from harm, as a mother would guard a favourite child from the fire.

The wedding feast was remembered by the bride as sumptuous, with bride and bridegroom enthroned in the flower decked chairs. Max was particularly delighted that his favourite food syllabub was served. Herbert intoned in a parsonical voice, 'And Sillabub, the son of Sillabub reigned in his stead' which shocked Max. To Herbert everyone from paupers to bishops was grist to his noticing eye to be reproduced later. At the beginning of his marriage from his letters he obviously had the kind of religious feeling expressed by a carelessly written C. of E. on an official form, but his natural feelings were those of the agnostic who prefers to see sermons in stones and books in running brooks. He said he found it difficult to believe in things which his common sense told him did not exist. 'Oh God, give me faith to believe in those things which the common sense thou hast given me tells me are not true.' Perhaps, as he later wrote, he felt it easier to compromise with God in order not to offend the Devil. Maud accepted conventional respectability and morality on its face value, and believed in it.

Herbert was a more complicated character. While on the surface he appeared vague, and even childish, he would confide thoughts of self-questioning to his diaries. He was always sceptical of appearances, and on that account had a penetrating insight into the real characters of people. His vagueness deceived them, and while seeming not to be aware of what was going on, he was able to sum up men and women when they were off their guard.

The main differences between the young couple as they set off under the flowery arches and showers of rice and rose petals were fundamental. Maud was conventional and had more than a touch of the puritan in her make-up. Herbert found it impossible to differentiate between dukes and dustmen. Both men could have points of view which Herbert might find interesting. He was like a child discovering everything new every day, but the child with the penetrating eye, who was not deceived. '*You're* a tiddleywink— and a rascal too.'

The sharpest difference between Maud and Herbert was their sexual temperament. Herbert was a physical man—he liked he said 'the modesty of passion', adding that to the puritan all things are impure. Maud generated what Herbert called temperature without temperament. Maud had been very strictly brought up by her family in Richmond but she became bored with the restrictions imposed by her parents and her brothers and sisters. Though she longed for a larger life she still retained the narrowness of outlook with which she had been surrounded when she was young. Though Herbert's upbringing had been equally strict it had perhaps been enlarged in the sense that his father's Continental background gave him a different view of small things. With Maud's marriage her outlook became more and more 'social' while Herbert always retained his ability to be as interested in a cab-driver as in a count. But as they set off on their wedding journey, and Herbert anticipated delicious days and nights without chaperones, all this was to be discovered.

In the beginning Maud, as the adored and adoring bride, got her own way. By January 1883 she had her first part on the professional stage and they had set up house to begin with in rooms in Old Burlington Street and then in various hotels. Their first home together was in the fashionable district of Belgravia at 4 Wilton Street. There Maud began serious housekeeping with the aid of a house parlourmaid, Leah, and Mrs. Pellatt, a cook. Soon afterwards Maud became ill. Herbert was at once all attention and devotion. His grief over her pain flowed over in self-reproach that perhaps he had been lacking in love. So overwhelming was Herbert's devotion that when Emmie, Maud's sister, finally died, Maud felt herself so cherished and cushioned in Herbert's love that the blow was softened and the sorrow touched her only lightly.

In spite of her marriage, Maud was often drawn back into her family circle, and during one of her absences Herbert wrote a letter which seems to prove that even the shortest of absences caused him speedily to revert to his bachelor way of life.

His guests had been Hermann Vezin, the actor, Claud Ponsonby and Godwin, on whom Maud's disapproval had fallen so heavily. Whether Maud was delighted to learn that they had had a pleasant chatty evening with plenty of scandal is open to doubt. That soda water bottles and the relics of departed spirits were strewn all around Herbert as he wrote was certainly unpleasing.

Although he was alone he was not lonely, Maud was with him in spirit he solemnly averred, but in what kind of spirit he did not specify. He found he had no stamp and resolved to post the letter without one. She would get the letter in the morning and then be reminded of him *doubly* by having to pay twice the postage. He hoped she had spent a happy evening but not too happy to make her grieve to return to her loving Herbert. What Herbert's darling replied to this truthful account of the evening's entertainment is not recorded. It is possible that Maud determined not to leave her boy too often, or he might fall into evil company.

Shortly after this an unexpected misfortune fell on the young couple. Herbert was without an engagement! She had been used to Herbert giving her his twenty pounds every Friday and as speedily spending it, but suddenly the golden sovereigns did not appear. They decided to let their house and retired to gloomy lodgings in a sad grey road in a sad grey neighbourhood where genteel Haverstock Hill masquerades as salubrious Hampstead. They had come down in the world.

But Herbert did not complain for the art of grumbling was not in his nature. They got into debt. Maud was to run up debts very easily during her life, the fact of being in debt was not something which worried her. Creditors had to shoulder the burden. She found it difficult to differentiate, or to focus her attention on essentials. Looking back over their time of poverty she remembered them walking light-heartedly down Haverstock Hill, singing and laughing and buying clean collars and snowdrops. Presumably the landlady was expected to concern herself with the mundane mutton chops and potatoes, and Maud's contribution to financial penury was to borrow from her sister who was later to be paid back with a set of chairs.

Maud never seems to have taken housekeeping over seriously. When Frank Benson's wife was consulting her about the complications of cooking, Maud asked her what she fed her husband on. On hearing the long list of heartwarming foods which were poured into the athletic Frank, Maud replied succinctly: 'You feed him too well! I give Herbert a rasher of bacon, and he thanks God he has got a wife.'

In the springtime of their marriage Maud's blue-stocking disdain of housewifely duties could be disregarded. By the summer they were back in Wilton Street and Maud was ill again. Were these 'illnesses' miscarriages? She does not say, but the intensity of Herbert's worry over her, and his constantly reiterated 'I have not loved you enough!' leads to the thought that they might have been. The reticences of the Victorians lead to many speculations, and though they were married in 1882, their first child was not born until nearly two years later, a little unusual in times when most first children followed promptly nine months after a wedding.

Maud went down to the Isle of Wight to recover from her mysterious illness and Herbert was once more rehearsing. The play was *The Glass of Fashion* which opened at the Globe, Herbert playing, as was usual for him at this time, a dubious foreigner, the Polish Prince Borowski, a dastardly seducer of women, a part which set a fashion for the wearing of caddish brown plush smoking-jackets.

Herbert was still adamant against Maud's going on the stage. But when she had recovered from her illness, she managed to persuade him to let her act in a 'curtain raiser' to Herbert's play. He gave as his reason for disliking Maud's becoming an actress that there was so much *else* she could do. But Irene Vanbrugh, who knew her later in her career, stated quite categorically that Maud 'was not a good actress' and some of her notices seem to testify to this point of view. Yet it was hardly something which a husband could point out to his young and pretty bride. The stage had first attracted Maud to Herbert and she was determined to act. Her first chance came with a part in a play called *The Millionaire* in which she played an adventuress called Hester Gould. Her approach to the part was the intelligent one of going back to literature to find the character. She wrote: 'I donned scarlet hair, and modelled my demeanour on that of Wilkie Collins's immortal adventuress, Miss Gwilt.'

The result was a success which surprised and did not entirely please Herbert, who on reading the notices rushed in to Maud, shaving-brush in one hand and cut-throat razor in the other shouting, 'I hope this doesn't mean you will be more famous than I! I couldn't have that.'

Maud was beginning to earn her own money which she spent on hansoms, flowers, intimate suppers at Wilton Street, parties and week-ends at the sea, or in the country. Maud's money was for spending.

But in March of 1884 came Herbert's first break with playing sinister foreigners—and his first real success. It was the farce *The Private Secretary*.

Tree did not want to play the part of the foolish bun-eating, milk-drinking curate. Consequently the play became filled with his inventions, and it was the first time that his passionate flair for 'business' came into its own. The part of the Rev. Robert Spalding was taken over and recreated by Tree. At the last minute he decided to make the terrified curate a teetotaller, marked by wearing a blue badge. He suddenly told Maud he must have a piece of blue ribbon as a buttonhole. Maud tore a piece of material from her sleeve and dipped it in blue paint and from the moment of Herbert's appearance the curate was created.

The play, an adaptation from the German by Charles Hawtrey, was found by the critics to be weak and silly, with a stupid plot. All the actors were described as ineffective, or ridiculous. 'The most important exception is Mr. Beerbohm Tree, who takes the part of the curate, and interprets it in a manner that can only be described as masterly. It is an excellent quality in Mr. Tree that he always merges his own identity in the character he undertakes, not only does he look the part but he throws in a number of little touches which are consistent and immensely funny.'

But in spite of Herbert's little touches, the farce languished for a fortnight. Maud, who was acting in a curtain raiser called *Six and Eightpence* written by Herbert, sat miserably in the stalls during the main play, trying to make the theatre seem less empty.

Then suddenly the breakthrough came. One of Mrs. Leigh Murray's petticoats dropped off, and with great and blushing embarrassment she had to throw it into the wings—in full view of the audience. Herbert as the Rev. Spalding (making his entrance in the second act) said nervously, 'I beg your pardon, I thought I met a petticoat on the stairs.'

The cast broke into laughter at Herbert's magnificent impromptu. The petticoat had saved the situation—and the play. Success and failure in the theatre are the difference between the flight of a butterfly in the sun, and its destruction by a quick flick of a cat's paw. *The Private Secretary* became the talk of the town. The part which Herbert did not want to play gave him his first taste of fame. The theatre filled and the farce became what he was later to call 'an obstinate success'.

It was still being played fifty years later.

But from the very first Herbert was never attracted to playing the same part night after night. He had not the dedicated actor's capacity for using his technique for staying the course. He had succeeded. He had proved that he could do it, and after a few months he happily passed the part on to W. S. Penley who went on playing it for many years, gathering the corn which Herbert had sown. Penley is often believed to have created the part, although Maud wrote that he had not only taken over the part, but all Herbert's business and characterisation.

Herbert, as if to show from the beginning his capacity for

delineating sharply contrasted characters, went on to play in a thriller, *Called Back* by Hugh Conway. Up to this time stage villains had been melodramatic. Tree's Paolo Macari was subtle, cynical and well-observed, a handsome, confident Italian spy. By abandoning the Rev. Robert Spalding he had in one step managed to enhance his reputation and draw attention to his versatility. He had an instinctive feeling for the right things to do. He always knew why a man failed.

By the summer of 1884 Maud was pregnant with her first child, and they had moved to Cheyne Row. Maud was one of that great band of irritatingly dedicated movers. Tree, like many men who leave the details of life to their women, put up with being shifted from Chelsea to Chiswick, from Hampstead to Sloane Street, and once they began to be rich, Maud enlarged her sphere, adding country moves to town moves, doubling the expense and the inconvenience. Like other movers, Maud seldom made money on her moves. She re-decorated and re-arranged, re-built and repaired, but she never bought her houses, and all the money she spent disappeared like snow in the sun.

Cheyne Row was the first of her real moves, and she remembered it with affection. There was not a sweeter place on earth than the Cheyne Row that summer. Their circle of useful friends was enlarging—playwrights Hamilton Aïdé and W. S. Gilbert, Oscar Wilde—and Maud in her new-found prosperity and happiness was even prepared to tolerate the dreadful Godwin. She had perhaps misjudged Godwin she felt, she admitted to having had a narrow-minded jealousy of him. She could not put Herbert in a glass case and she had an instinctive feeling that if she did, Godwin might try to get him out, but in the complacency of her marriage and pregnancy, even Godwin could be accepted as a friend. Let him take Herbert out of his glass case; it could do no harm.

In July 1884 Tree's first daughter Viola was born. She always seems to have been his favourite child, perhaps because she was the child of a new love, possibly a first real love. Her childhood sayings were often quoted by her father. From the beginning he found her clever and amusing. At the age of two she refused to kiss W. S. Gilbert, and when reproved by her father who said: 'Oh, kiss Gillie, Daddy loves Gillie', Viola replied pertly: 'Then Daddy kiss Gillie.'

Herbert found this precocious remark full of a depth of childish and profound philosophy in so young a child and quoted it with love and admiration. He felt he had produced a genius. Maud tended to be less impressed. When Viola, playing on the beach gave her mother a pebble, Maud said: 'Clever, clever girl', and in a down-to-earth aside to Frank Benson's wife added, 'You always tell children—and men—they are clever, I don't know why.'

During the two years between 1884 and 1886 Tree acted in a variety of parts without regaining his initial popular successes. He was held to have failed as Joseph Surface although one critic noted that 'Mr. Beerbohm Tree made Joseph Surface a very much more probable individual than usual' adding that the public seemed to take more interest in Mrs. Langtry's dresses as Lady Teazle. In *Peril*, an adaptation from Victorien Sardou, he was said to have been the best thing in the play, his make-up was a study in itself, 'he is becoming one of our finest character actors'.

But there were also critical failures. Mr. Poskett in Pinero's farce *The Magistrate,* and in Gilbert's *Engaged*. This funny, but much under-estimated, play was not to the taste of the audience, they expected funny rhymes from Gilbert. Nor was Gilbert himself pleased with Tree. When he went round to see him after the first night he found the actor dripping with sweat. 'Your skin has been acting at all events,' said Gilbert drily. Tree was worried about his false moustache, and debating whether to grow a real one for the part, but Gilbert, not admiring of the way Tree had served him, said: 'You will be able to grow an *enormous* moustache before you can play this part.'

But in spite of his failure Herbert was not going to be driven to doing things of which he did not approve. He had a clear view of what he wanted and the determination to get it. When he was spending a week-end with the Gilberts, the playwright asked him if he had had any offers that week. Herbert said he had had three. 'Which have you accepted?'

'None,' said Tree.

Gilbert, with Victorian prudence, considered that Tree was behaving in a very irresponsible manner. He had a wife and child to support and was in no position to refuse offers. But Tree remained firmly set on his course.

'My ambition is in a different direction,' he said simply. He was determined on aiming higher than mere bread and butter parts.

While Herbert fixed his eyes on his goal, Maud was happily

engaged in moving from Cheyne Walk to North Audley Street, a more fashionable district, finding it was too expensive and moving to a flat over the Prince of Wales Theatre, and later to a dark house near Ascot. Herbert went up to London looking for work. Finally he was offered a part in a play which was being recast, called *Jim the Penman* by Sir Charles Young. The plot was the usual complicated farrago of wicked forgeries and wronged innocence. Herbert was expecting to be given the principal role, but in the disappointing way of theatre careers it went to Arthur Dacre. He was made to take over from a Frenchman called Marius the part of Baron Hauteville. Even worse, M. Marius had very good notices, 'His nationality prevented him having any trouble with the part, which could hardly be improved on for make-up, and artistic effect. The many little touches introduced made his portrayal one of the most quietly perfect and humorous character sketches we have seen for some time.'

For the first time Herbert was despondent: 'My soul is dark,' he said to Maud. But he thought of a way round the problem—he turned Baron Hauteville into the Baron Harzfeld, changing his background and nationality and, like the petticoat in *The Private Secretary,* the Baron became the hit of the play.

When the season came to an end both he and Maud were asked by Frank Benson down to Bournemouth. Frank Benson and his wife were about to start out on their long years of acting and touring. But that was in the future, Frank's eyes like Herbert's were set on a London success, and he wanted an attraction for the start of his tour. He knew that Tree's ambitions lay on higher things than foreign barons and comical parsons.

'How would a week at Bournemouth suit you for experiments?' As an added attraction, he suggested that Maud might care to play Portia and Lady Teazle. 'Provincial business is very small', wrote Frank Benson modestly, 'but I presume that is not so much your object as an artistic experiment? How would half my profits suit you, £10 guaranteed? That seems to me to be a fair thing.'

His wife would be able to show Mrs. Tree some of the stock business for Lady Teazle and he ended 'P.S. I can make this off. definite. I shall want to know about Bournemouth by Tuesday. It is a nice little theatre and a nice place, and I think it will be the best place for it.'

Tree also felt it was a 'fair thing' and accepted. They played

Othello (Tree as Iago), and *The Merchant of Venice* adding *The School for Scandal* for good measure for, as Benson said, 'The old comedies never fail to attract and please an audience singularly quick in entering into the spirit and appreciating the wit of the "powder and patch" period.' Maud happily plunged into her leading parts, but she does not appear to have thought her performances a success, for she quotes a critic as saying that she had played 'with all the airy complacency of ineptitude'. Mrs. Benson's stock business does not seem to have been enough to make an instant leading lady of Maud.

Benson transferred *Othello* to Oxford. Tree was still acting the Baron Harzfeld while playing matinées at Oxford, and used to travel to London dressed as Iago, arriving just in time to change and appear as the Baron in *Jim the Penman*. 'Narrowly escaping arrest as a lunatic,' according to Benson. In his nervousness about the part of Iago, Tree asked Hermann Vezin to coach him in the stage business needed for the part. Vezin was astonished at this approach—the conception of the character came first, said Vezin, the business was secondary. But from the first, Tree's parts were built up with a proliferation of business, as pointillist painters build up a picture with a mass of dots of colour.

By the spring of 1887 Herbert's chance to lift himself out of the rut of being merely an actor came—he took on the lease of the Comedy Theatre. This venture was financed by Stuart Ogilvy. J. Comyns Carr, the playwright, whom Shaw called 'an encylopaedic gentleman', had previously attached himself to Irving. He had now become self-appointed literary adviser to Tree. He was gradually transferring his talents to a rising star.

Herbert had become that man of the period—an actor-manager. Maud celebrated by moving yet again. She later remembered the lonely hours she spent at Rosary Gardens, Chelsea, while the three men plotted their success.

Chapter 3

Actor-Manager

'I can always get what I want.'
HERBERT BEERBOHM TREE

The Red Lamp, a melodrama, was set in Russia with romantic settings such as 'The Princess Morakoff's Palace in St. Petersburg', and Tree playing Demetrius, the head of the Secret Police. The best description of him in the part is given by Kate Terry Gielgud, who brings him to life as if she were seeing him on a re-run film.

'With loose-lipped, fleshy face, the white eyelids, low, over expressionless pale eyes, cat-footed, though rather ponderous in build he walked on to the stage, stick in hand. For just one moment the eyes flashed, he thrust the stick viciously beneath the sofa—an action incredibly swift, and he was again immobile enigmatic and unrecognized in his own theatre, until an individuality of enunciation revealed the amazing disguise, and cheers rang out.'

The play opened in April of 1887. Herbert, as he was always to do, chose his cast with care—it included Marion Terry and Janet Achurch. It seems to have been a melodrama with Tree's subtleties triumphing over such phrases as 'One touch to the communicator and oh! how hideous a ruin!' and 'It is the dawn, mad woman—it is the dawn!—ay the dawn of blood!'

But Tree was aware of his power. Acting, he said, was largely a matter of hypnotism. 'It signifies little to have faults so long as we have the little bit of radium.' He had that quality to make dross glow and to make a villain believable and lifelike. The Red Lamp grew into a success. Maud described Herbert and Comyns Carr hiding in the Box Office listening to the merry chink of coin paid for seats. But in spite of this, actual profits failed to materialise. The profits were always going to be seen in the following week.

In the autumn Herbert took another step upwards. He took over the Haymarket. It had been in decline since the Bancrofts had left it some two years before. But Tree was not deterred. He was thirty-five years old and he knew what he wanted. It was not a theatre encrusted with tradition. The theatre public was changing and he was going to change the theatre to suit them. He put in electricity, cut the price of seats in the upper circle, abolished a number of old-fashioned boxes, and made the gallery and dress circle larger. His new public were no longer divided into gentry and the rest who would put up with benches. The buses and trams were bringing in customers from the growing suburbs and they were his new audience.

The installation of electricity caused a fluttering in the public dovecotes. It was regarded as a very dangerous thing. There had recently been disastrous fires in Paris and Exeter; anything which might risk a fire was worrying. Tree wrote a long letter to *The Times* defending electric light. A week or so later the *Daily News* recorded that 'Mr. Beerbohm Tree is going to take the highly practical and sensible course of stationing a fireman with a hose attached to a hydrant in the "flies" during every performance'. Public agitation died down. The solitary fireman reassured them, and the theatre ceased to be regarded as 'ill starred'.

The Red Lamp continued to draw the public. Maud, to her delight, had taken over Janet Achurch's part and been rewarded by the critical accolade that 'she showed much feeling and power'.

The next play he put on was *Partners* adapted from *Fromont Jeune et Risler Aîné*, a work of Daudet. It was considered to be too risky in its original form. Tree himself commented, 'With Daudet's work the adapter had to face the terrible situation of a brother being one of the lovers of his own brother's wife. This is a situation which it is obvious no audience would tolerate, therefore any adaptation would have to be a free one.' Tree was always to be delicately sensitive to his audience's prejudice. Whatever they did in private, when they were in the theatre they adopted a public morality, and so did Tree.

Punch did not take to the play remarking that 'Mr. German Christmas Tree had been cut down to a shrub', a sarcastic reference to the fact that the adapter Mr. Buchanan had had to cut the play, 'which now commences at half past eight and concludes before the magical hour of eleven'. *Punch* patted itself on the back, evidently there were some managers who were so 'umble as to take a critical slashing cheerfully and profit by the process.

But the play does not seem to have suffered as much as *Punch* might have hoped because 'in spite of the fog' it was still running in February of 1888 and business was said to be excellent.

Tree had now become a personality and was giving extensive interviews. He had already cultivated an easy, pleasant relationship with the press which was to stand him in good stead over the years.

During the run of *Partners* the reporter of the *Society Times* sat by fascinated as he changed from the middle-aged untidy German he portrayed in the play, to a trim slight young man, 'very smartly dressed in garments of exceptional cut'. Tree suddenly interrupted the interview and said: 'Excuse me—I am just about to poison myself', and produced two small black bottles and carefully poured out nine drops into a tumbler of water, explaining that it was some sort of homœopathic stuff for the nerves. He was not, he explained, a homœpath 'but this stuff seems to pull me together wonderfully when I am tired after the performance, or before if I am feeling nervous'. Tree then made the usual remark that it is not possible for an actor to be good unless he is nervous, gave a brief run-down of his career and put on a handsome fur-lined overcoat. Then, as if to explain away so much magnificence, Tree told the reporter (in confidence) it was the one he had worn in *Nadjeska* and went out into the street.

To another interviewer he was equally confiding—the life of an actor–manager was not a life of idleness, but he would try to spare the *Topical Times* a few minutes after the performance. While the audience departed for Gatti's, the Café Royal and the Continental Café, Tree was still working at his publicity. The play managed to keep afloat and the Princess Mary of Teck, the future Queen Mary, attended the last night.

On the domestic front *Partners* had less happy consequences.

Herbert had chosen Marion Terry for the wife in the play. This did not please Maud. She had had very good notices for her performance in *The Red Lamp* and expected to be the natural heiress of all the leading parts of Herbert's theatre. What else were husbands for?

Marion Terry! Maud demanded angrily why he had not chosen his own wife.

Herbert explained that Miss Terry seemed to him to be more suitable for the part. She had not only the appearance but the personality. And here Herbert made his fatal mistake. Untactfully he pointed out that great sympathy was the quality the part demanded.

Maud exploded with rage. On Herbert's head fell the double-edged anger of the thwarted actress and the infuriated wife.

He did not stay to bear the brunt of the full fury of the storm. He decided on retreat and left the house. Drama had moved over from the Haymarket to New Cavendish Street where the Trees were living in what Herbert called 'The house of the Seven Stables'.

Maud found she had pushed him too far. Would he come back? Herbert had many bolt holes, he belonged to a number of clubs, there were always good fellows about who also wished to avoid domestic situations. What were clubs for if it were not to be refuges from women, whether wives or mistresses? Hours of heart broken sobbing, keeping watch for Herbert's return, reduced Maud to a suitable frame of mind for a tender reconciliation to take place.

In spite of Marion Terry's sympathetic handling of Maud's coveted role, the play did not succeed and Herbert's next project was *The Pompadour* by Sydney Grundy—from a German play suitably glossed for the English public. Herbert's plans for *The Pompadour* were thrown out of key by Maud. She had been promised—and lost—a leading part in another play. Maud's disappointment and chagrin dissolved in bitter tears which Herbert could only mop up by promising that she should be Pompadour and go to the Ball.

Although Herbert chose to play Fairy Godmother he could not turn Maud into an emotional actress overnight. Herbert's rehearsals were never zones of sweetness and light, but *The Pompadour* with Maud and Herbert at loggerheads was hardly an eighteenth-century gavotte. Maud did not want to be thrown down a flight of steps, she might get hurt. Herbert incensed could only yell at her to act! She would not *get* hurt if she would only act! But Maud did not fancy being thrown down and plumped to be pushed off the lowest step—a fact to which she attributed her failure.

But the unsporting *Sportsman* remarked that Mrs. Tree's Pompadour was apparently devoid of any fascinating qualities, and it was incredible that even Mr. Ashley's comical Louis XV could be affected by her to the point of becoming her devoted slave.

The settings and the clothes were after Watteau, Boucher and

La Tour and the boys and girls ballet full of pre-revolutionary charm. The critics disliked all this pishtushery and continued to carp, complaining that Wills and Grundy had taken an old German play by a 'person' called Brachvogel and adapted it into English 'after a very colloquial fashion'. Eighteenth-century characters were expected to display some nobility of phrase. *Vanity Fair* complained that hoops and petticoats do not make a play. But it was generally admitted that the play was beautifully mounted. The pictures show rich settings in the Edwardian-Ritz style of Louis Quinze much to the popular taste. 'Frocks and sets' were said to have cost a cool £4,000. The play drew the town and became 'the chief piece of the season—though that says little for the discrimination of the London playgoer'.

But on and off stage Maud sparkled. 'Mrs. Tree is one of the best dressed actresses *on* the stage—and one of the best dressed women in London *off* it', remarked the *Star* approvingly. It was a reputation to which Maud, a woman of her era, attached great importance, whether she could afford it or not.

Herbert, nettled by some of the criticism, did find a chink in the critics' armour. 'It is not for me to argue as to the utter worthlessness of such authors as Messrs. Wills & Grundy', he wrote to the *St. James's Gazette*, 'but when your contributor proceeds to point out that no one was called before the curtain', he would in his turn like to say that 'the space in front of the curtain has been abolished since 1879 [nine years before] and no one can appear before it without falling into the stalls. As Mr. Puff puts it, "The Spanish Fleet you cannot see—because it is not yet in sight".' The play continued to run, and even the press admitted that Mr. Tree could afford to chuckle when he received Mr. Bashford's good reports from the front of the house. His diary for 1888 begins with a careful list of takings for *Pompadour*, varying from £84 at the beginning of the week to nearly £300 for the two performances on Saturday. But Tree's dedication to his financial progress did not endure. The expenses continued for several pages of the diary and then stopped abruptly, as if the whole idea of careful accounts bored the diarist, as indeed finance was always to do.

Pompadour had been a modest success but Tree's next production was to bring prosperity. *Captain Swift* turned the financial corner for Tree—suddenly his management had begun to blossom and to be acclaimed. But not without preliminary birth-pangs.

The writing of the play was typical of Tree's haphazard intuitive methods. He had met Haddon Chambers, a young Australian who was scraping up a living writing stories for magazines, with a marked lack of success, for he was living in one room over a dairy in Bayswater. Tree, who knew him slightly, ran into him outside the Comedy Theatre one day, and suddenly asked Chambers, 'Have you ever thought of writing a play for me?'

It was an astonishing question from a theatre manager to an unknown writer. Like any struggling writer Chambers replied promptly: 'No, but I will.' He went back to his eyrie over the dairy and after a four months' struggle produced a play. Captain Swift (the bushranger) was one of the oldest of stage types—the scoundrel with the heart of gold. He arrived to blackmail, and stayed to be redeemed by the sweetness and light of an English home, and the loveliness of love and duty. It also had some very long arms of coincidence to pull the plot together. Having saved his hostess's husband from being run over by a cab, the bushranger turned out to be her illegitimate son.

Haddon Chambers, the author of this powerful piece, was an amusing Australian whom Bernard Shaw called 'a rough and ready playwright with the imagination of a bushranger—but it *is* imagination all the same—and it suffices.' He amused Tree, and had an easy-going temperament which appealed to him. There was something in Chambers which struck an echoing chord in Herbert's vagabond nature. He was prepared to encourage the young man, and agreed to hear the play.

At the inevitable reading, Tree fell asleep in Act II, woke up and decided he needed a Turkish bath. But Chambers was not to be deterred. He followed Tree from cold to medium, to hot rooms, and when finally cornered in a cloud of steam, Tree consented to do the play.

Comyns Carr predicted financial and artistic disaster. Hastings, the stage manager, was more succinct and voted the whole thing 'damned rot'.

It was put on for a trial matinée with Tree playing the cad with the heart of gold and, like much damned rot, succeeded brilliantly with the public. Tree's cool adventurer appealed to the women and for perhaps the only time in his career caused the ladies to mob him at the stage door. He had transformed his pale face into that of the outdoor man and by darkening his eyelashes managed to give his audience the feeling that he had black compelling eyes. With these newly flashing eyes Herbert suddenly took on a new and dangerous dimension to his audience, and to Maud. He seemed handsome, even poetic. There had never been a finer study of a real cad. There remained a nagging little doubt in Maud's mind. Was it perhaps a little worrying that he played the cad so masterfully?

Maud played opposite Herbert and was voted graceful and tender. Although *The Country Gentleman* remarked that if Mrs. Tree's four frocks came with the play from Australia, 'the best groomed ladies of the day had best go to Queensland for their dresses'. The lady gossip writers were ecstatic over Maud's snaky, flowing aesthetic dresses which so set off to advantage her graceful figure. 'In the conservatory scene she wore a white dress with a wonderful vest composed of frills upon frills of rose crêpe lissé, the skirt so thickly embroidered with white braid that, even with strong glasses, I could not distinguish the nature of the material underneath, round the bottom was a deep edging of handsome gold embroidery appliqués to the dress which had a *very* good effect'.

The Trees in their own theatre were a financial, social, and sartorial success. It was all very pleasant.

Captain Swift was also held to have uplifting sentiments. One of Maud's sisters had suggested a motto for the play which was used on the programme: 'There is some soul of goodness in things evil'. There were also some financial pickings for the Trees in purveying romantic rubbish—provided that the settings and dresses were elegant.

From the beginning of his career as manager, Tree had a delicate instinct for the right sets for his plays. If the Bancrofts had got away from badly painted cloths to solid drawing-rooms with recognisably good furniture, Tree carried this a stage further. It was said of his sets that he managed to differentiate between the drawing-room a bank manager would choose and that of a stock-broker. His noticing eye fell on everything from people to props. The English home into which the adventuring Captain Swift stepped—to try his blackmail—and to be reformed was perfect of its kind.

With the new-found prosperity Herbert's little family were able to flaunt their prosperity. Maud had a carriage and Herbert began to ride every day. New prospects had opened before them and the partnership of Maud and Herbert was evenly divided—according to Maud. She had only to live, to act and to amuse herself. Herbert was only too happy to see his wife elegantly turned out—unlike most husbands he was never angry at her extravagances. Herbert's share of the partnership was bounded by ambition and enterprise.

Their social circles were expanding—and becoming grander. It was an age when the aristocracy liked to patronise the stage— Maud mentions two of their new hostesses, Lady Waterford, Lady Dorothy Nevill. Suppers, receptions, balls, luncheons and all the gaieties of the London season were there to enjoy. Herbert had bought a carriage and Maud with her elegant clothes was able to lure him into enjoying the fruits of his success and to become at last Queen to his King.

Success bored Herbert and as soon as a play was running his busy mind was ready to try something new. He produced the old Tom Taylor favourite *Masks and Faces*, playing the starving playwright Triplet with Mrs. Bernard Breere as Peg Woffington, and Maud as the noble heroine, Mabel Vane. Tree then produced the first of his Shakespeare plays, *The Merry Wives of Windsor*, for a series of matinées.

Then in the autumn of 1889 came *A Man's Shadow*, one of those plays which had such an appeal to Victorian actors, in which a double performance enables the principal performer to show his capacity for portraying good and evil in one grand *tour de force*. The play by Robert Buchanan was the usual adaptation from the French with Tree playing both the bewildered, tortured and falsely accused hero and the debauched absinth-sodden villain with his harsh singing of *'Plaisir d'amour ne dure qu'un moment, Chagrin d'amour dure toute la vie—e'*. The climax came in a trial scene which Tree had produced with infinite care. Julia Neilson, whom Tree had brought in to play 'the bold bad woman', the advocate's wife, had her first chance in this play. She wrote, 'When I think of Tree I bring to mind his eyes, the bluest eyes I have ever seen, and his expressive hands which he used incessantly.'

Outside the theatre, she remarked, he was like a schoolboy, but once in his natural element at a rehearsal he never rested until he had fined down the actors' performances to his satisfaction. It often appeared to outsiders as if his rehearsals were chaotic and that the effects he managed to achieve were happy accidents, but inside his head he retained the picture of what he wanted. He worked his cast at rehearsals sometimes until dawn, and expected them to turn up in the morning as if they had had ten hours' sleep.

He never liked to see anyone on business during rehearsals. He wanted to keep the picture of what he was trying to achieve in his mind.

Rehearsals did not stop for meals—the actors were expected to picnic on the stage. Tree had his modest lunch of a hard-boiled egg and bread-and-butter brought to him on the stage. He ate the bread-and-butter and solemnly cracked the top of his egg and— left it at that. He was never seen actually to eat it. The joke in the theatre was that the egg was the work of the property man, merely a show egg and not for eating.

The run of *A Man's Shadow* was graced by the presence of that dedicated playgoer, Mr. Gladstone who, on going round to see Herbert after the show, took the opportunity to do a little canvassing. What were the political opinions of the theatrical profession? 'Conservative on the whole,' said Herbert cheerfully, and then catching sight of Gladstone's gloomy Liberal face added hastily, 'but the scene shifters are Radical to a *man*.'

There is something about dear old vicars and village priests which seems to attract actors. Irving drew tears for the Vicar of Wakefield, and Tree was drawn to his French equivalent in *A Village Priest* from *Le Secret de la Terreuse*, adapted by the hardworking Sydney Grundy.

The gentle, humorous, absent-minded old priest, browbeaten by his shrewish housekeeper, gave Herbert the chance to disguise himself completely in cassock, skull-cap and white wig, pottering about his garden amongst his blossoming apple trees, with a long curving pipe and watering-can. So well had he achieved his disguise that the principal of the Royal Academy of Music— meeting Herbert in the corridor—mistook him for the Abbé Liszt.

The play had a mixed reception. The *Morning Post* found the character singularly attractive and the actor 'by his sympathetic treatment enhances its most engaging features. Even in appearance and manner the Abbé captivates us.'

The plot hinged on the dear old Abbé breaking the seal of the confessional (for very good and cogent reasons). But this did not please the *Catholic Times*, which attacked him and then ended: 'We acquit the dramatist at once of any intention to attack the

Roman Catholic priesthood. He has erred in ignorance and his error is also false in art. A noble drama could have been made of the subject if the Abbé had been kept faithful under *all* trials to his duty.' Even the *Sporting Review* did not take a sporty attitude— their critic wrote that it seemed a pity that Mr. Tree's splendid powers should be devoted to a character which had excited such a storm of indignation in the religious breasts of many well meaning and tolerant people.

Some English Catholics were recovering slowly from the feeling that they had a priest hidden in the cupboard and remained touchy. In France they took their religion more lightly. Herbert wrote many indignant letters to the Press which Maud persuaded him to tear up, remarking wisely that a little controversy never did a play any harm. With her social flair and natural instinct for publicity, she was becoming her husband's best public relations adviser, long before public relations had become a profession.

A great deal of heat and little light sprang from the controversies. Herbert's attackers bombarded him with letters on knotty theological points and he, though hardly a devout churchman at heart, was forced into lengthy replies. He was being attacked from both sides of the confessional box, although he had found a few broadminded Catholic defenders.

To one correspondent he wrote that he had never categorically stated that the Abbé was justified in his course of conduct. But one Catholic priest whom he had consulted had taken the view that in the difficult situation in which the dear old Abbé found himself, it was hard to see what else he could have done. Herbert pointed out that it was impossible for him to divulge the name of this priest as it must be regarded as a secret between the confessor and himself.

He ended his letter by remarking that the drama was not a place for nursery twaddle and music hall buffoonery, and he felt it his duty to drag it out of the slough of suburbanism. He was sorry if a serious work offended the susceptibilities of his correspondent, but it was impossible to do worthwhile things without ruffling someone.

Herbert's portrayal of the Abbé, according to Maud, diffused an atmosphere that hung between earth and Heaven, but Herbert's defence against attack was his public and the Box Office returns.

In the spring of 1890 Herbert took Maud for a country drive to

Hampstead and here, unfortunately both for Herbert and for
Maud, she found a charming old manor house with three acres of
garden and surrounded by meadows. It was to let unfurnished.
Herbert noted gloomily that they moved to Hampstead on
30th May. Maud waxed lyrical about spending a summer amongst
the roses in their garden.

Herbert was preparing for his autumn tour. But there is a small
entry in Herbert's diary which leads to a question mark. On one
Sunday in August he seems to have escaped from Maud's paint
pots and re-arrangements at the Grange. He visited a Miss Carew
at 13 Shrewsbury Road, Bayswater, adding that he went with the
possibility of giving her a part. Admittedly Herbert did not like
discussing business during rehearsals, but the entry is somewhat
invalidated by being accompanied by a solitary pressed pansy.
Perhaps Maud was not wise to move so far away as Hampstead.
Theatre managers, like secret service agents and detectives, always
have a valid excuse. But Maud's heart was full of the joys of
success. There was not a cloud in the sky. Maud and Herbert
began their tour on August 3rd at Brighton where *A Village Priest*
was acclaimed. Dublin, Edinburgh, Glasgow, Liverpool, Manchester—what success, what friends, what wonderful experiences
greeted them everywhere! Maud was ecstatic. The utmost luxury
and indulgence were hers. One small cloud was in the sky. She had
had to leave Viola, her child, behind at Brighton. But when they
got to Birmingham Herbert pretended to have to go to London
on business, returning with 'luggage' which turned out to be
Viola. He always liked 'larks', surprises and hidden presents.

There was another cloud at Birmingham, the *Daily Gazette*
reported Dr. McIntyre as preaching at St. Chad's giving a clear
firm answer to the question posed by *A Village Priest*, should the
priest break the seal of the confessional? From St. Chad's came a
firm authoritative 'No'. The newspaper in reporting Dr. McIntyre
professed a lofty disdain for these niceties of 'the Romish Church'
and blamed it entirely for the troubles in Ireland.

At the end of September the tour ended, and Maud recorded
that the dear Company presented Herbert with a piece of silver,
Mr. Fernandez made a charming speech, both she and Herbert
cried. How sweet they all were, and how they loved and respected
Herbert, and above all how proud they were of what he had done.

During Tree's first successes at the Haymarket, he began a

series of matinées and try-outs. Granville Barker has been credited with beginning the repertory movement in London. Tree's Monday evening try-outs and Wednesday matinées long preceded the experiments at the Royal Court. For these try-outs he followed the ideas expressed in his letter to the infuriated Catholic and put on plays which he did not think would draw the town and were perhaps in advance of its thinking.

Henley and Robert Louis Stevenson had written a play called *Beau Austin*. Henley wrote a prologue to it to give it the right period flavour:

> To all and singular, as Dryden says
> We bring a fancy of those Georgian days,
> Whose style still breathed a faint and fine perfume
> Of old world courtliness and old world wit,
> When speech was elegant and talk was fit,
> For slang had not been canonized as wit.

Unfortunately the play was hissed and not canonised. The very eccentric costumes of 1820 in *Beau Austin* offended the fashion-conscious nineties. They do not seem to have appreciated any English period but their own, for in *Trelawny of the Wells* the foolish crinolines were treated with equal scorn.

Maud Tree played the innocent young girl to Herbert's elderly seducer against a background of old Tunbridge Wells. When the beau's 'iniquity' is revealed, Maud, as Dorothy, spurns him: 'I have been your mistress, I can never be your wife.' This sentiment ran against the accepted canons of the stage. Betrayed maidens either had to get married—or commit suicide.

When the autumn and winter came, Herbert was rehearsing Henry Arthur Jones's *The Dancing Girl*, Maud's flower-embowered Grange on the heights of Hampstead had become a liability. There was no public transport to such a remote country spot in those days. By the end of the year Herbert was running in thick snowstorms down to the cabstand, or having to leave his hansom cab to walk up Fitzjohn's Avenue because the horses were slipping on the frosty road. Added to which Jones and Tree quarrelled incessantly. When memories had faded into the background and the successful box office returns were the only things which could be remembered, Jones murmured how much he owed to Tree. *The Dancing Girl* had been one of Jones's greatest successes. But the rehearsals were punctuated by bitter quarrels, by threats of solicitors' letters, by the author rushing out of the theatre, and Tree rushing into his dressing-room to take a few drops of his mysterious tonic.

One of the exchanges between the two men turned into farce, with Jones shouting, 'No, no, No!' and Tree replying 'Don't repeat yourself'. Jones, a rough diamond who dropped his aitches shouted back, 'I must if you 'aven't listened.' Tree became dignified. 'Repetition breeds listlessness. By the time you said your last 'no' I had forgotten what the first one was about.' Jones said he would content himself with a solitary 'No!'

But Tree had the last word: 'No what?'

Jones stormed out of the theatre.

On being asked by a friend how he was getting on with Tree, Jones said 'Excellently! I had to send my solicitor round to him this morning, but apart from this—everything is going smoothly.'

The plot seems to have suffered from extremes and it is possible that it was only Tree's performance which saved it. *The Dancing Girl* was Drusilla Ives (Julia Neilson), a humble Quaker girl from Cornwall, pretending to have a good situation in London, but actually the mistress of the fashionable libertine, the Duke of Guisebury. The play centred round these two. While the Duke was entertaining in his magnificent mansion with its vast cere-monial staircase and sumptuous furnishings, David Ives, the girl's father, dropped in to ruin the party by denouncing the Duke and pronouncing a curse upon his daughter. But vice was not to be permitted to get away with it, for the Duke—having squan-dered the last of his fortune—is about to commit suicide by drinking poison when there is a pathetic touch. He is saved at the last moment by a girl he has rescued from being run over by a cab. There is after all some good in everyone.

The critics were ecstatic over Tree's portrayal of the Duke. It combined lightness of touch, easy comedy and an exhibition of high courage, contempt of danger, and a grim sardonic humour as the Duke's troubles encompassed him.

A synopsis of the scenery gives a good idea of this drama.

Act I: The Beautiful Pagan (Scene, the Isle of St. Endellion)

Act II: The Broken Bowl—A Villa at Richmond

Act III: The last Feast—Guisebury House, St James's Park

Act IV: The Isle of St. Endellion

With all these monstrous scene changes it was not surprising that the first performance took four hours. In spite of all this and Julia Neilson's dress coming undone, the play received universal acclaim, but possibly not from Maud for it was remarked by several critics that Mrs. Tree was not in the play. Maud later remarked that by the autumn of 1891 she had learned to love and admire Julia, but by that time dear Julia was safely out of the emotional way and married to Fred Terry. Maud admitted that in the beginning she did not harbour tender feelings towards dear Julia.

Maud had many admirable qualities, not the least being the truthful way in which she made no secret of her jealousies public or private, marital or professional. But jealousy is tiring to live with and often provokes the very things which it fears. This was to be the case with Maud and Herbert.

Chapter 4

A Secret 'Wife'

'To perpetuate his race is the natural instinct of man.'
HERBERT BEERBOHM TREE

Some time in the late eighties or early nineties, Herbert met
Beatrice May Pinney. She seems to have been born on 23rd May
1871 in Ramsgate, Kent, the daughter of a Professor of Music,
William Pinney. How he met her and what she looked like
remains a mystery. She was a sphinx who kept her secret. But she
obviously had some quality which attracted Herbert towards her,
and kept him attracted, because he had six children by her.
Possibly she had that cosy *gemütlichkeit* which Maud lacked, so
that his wife was the *maîtresse en titre*, while May was the soft
weibchen which the German side of his nature needed. She must
have been a lady of a long-suffering character because her large
family was stretched out from the 1890s to the coronation of King
George V in 1911 twenty years later.

Had she, like the woman described in one of Tree's short
stories, the peculiar fascination, when engaged in conversation,
of saying with her eyes: 'This is the moment of my life: I have not
lived in vain'? Or had she some extra qualities? Tree wrote:
'Ever since I first beheld the generous curves of Mrs. Noah, and
first tasted the insidious carmine of her lips, have I regarded the
wife of Noah as symbolical of the supreme type of womanhood.'
Was Miss Pinney the living embodiment of the Mrs. Noah of
Herbert's dreams?

Four of her children were born at Daisyfield, a house in a
respectable part of London, where Wandsworth runs into Putney
and verges on to Wimbledon Common. In its day it was regarded
as the upper-class end of Wandsworth and the massive detached
houses standing in their large gardens were prosperously and
respectably Victorian. But Daisyfield seems to have been different.
It had belonged to a painter called John Brett, an Associate of the

Royal Academy. Beatrix Potter refers to it in her Journal. 'Went to Mr. Brett's Daisyfield, Putney Hill. His house is a curiosity, planned by himself, all on one floor, in the ecclesiastical cruciform, without fireplaces—or originally doors, but it was so uncomfortable that they added some. According to Mr. Wilson, Mr. and Mrs. Brett repose in the Lady Chapel.'

Herbert must have bought, or rented, the house some time in the late nineties, for the Byam Shaws referred to his having a house on Putney Hill in the early 1900s. Most of the old houses have long since been demolished to give way to blocks of flats and Daisyfield, with its ecclesiastical architecture and cruciform shape, has also disappeared.

The eldest sons of May Pinney and Herbert were born some time in the late eighties or early nineties between Viola and his younger legitimate daughters Felicity (1894) and Iris (1896). These two sons were certainly not born at Daisyfield because Mr. Brett, who also had a very large family, was living there in 1895.

It has been recorded that Maud was furiously jealous of Tree's 'American' sons, but the sons she was jealous of were not American, they were English and living within a few miles of his legitimate family. Possibly Maud had found out about his liaison with May and there was a loving reconciliation, a renunciation of May and a temporary return of Herbert to the marital bed. Maud may have hoped that she might have sons herself, as obviously Herbert was capable of achieving this. To the Victorians sons were a crowning achievement, necessary because they were the inheritors and in an age which attached great importance to inheritance and to material goods, sons to take over were a stake in the future and an assurance that the inheritance could be secured and held. Herbert's family was not an insignificant one and it was natural that he should wish for sons.

Not that the perpetuation of his race was the sole reason for Herbert's extra-marital activities. He felt, as he wrote in one of his short stories, that he was a slave to his sense of beauty, and 'excused his flitting temperament to a friend by lamenting that he resembled the cherubim which have only wings—they lack the wherewithal to repose'. Perhaps Herbert found repose in the Lady Chapel at Daisyfield. Herbert's excuse was that he was unable to hurt a woman's feelings. Maud's comment was wittier.

'Herbert's affairs start with a compliment and end with a confinement.'

Being everything to everyone by turns, and everything sincerely, leads to certain subterfuges, and to lead a double life, in an age which valued respectability above everything, was not an easy double to achieve.

Herbert, while being sensitive to public opinion in his theatre, even to the point of puritanism, yet managed to father his large family, and keep his public reputation intact. It was no wonder that on being asked how he was, he replied 'Radiant!' He had a good deal to be radiant about.

How he managed it leads to interesting speculations. He liked to give the impression that he was much less astute than he was. This facility became a useful cover. He was constantly leaping into hansom cabs and supposedly being unable to remember his destination. One cabbie asked 'Where to?' and Herbert replied, 'Home.' 'Where's that?' asked the cabbie peering through the hole into the hansom cab. 'You don't think I am going to tell you where my beautiful home is?' But after any companion had got out of the cab, he would be able to tell the cabbie to drive quickly to 'Daisyfield'.

Herbert, it was said, lived in and for his theatre. But he also had time to visit the loving arms of May Pinney.

In 1891 Maud had moved to 77 Sloane Street, a tall Georgian house which faced Cadogan Gardens. Once more she set to work with interior decorators, and achieved a white dining-room, a green drawing-room, a blue drawing-room, nurseries and a study for Herbert. The bill of poor Mr. A., who had re-done the house, hung heavily on Maud's hands. But she wrote happily, that she felt that its burden weighed more seriously on Mr. A.'s mind than on hers.

The house was dainty, there were three or four servants to minister to the needs of the family including the dear cook, Mrs. Browning, who produced not only dinner for the family at five o'clock, but supper for whoever Herbert cared to bring home after the play.

While Maud was busy with decorators to provide a setting for social activities and the furthering of Herbert's fame, Herbert was fathering his other family.

There were no children of his marriage for the ten years after

1884 when Viola was born, 'a constant joy', as Maud called her. She was also a constant joy to Herbert who revelled in her precocious wit. But Herbert's temperament was hardly destined for sexual abstinence and Edwardian women who wished to retain their elegant waists and their full social lives very often took refuge in headaches, 'delicate health', or memories of difficult confinements to achieve their ends. Husbands outwardly submitted to chaste kisses and separate bedrooms, while making their own arrangements. Whole quarters of London were given over to discreet ladies who fulfilled functions too coarse or inconvenient for Edwardian wives and mothers to consider— except as a treat. St. John's Wood was the best known of these districts. When James Davis (Owen Hall, the writer of musical comedies such as *Floradora* and many others) died someone remarked, 'He was much loved—there was not a house in St. John's Wood without a drawn blind.'

Tree chose a less obvious district. May Pinney was a different type of woman. Herbert was a man who was always on show, always planning, constantly writing down amusing remarks to be popped into plays, used to liven up dinner parties, or keep a restaurant table laughing. He wrote astonishing numbers of letters, his brain was never inactive and he was soon bored. But in everyone there is a public and private face. There must be moments, and people, who help to relax and revive the soul. For a man with a dozen masks, and a bubbling radiant public personality, and a wife who courted the rich and the aristocratic, there were moments when he wanted someone who said nothing when he sat by the fire in the winter, or watched a child at play in the sun. A comfortable easy woman who was prepared to share a feather bed and did not demand to be seen in public and above all was always there, always available and always undemanding.

Sometimes it is the woman who demands nothing and who accepts in simplicity who can attract and keep a man. Herbert wrote that it is for the man to give and the woman to forgive. His women had a great deal of forgiving to do. His first successful stage part had been founded on the words, 'I thought I met a petticoat on the stairs.' Herbert met many petticoats both coming and going on the stairs, the trouble was that he never was able to let them pass by.

But it seems as if Beatrice May Pinney had some especial quality for Herbert, for even in the last year of his life he was still in touch with her and still making plans for her comfort, as perhaps she had always made plans for his.

It would be pleasant to be able to recapture the pseudo family life which May led with Herbert. In the days before telephones were universal it was perhaps easier to trot off to a rendezvous without being traced. On the other hand it was more difficult to set times and dates of arrival. Did he have set dates when he always went to see her? Did he have special messengers who arrived in hansom cabs with loving messages for her, or excuses for his absence? Edwardian plays are full of marital infidelities discovered by the fatal letter and in the absence of telephones it is easy to discover why.

Herbert wrote himself a firm reminder—he must arrange the hours when he would be at the theatre. He must also have arranged the times when he was always to be with May. The summer break from the theatre was long, but it was not so easy to slip out of the family and social round once the season ended. On the other hand Maud was inclined to drift off for holidays with grand friends. Even in the first years of her marriage she had spent six weeks touring Egypt with W. S. Gilbert and his wife.

Long visits with aristocratic or theatrical friends in the country by wives gave husbands plenty of rope—and plenty of scope. Yes, he would be quite all right. No, there was no need to trouble the servants, they could be put on 'board wages'. He would have supper at his club while his wife was away. What a gentle, understanding and above all easy husband such a one might seem.

And while servants could put up their feet round the kitchen fire and read of murders in low life and scandals in high life, a handy hansom could carry the unattached male off to the other side of the river, where cosy comfort and willing arms waited, where supper was always ready and there was someone who listened and understood the need for a quiet life.

There is a tendency for actors to carry their parts into real life. When playing in witty comedies they will be gay, airy, debonair, and easy to live with. But wives who find Hamlet at breakfast, or Macbeth in the stilly watches of the night begin to regret the disappearance of Jack Absolute or Benedick. In the early nineties Tree had played seducers in *Beau Austin* and *The Dancing Girl*. No doubt these were reflections of his private life. There is always an excitement about carrying on a double life successfully, especially in a censorious age. Herbert was well aware of the two sides of himself. He realised children were taught that to tell lies was wrong, he had been told that himself, but as he went through life he had found that telling the truth was apt to be equally wrong. Sometimes he admonished himself with a word or two from Wordsworth, 'Avaunt all specious pliancy of mind' but on second thoughts he realised that a man's moods could vary. He might perhaps decide to come to terms with Mammon. Life was simpler if the webs of lies and intrigue could be avoided. Clean, fresh, renewed he could breast the winds of life with a clear mind and a clear conscience. That might be the man's mood after breakfast on a fine day. But his real nature would be there all the time. The inner man would scorn the cautions mask he had donned. He would spring naked into the battle of life.

Herbert did not only get on with the Mammon of unrighteousness—he made a friend of him. He slapped him on the back. There was no one who did not find Tree kind and willing to help. He had none of the censoriousness of his age, though when it came to his plays he respected its standards, while ignoring them himself.

The question that poses itself was what Beatrice May Pinney (Mrs. Reed by deed poll) told her children? It was an age when children were not expected to know anything about the lives of the godlike adults who surrounded them. Secrets were easy to keep. Did Herbert pose as the inevitable 'uncle' or 'guardian' of so many stories of the period? Did Mrs. Reed invent some exotic occupation for the man of her choice. When registering the births of his children it was stated that Herbert Reed was 'of independent means', a nice gentlemanly phrase which could cover a multitude of sins and omissions. Did Mrs. Reed tell the neighbours that Mr. Reed (of independent means) was an intrepid traveller who spent much of his time abroad? How did she explain his constant comings, and equally swift goings? Or did she live a quiet domestic suburban life keeping herself to herself, as it was possible to do in those days, with a faithful servant or two to keep her secrets and help her bring up her fathered, but fatherless brood.

*

In the summer of 1891 Herbert studied Hamlet, and according to most of his critics, not to his advantage. It was produced at the Haymarket at the beginning of 1892. Shaw was a music critic at the time and Tree asked him to the dress rehearsal to hear the music which Henschel had composed for the production. Shaw said that he had never heard of a tragedian regarding incidental music as having any interest. Usually the music consisted of the March from *Judas Maccabaeus* for the entry of the Court and the Dead March in Saul for Hamlet's death. But true to his character Shaw spent the intervals explaining to Tree how he should have played Hamlet to which Tree listened with the utmost patience.

Most of the critics found Tree's Hamlet simply Tree with a flaxen beard and wig. Alfred Sutro, the playwright, wrote that it was not a role to which he was suited. He over-romanticised the part, making of Hamlet the sentimental lover. After the 'get thee to a nunnery' speech, he came quietly back and kissed Ophelia's long tresses. It was an over-flowery Hamlet—in the grave scene Tree reappeared with flowers for Ophelia's grave and the church-yard scene itself was cheerful with blossoming trees, birds trilling, and flowery hills in the background. Yet Tree had noted the welling sadness of *Hamlet* as a play. It was as if he could not bear to make it as sad as it should be.

But there were a few voices raised in his favour. Frederic Harrison thought the production which had no scenery, only rich tapestries, was most effective. He liked Tree's interpretation and he had seen nearly twenty Hamlets, from Macready and Phelps to Irving and Sarah Bernhardt.

Tree was naturally anxious that his friends should appreciate his performance and asked John Hare to watch it, putting him in the Royal Box. Hare sat through the performance. Tree popped in during the intervals and still Hare did not say a word. Afterwards they had supper and still John Hare said nothing. Tree saw him to his carriage and as it was about to drive off, popped his head in at the window: 'At any rate it *is* a fine play, Johnnie, isn't it?' Then he waved his hand to the coachman and John Hare drove off.

Maud was ecstatic and with reason, she had been praised as Ophelia. Never in the world had there been an Ophelia or a Hamlet so religiously dedicated to their parts and with what reverential glory they handled them. She used to sit in the wings and watch Herbert over and over again as he played the Royal

Dane. It filled her with wonder that he could merge his own sunny character into that of the sweet Prince.

W. S. Gilbert took a less exalted view—remarking that he had never seen anything so funny in his life—and yet it was not in the least vulgar. But the public loved it and the theatre was full for the whole season.

As usual, Tree was bombarded with letters from every side, for there is no one who has read or seen *Hamlet* who is without a theory on its inner meaning. But the editor of *Punch*, F. C. Burnand, was more concerned about the effects, especially the ghostly effects. Tree admitted that he had been nervous about these, for the only realistic ghost is the reflected ghost. He ended his letter by shrugging off his critics with a joke. His daughter Viola had asked him for a pony, he had told her he could not afford one. She looked at him sternly, if he could afford to put on *Hamlet* he could surely afford to buy her a pony, perhaps if he acted Hamlet *better* he might have the money for a pony.

In 1893 Tree produced six plays. Four have been forgotten but the fact that they included Ibsen's *An Enemy of the People* and Oscar Wilde's *A Woman of No Importance* is testimony to the catholicity of Tree's taste.

Tree had known Wilde for some years and, before he had met him, had already written a skit for *Punch* which satirized his style: 'I took the Newdigate—some man gets the Newdigate every year, but not every year does the Newdigate get an Oscar.' They had been friends and Tree was one of the few people who took Wilde's talents seriously. He had been trying to get him to write a play for the Haymarket for some time. But Wilde countered Tree's requests by jokes. 'As Herod in my *Salomé* you would be admirable. As a peer of the realm in my latest dramatic drama— I do not see you.'

Tree remarked that he was playing the Duke in Henry Arthur Jones's *The Dancing Girl*.

'Ah,' said Oscar quickly, 'that's just it—before you can successfully impersonate the character I have in mind, you must forget you ever played Hamlet, or Falstaff, and above all you must forget that you ever played a Duke in a Melodrama by H. A. Jones.'

Tree said he would do his best. Wilde added that perhaps he had better forget that he had ever acted at all. Tree asked why. Wilde said: 'Because this witty aristocrat whom you wish to assume in my play is quite unlike anyone who has ever been seen on the stage—he is like no one who has existed before.'

Tree said: 'My God, he must be supernatural.' Wilde said: 'He is certainly not natural—he is a figure of art, indeed he is myself.'

Oscar went down to Norfolk to finish the play and while he was there he heard of the death of Tree's father, Julius. Wilde wrote to Herbert very kindly, saying how much he had enjoyed meeting Julius Beerbohm and how proud he was of his son's success. Irving, always devoted to sending telegrams, wired from Ellen Terry's house in Winchelsea, 'Sincere sympathy, dear Tree, have just heard sad news.'

But Tree himself simply wrote down the date of his father's death with no comment at all, as if he could not bear to elaborate on the inevitable parting with someone he had loved.

To Irving Tree wrote, 'My father's was a very sweet and at the same time deep and reserved nature. To him death had no terror, for he possessed the most precious of all gifts—a simple and staunch religious faith. . . . We buried him yesterday—my wife sent a wreath with the words 'wearing the white flower of a blameless life'. I believe it applied to him.'

Herbert and Maud set out on their autumn tour and when they reached Glasgow some time in October Oscar arrived to read his play. Tree was delighted with it and the contract was drawn up. Oscar and Herbert enjoyed one another's company and revelled in one another's wit. Maud remembered the days of the rehearsals and the endless luncheons and suppers as full of fun. When Oscar was present, there was sharp intellect, wit and a great heightening of life's gaiety. A delicious part had been given to her and for once there was no necessity for tears, wailing or gnashing of teeth.

There was less difficulty between author and actor than usual, and Wilde told Tree that he would always regard him as the best critic of his plays. 'I have never criticised your plays,' said Tree. 'That's why,' said Oscar.

The play was a great success and Tree revelled in the witticisms of Lord Illingworth. Wilde summed up his feelings about Tree: 'Ah, every day dear Herbert becomes *de plus en plus Oscarisé*—it is a wonderful case of Nature imitating art,' and when someone else mentioned Herbert to him, Oscar said: 'A charming fellow—he models himself on me.'

Three years later, in 1895, Wilde's last play, *The Importance of*

Being Earnest was produced. In the same year came his disgrace. But Tree did not forget Wilde. When he heard that he was in need of money—he not only sent it but wrote Oscar an encouraging letter. He remembered the brilliance of Oscar's plays, there was no one to match him in wit or distinction. He was sure that Oscar's talents must dazzle once more. Most of all he remembered the kindness and courtesy which Oscar had always shown him. Herbert's devout hope was that he should not be overwhelmed by the troubles which beset him.

Tree was not to be numbered amongst those who passed by on the other side of the road leaving the man set on by robbers wounded in the ditch.

*

Maud's acting career reached a high point in 1892 with the parts in *Hamlet* and Oscar Wilde. Perhaps her acting reflected her happiness, for she and Herbert had become closer again, and after ten years Felicity was born in 1894.

Had the renewal of their marital love been brought about by Herbert's grief at the death of his father and the contemplation of the blameless life of Julius? Or had Maud found out about Mrs. Reed, and her two sons, Claude and Robin, and wished desperately for sons of her own? The questions remain unanswered. The only fact is that the child was born at 77 Sloane Street. This house was to be the family home for ten years, quite a record for Maud. Perhaps it indicated a stability which she felt at the time.

It is curious that in her writings Maud weaves a web of sentimentality around her life, like a cocoon of spun sugar, and yet many of her recorded sayings are penetrating and perceptive. She was like a romantic writer whose writings drip with beauty and romance, and yet when it comes to the publisher's contract proves sharper than any agent. Real life did not enter into Maud's writings, which were purely for public consumption.

The Trees' second daughter was born in December. Maud called the baby Felicity, a name which reflected the overflowing feeling of happiness which filled her soul. In a curio shop called Juliano's, she discovered an amulet with the word 'Felicity' written in Arabic. What more perfect present for Herbert—while he wore it his days would be filled with great happiness. Herbert, not to be outdone, weighed in with a brooch with the same lovely name wrought in diamonds. But when the baby was only five weeks old, Maud had to leave this new miracle in her life. She was to start on her first American tour with Herbert. With regret Maud left Felicity and Viola surrounded by a host of devoted aunts, nurses and loving friends and set sail for America.

They left for New York and for the first time for many years Maud had Herbert to herself. Looking back on those eight golden days at sea she felt that they were the high point of her life. Their only two travelling companions were Max who, being a bad sailor, disappeared and was never seen on the voyage, and Lionel Brough, an actor in the Company who, although a good sailor, also kept out of sight. Herbert, for once, was not ill, but he trembled on the verge of feeling that he *might* be seasick and on that account he was wistfully inclined to be waited upon and looked after. How heavenly for Maud. What was nicer for a wife who had so often suffered under the moods of a husband which veered from dominating to elusive than to have him entirely to herself? She adored the long days with Herbert so submissive, so grateful for her ministrations. Maud pondered her jealousies and reflected that a wife could not be happy until she had her husband safely in bed—with a linseed poultice. What was this passion to monopolize? Was it love or hatred in its egotism? She could not answer her own question. She only remembered the ship which seemed so devoid of passengers that it belonged to Herbert and herself. They sat on the deck wrapped in fur rugs, watching the porpoises, seeing a shadow on the horizon which was said to be an iceberg.

And then suddenly it was over. The sun caught the statue of Liberty. They had arrived. The dream week was finished. The ship was swarming with reporters who surrounded Herbert and elbowed Maud out of the way. New York reporters had a tough reputation, but they did not deter Herbert who remarked that after being interviewed in America he feared no foe. When the interviewing was over, Herbert found Maud in their cabin, weeping, because her happy hours in sole possession of Herbert were over. He dried her tears and promised that the golden days would come again. But according to Maud they never did.

It is hard not to pity Maud. She was clever, pretty, intuitive and she made a splendid public wife for Herbert. But like many women she wanted to keep the man and eat him. She knew her ruling passion and could not control it. Herbert on the other hand was well aware of his failings and shrugged them off. Like a swimmer he plunged into seas of feminine emotions and like a swimmer as swiftly shook the sea water out of his eyes and went on with his life. He admitted that he was a many-sided and complicated man, and deep down had no intention of changing his ways. He could resist everything except temptation and a man in his position, running his own theatre, had plenty of temptation to choose from. His boyish nature was always ready for any diversion, and his strong sexual appetites made the gratification of those diversions easy.

It is fortunate for men, and unfortunate for women, that men who like women find them easy to collect. They also find them just as easy to discard. The attraction which Maud had felt, and still felt, so strongly towards Herbert, was also felt by other women and her possessiveness only made her case more acute. But as Herbert remarked ruefully: to be understood—is to be found out.

But she dried her tears and as Herbert was taken over by the New York reporters, she went to their hotel. It was the best hotel in New York, an amalgam of Versailles, the Winter Palace, and the best parts of the Vatican. Maud felt like Marie Antoinette in her heyday. The rooms were full of Parma violets, sheaves of American Beauty roses, giant cyclamen plants, and forests of lilies-of-the-valley.

*

While Maud revelled in the luxury of her Louis XVI suite, May was leading her quiet domestic life in the suburbs. It is possible to wonder what she felt. Had Herbert given her to understand that all was over between them? Or had she been left with money in the bank and hope in her heart?

The difficulties of tracing Herbert's complicated life are made all the greater because Maud was concerned to keep his public image shining and his halo polished. A discreet mention of 'affairs' is one thing, but troops of under the blanket children are quite another. It is a curious thing that a large family of small children seemed to Herbert some sort of odd joke. For some reason, remarked Maud sharply, there were a great number of children in *Hamlet*.

But in 1895 Maud and Herbert were, temporarily, as one, and being fêted in New York. They had arrived at a moment when America was becoming itself, it had all the refinements of Europe, and was very much richer. It was the height of the New York season and even Maud was impressed. The beauty, the clothes and the tiaras glittering on every graceful head to her made London seem pale in comparison.

Herbert and Maud joined in the gaieties for six weeks and were overwhelmed with parties, people and publicity. It all seemed as if Tree had simply fallen on his feet as usual. But he had made careful preparations for the trip. He had already been extensively interviewed in London. He had read the American papers to get an idea of the tastes of New York and the type of plays which were likely to appeal.

A long article by Gilbert Parker appeared in *Lippincott's Magazine* before his arrival.

It started with a fanfare of trumpets.

America has seen several of the notable actors of England . . . she has yet to see and she will see soon Mr. H. Beerbohm Tree and I venture to prophesy not a hospitality which will spring alone from the generous courtesy which the American people extend to the illustrious but from a sound intrinsic appreciation of a distinguished and powerful actor. It is a common thing to say of Mr. Tree that he is singularly versatile; but the word versatile has the feeling of smartness, of juggling with the talents as it were; it does not express continuity, consistency, the force of a masterful temperament—searching, glowing, attractive. These are the things concerning this outstanding man which should be seen illustratively through this article. I want to give the idea of a man who has an individuality which must be taken into large account; an idiosyncrasy in his art which is at once a style and an impulse, a stage manner which is not a mannerism even when it comes at times near to the fantastical, but is rather a kind of idiom of— shall I say the word—genius?

The article ran to over 2,000 words, for in an age when journalists were paid badly, they were given plenty of space to expand.

It was a paean of praise and, even allowing for the fact that it was advance publicity and that Parker was an aspiring playwright, it does give a contemporary view of the attractions of Tree's acting and explains his hold on his public. The writer went on to say that when he used the word *genius* in writing of Mr. Beerbohm Tree what he wished to emphasise was that it signified 'presence'. The general effect of a personality, the vital influence which produced effects, by simply being, not acting. 'It is that persuasive something which fills a room, a place; which bulks materially almost as much as it suggests. . . . Mr. Tree himself touched upon this in his well-written, pungent, and wise lecture on "The Imaginative Faculty".'

Parker then quotes Tree's idea on acting: 'By the aid of his imagination he becomes the man, and behaves unconsciously as the man would, or should behave; this he does instinctively rather than from any conscious study, for what does not come spontaneously may as well not come at all. Even the physical man will become transformed.'

But while Tree was giving the impression that everything was plucked out of the air, he was busy scribbling in his notebooks a jumble of ideas, impressions and even replies to be used when he was interviewed, foreseeing possible questions from sharp New York reporters. There was no point in walking off the gangplank unprepared.

Yes, he had hoped to travel with the company. He asked himself the reason why he had not gone with the company. He could not answer his own question and passed on to other possible topics. He told his imaginary interviewer that he not only had many American friends in England, but that America seemed to him to be the promised land of the theatrical manager. Although he had always hated and dreaded the sea, it was worth crossing it to reach a promised land. He would give his interviewers a quick idea of the plays his company would act, adding a rider that versatility was of the essence. Maybe the American idea of versatility was different from the English, but as far as he was concerned he saw his mind as a blank page. That was it. A blank page. It was the same with acting. He might not be able to carry out his ideas when he was acting a part, but what he felt was that the whole being must be poured into the part, the actor must *become* the character. He would become the man—without study.

But Tree did study when he was abroad or on long sea voyages. He had been reading, while he was on board, *Studies of Shakespeare* by Richard Grant White. Some things in the book pleased him. The study of Iago had hit the nail on the head, but in the essay on Hamlet, White did not seem to soar as a critic to the imaginative height of the character. The eye of the critic was cabined and confined compared with the illimitable standard of the imaginative artist. Then Tree wrote down a phrase about Hamlet which he was later to use in a short story: 'He was everything by turns and everything sincerely'. To Tree that seemed to sum up the tragedy of Hamlet. He goes on to copy out the writer's idea on Iago, 'Yes, Iago is essentially the man who slaps others on the back. He was orally colour-blind. To such men it is no shock to do ill—it costs them nothing—they do not blush as they look at themselves in the looking-glass—while to others to *do* mean things is, as it were, more expensive than to suffer in not getting what they wanted.'

He then makes a note about the Elizabethan habits of wearing miniatures, and draws a picture of 'fardells' (*sic*) and another little caricature of a plump, nearly naked, man carrying them, as if to imprint on his mind the feeling of carrying them. Herbert thought that nothing was so fatiguing as rest and even when he was resting, being cossetted on board his Atlantic liner by the loving, if possessive, Maud, his mind was busy.

Once arrived in New York, he became the theatrical manager. Deep thoughts were put aside for the *sturm und drang* of rehearsals and the necessary publicity for his first visit to the United States.

He had chosen his plays with care. Versatility being his forte, he was out to astonish. The first two were *Gringoire*, in which he played the starving revolutionary poet, followed by *The Red Lamp* with himself as the loose-lipped cat-footed Demetrius.

Most actors like to play *Hamlet*. Tree's Hamlet had not been well received in London. Judging by his notebooks he had thought long and deeply about the character, but in spite of that and what was called his 'seeing himself as a sensitive physical machine', Hamlet was not one of his successes, but to a foreign audience it might be new and better received. The Americans had not seen quite so many Hamlets as the critics in London and, with any luck, they might not know the play quite so well.

There was also another reason for playing Hamlet—Maud was

to play Ophelia. When playing the part Maud insisted on having fresh flowers at every performance for she felt that tearing the living flowers to pieces would give that extra edge to her acting. It also added considerably to the cost, but that was never a consideration which weighed heavily with Maud.

Tree also played Falstaff in New York, with Maud playing Mistress Ford, and then finally a new play given in London the previous year, *A Bunch of Violets*, one of the usual adaptations from the French by Sydney Grundy. When one reads the words 'adapted from the French' in connexion with Victorian and Edwardian plays, it is always tempting to substitute the word 'bowdlerised' for adapted. But Gilbert Parker in his article on Tree's acting brings his performance in this play sharply to life.

You can guess what most actors will do in given situations; you cannot guess by what singular, sometimes masterly, touch Mr. Tree will make a situation powerful. Possibly it will be the touch of total inaction, of an apparent arrest of every function of movement and purpose, the seeming numb silence of mind and body. One of his latest *A Bunch of Violets* affords me an evidence of this particular thing. In the third act, when all the schemes of the central figure have gone agley, his villany [*sic*] discovered, his wife and child vanished, ruin and vile shame staring him in the face—he does nothing. That is it. There is the secret force of the scene; no melodrama, no moaning, no trepidation, no violence of manner or words, no distortion of sense or sentiment to produce an unusual stage effect, but something silent, stricken, amazed, dumbed, distressfully awry: a guilty man, having played big game and lost, paralyzed as he faces the future.

So Mr. Tree presents him, sitting haggard and stony; and the effect is much finer than the play itself gives warrant for. That is something of what I mean by the action of presence: the inner man, the imaginative, the being with the temperament, producing effects by the sheer power to chill the stage—that is, to fill the eye and the receptive sense of an audience; the great actor has this quality always, for he has that distinctiveness, that outstanding something, which attracts.

Mr. Tree had obviously fascinated Mr. Parker and not only Mr. Parker. He had chosen a programme which fascinated his

New York critics and the American public. *Quel tour de force*—
Hamlet, Falstaff, the spy Demetrius and the defeated husband in
A Bunch of Violets.

Maud watched with pride as Herbert conquered New York. He
had cleverly chosen his parts for contrast—the starving poet
Gringoire and then the cat-footed Demetrius in *The Red Lamp*.
His disguises were perfect—how could anyone find Herbert in
either part? Even the critics rose to him on the first night. It was
small wonder that his acting became the rage of New York. For
Demetrius was followed by his strange silent playing in *A Bunch
of Violets* and finally Falstaff. Such versatility had never been seen
before.

Maud gave herself a modest pat on the back. She had been
praised, perhaps not overpraised, but to play the Princess Morakoff, Mrs. Murgatroyd, Ophelia and Mrs. Ford in *The Merry Wives*
did prove her ability to portray a range of parts. She may have
been playing second fiddle to Herbert, but at this moment in her
life even the second fiddle was playing a sweet melody.

Maud and Herbert took New York to their hearts and New
York opened its arms to them. Maud was instantly impressed by
the chic of the women. She had been lent all Lady Granby's
jewels, and even with those and her best brocade she still felt
shabby. There were many grand ladies in the city but they did not
move stiffly about their grand houses as they would have done in
London—they moved with cheerful *élan*, as full of wit and gaiety
as Margot Tennant; they danced with grace and verve, they did
imitations, they were as cheerful and carefree as children. Even the
correct young men in their correct clothes were equally light-
hearted—Maud felt perhaps that it was their electric climate which
made them so carefree.

Max gives a sharply observed picture of Herbert's attitude to
fame and to reporters. He never became used to fame and was
constantly amazed at the interest of his public, invitations from
the illustrious and innumerable 'fan' letters. They always took
him by surprise as if the sun had come out in bleak mid-winter.
'It was characteristic of his complexity,' wrote Max, 'that he was
greatly bemused at his own naiveté. He once handed me a letter
from a stranger who had seen him act on the previous night.
"That's very nice" I said after reading it. "Very," said he. "I can
stand any amount of flattery so long as it's fulsome enough."'

He arrived in New York in January and liked everything he saw. The overheated rooms and the over-iced street, the low voices of the men and the high voices of the women. He never grumbled at different customs, not even at having to make a speech at the end of the penultimate act. If members of his company grumbled, he was not of their number. Max remarked that he had never admired Herbert more than on this first trip to America.

Max had reason to be grateful, he was being paid for the trip—as a secretary. But a very bad one he turned out to be. By the time he had polished every shining phrase, the pile of letters to be answered had grown ever higher, and Herbert had to engage a professional secretary—but he still went on paying Max.

Herbert liked the company of men younger than himself and with them he lost his vagueness, he seemed more at ease. The young men of the nineties suffered much from pomposity and Paterism, and this amused Herbert. He was prepared to sit up until the early hours of the morning listening to Max and his friends. 'We did not know how much we amused him,' said Max.

There were moments when even Herbert's radiance failed him. When Tree's company had been playing for a week in New York, they were summoned to give a great Charity matinée at Washington. The idea was that Herbert and Maud should travel by night, act in a scene from *Hamlet* in the afternoon, and be back in New York for the evening performance. Herbert once remarked that wherever he went in the world it always turned out that the weather was 'unusual', as if all countries felt that their weather was predictable. Unfortunately for the Washington trip, the weather turned out to be very unusual indeed. Maud and Herbert boarded the train, had a leisurely luxurious supper and went to bed. They slept soundly and when they woke—it was still dark, the train was not moving. They looked at their watches—it was ten a.m. They heard dull thuds. And then the news broke. They were totally encased in a snowdrift and had been for some hours, the dull thuds were the rescuers trying to dig them out.

Herbert gave a very good performance of a trapped lion, raging up and down the train corridor, fretting and fuming. No doubt had he possessed a tail he would have lashed it.

They arrived in Washington in time for the matinée, but the evening performance in New York was off. Maud, always alive to publicity possibilities, was well aware that the bills which had to be posted up all over the town did not harm their success in New York, but rather drew attention to the plays. They returned to even better houses. She could afford to regard the whole affair philosophically, but it was obvious that there were better ways of passing one's time than being snowed up with Herbert for several hours. She may have regarded it as a happy accident, but Herbert took a different view.

They were six weeks in New York and then left for Chicago. New Yorkers had warned them about Chicago—an uncivilised place with its million factories, noises and lawlessness (sandbagging a stranger in the street was current fashion). But they had a wonderful success there, according to Maud, as the city had become eager for culture and beauty, to add jewels to its wealth. Two weeks at Chicago was followed by a week at Philadelphia and so to Boston.

At Harvard Herbert gave a lecture. Here he was in his element surrounded by bright, intelligent youths. He made the point to them that the sentence, 'Whom the Gods love die young' did not mean that those loved of the Gods died in their youth, but he took it to mean that those whom the Gods love never grow old. It was certainly true of Herbert.

Herbert gave for the first time a performance of his view of Shakespeare's philosophy. He often spoke, and wrote, of the 'darling intelligence of Shakespeare' and here in Harvard he gave his own quirky view of this intelligence. He delivered Hamlet's speech 'To be or not to be' in the voice and manner of Falstaff, and in the voice of Hamlet, Falstaff's speech on 'Honour' in Henry IV. Kean once remarked of one of the high points of his acting 'the pit rose to me'—so did the students at Harvard rise to Herbert. He had his own darling intelligence which was ever new and ever lively, something which appealed to the young because it was never pompous and never stale.

Maud went to Vassar and felt that it out-Girtoned English women's universities. Here she saw the kind of life she would have liked had she continued in her career. The libraries weighed down with the carefully garnered wisdom of many poets and philosophers and on the walls reproductions of old Masters. What a setting for a girl to acquire beauty and culture!

From Boston they went again to Washington. The President

came to their opening night and they were bidden to be presented at the White House.

The ceremony was far greater than it had been when they had met Queen Victoria. Past endless policemen, soldiers, servants they were ushered through room after room, reception chambers, ante-rooms, corridors, staircases—and at every turn arms were levelled and pistols presented. Then finally they came into the Presence—and met President Cleveland, a large man of great charm, simple, affable, and amusing.

Two weeks later they left America—loaded with toys for their children.

The tour had not been a financial success. The parties, the receptions and the fêting in America often give the impression of success, but when the accountants get to work, it is discovered that the profit is small. Nor had the American critics been universally acclaiming.

Unfortunately actors are not as a rule very interested in accounts, and Herbert was no exception. It was the project which interested him, and not the profit.

But in America—by one of those happy accidents which seemed to come to him—Herbert found his greatest success, *Trilby*.

Chapter 5

'Come Svengali, Play us
some Music'

When Herbert was acting in Philadelphia, Paul Potter's adaptation of du Maurier's *Trilby* was being played at one of the theatres. As it was drawing the town, Herbert suggested Max should see it. It was hardly to be expected that the dapper Max with his neat classical taste should be able to see *Trilby* as a potential money-maker—even if he had been interested in the making of money, which he was not. Sent to report on the play, he managed to sit through it. When the brothers met after the theatre Max said that the play was the greatest nonsense and could not do anything but fail in London.

Herbert forgot all about it, but on the last days of his American trip the company were having a day off to see Niagara Falls. Herbert stayed behind to see *Trilby*. It was a wise decision. For when he finally did see the Falls, some years later, he looked at them and remarked, 'Is that all?'

On this first trip, he skipped the wonders of nature to watch two acts of *Trilby*. He left Maud in their box and went round and bought the play at once. The following day he sailed for England with the manuscript in his pocket. He may not have made money in America but he had the means of making money in his grasp.

But at the moment of getting back to London he had ideas of planning a more certain success than *Trilby*. What better than the combination of Victorien Sardou, the most popular playwright of his age, Mrs. Patrick Campbell, the return of Mrs. Bancroft to the London stage, and himself as an evil villain? Tree chose to open his London season with *Fedora* (adapted from the French of Sardou by Herman Merivale).

Tree had come to the realisation of Mrs. Pat's drawing power rather late. She wrote that she had called to see Mr. Beerbohm

Tree a year or two before her great success as Paula Tanqueray and asked him for a small part at £4 a week. He was, she said, rather hurried and nervous in manner, and said there was no opening for her. Later he excused this lapse by saying that it was dark, and he had not seen her face.

But during the run of *The Second Mrs. Tanqueray* he offered her £60 a week. Actors can be forgiven for thinking that other actors are only worth what the box office brings in. Besides, Tree was never a manager who surrounded himself with nonentities. As Shaw wrote to Ellen Terry: 'He surrounds himself with good actors and does not mind if they act him off the stage—look to it, Ellen.'

There were other things which Shaw admired about Tree. He had an open mind, he had even had the courage to stage Ibsen's *An Enemy of the People*. Shaw's passion for Ibsen had perhaps fatigued the easily bored Tree, for later Herbert wrote in his notebook, 'What do they know of Ibsen who only Ibsen know?' It sounds as if he had had a session with Mr. Shaw and his obsession. But on his return to London Tree put the idea of Ibsen out of his mind. Sardou was a draw, and so was Mrs. Pat. Besides, Tree had her under contract and although she was acting in the successful *The Notorious Mrs. Ebbsmith* he claimed her. 'I was bound by my contract, and he refused to let me break it but Mrs. Ebbsmith did not survive the change of cast,' wrote Mrs. Pat complacently. She was notoriously difficult, and the fact that she was playing Agnes Ebbsmith and forced to rehearse *Fedora* probably did not put her in the best of moods.

The play opened on 25th May 1895. Shaw had been writing for the *Saturday Review* for five months and he was at the peak of his form. He did not like Sardou's plays. It gave him a splendid chance to demolish the piece. He had, he wrote, never seen *Fedora*, 'To see that curtain go up again and again only to disclose a bewildering profusion of everything that has no business in a play, was an experience for which nothing could quite prepare me. The postal arrangements, the telegraphic arrangements, the police arrangements . . .'. The way in which Shaw describes the play gives the impression of an old-fashioned detective story in which the reader is so bewildered by time-tables and whether the murderer could have wriggled his way through the hedge in time to catch the 3.45 and re-appear at dinner immaculately clad in his dinner jacket, that he quite loses interest in the murder.

Nor did Shaw like the characters any better. Tree played Louis Ipanoff, 'a vulgar scoundrel—as far as he is credibly human at all, and Fedora . . . sinks to his level, when on learning that her husband preferred another woman to her, she gloats over his murder.'

Shaw remarked that bad as the play was, Mrs. Campbell's acting was even worse. He was not so censorious of Tree.

Mr. Tree, confronted with the impossible Louis Ipanoff was forced to take the part seriously, and with the help of a Polish make-up, try to pull it through by a creditably awkward attempt at conventional melodramatic acting. . . .

Besides Mrs. Campbell ruined his clothes. Wherever her beautiful white arms touched him—they left their mark. She knelt at his feet and made a perfect zebra of his left leg with bars across it. Then she flung her arms convulsively right round him; and the next time he turned his back there was little to choose between his coatback and his shirt-front. Before the act was over a gallon of benzine would hardly have set him right again.

But Tree had his revenge, according to Shaw, because when he fell on her body at the end of the play he managed to transfer a large black patch to her face. Shaw suggested to Mrs. Campbell that she might try soap and water—it was an excellent cosmetic and had the added merit that it did not mark coats.

When looking back on *Fedora*, Maud took a rose coloured view of the disaster—the play had seemed to her a success without parallel. Mrs. Patrick Campbell at the height of her popularity, her mysterious beauty, passionate wilfulness, and grace, brought the play to wonderful life. For Mrs. Pat, *Fedora* was less gracefully veiled in tulle. She remarked that after two weeks she had *unfortunately* lost her voice, and Mrs. Tree took up the role.

The tone of Mrs. Pat's remarks seem to suggest a certain satisfaction that although Mrs. Tree took up the role, she had almost as speedily to put it down again. Maud had learned the part in one night and played it on the next. While she was pleased with this feat, she was shrewd enough to realise her limitations. In Sardou's tragedy it was only the heroine who counted. Maud knew she had failed. She admitted she had talent, but nothing could match the blazing talent of Stella Campbell. But Maud was

able to recollect her failure, in tranquillity, many years later
when by sheer hard work she had added technique to her talent
and could look back on the past without recrimination.

While keeping *Fedora* afloat with yet another of his sinister
foreigners, Tree was busy with plans. They included the building
of a splendid new theatre.

Opposite the elegant Haymarket Theatre with its classical
façade, there was in Tree's day a decaying theatre, which was
about to be pulled down. It was this site to which Tree turned
his eyes.

It has generally been thought that the success of *Trilby* pushed
Tree towards the realisation of his grandiose schemes, but Maud
makes it clear that he was already busy with the plans for his new
theatre before he bought the play. He was spending his usual
holiday in Marienbad and wrote to Maud, who was obviously
very nervous about his finances and also despondent about her
acting: 'You will only feel bye and bye what an enormous impression you made in *Fedora*. . . . Now dear Maud, *do* enjoy yourself—make up your mind to, and you will, and don't make
troubles for yourself.'

She must not, he wrote, allow herself to mope. There never
was a time when there was so much hope for her future in regard
to the stage. She had made enormous strides during the past year
—and especially this season. He himself was full of hope. The
Marienbad cure would set him up for the entire year. The town
was quite beautiful, the air fresh and cool.

She must leave everything to him. They must see how *Trilby*
turns out, he has been working a good deal at it. Yesterday he had
read the play to a German manager and, feeling very well indeed,
had decided to take mud baths to get rid of his rheumatism. He
had sent some of his suggestions for *Trilby* to du Maurier. In fact
he wrote two or three new scenes of a melodramatic nature to add
to the thrills in the play. Du Maurier had approved his changes.
Then Tree added a note: 'Do tell Viola not to swim or float too
boastfully'. It was a curious phrase and yet it brings to life a
spoiled child who likes to show off and to dare.

When Herbert returned to London, refreshed from his mountain holiday, he went straight to Folkestone and went through
Trilby again with du Maurier, and Tree's scenes were put in.

The next step was to find a Trilby. This was more difficult. The book was so well-known and the character so well described and so idealised, that it was difficult to make a girl of flesh and blood bring to life the fervent, if not fervid, imaginings of so many readers. She had to be tall, with a lovely head, a perfect body, youthful with glowing health, brown hair, blue eyes and the figure of a Venus de Milo. Where could such perfection be found?

With Tree's usual luck he found a girl suited in every particular to the novel's heroine, Dorothea Baird, later to become Irving's daughter-in-law. She had been acting for a year with Ben Greet, touring with his Shakespearean productions, and when Tree and du Maurier met her she was discovered, like a character at the rise of the curtain, lying on a sofa surrounded by books, studying Desdemona.

They engaged her at once.

A gossip writer who went to interview her waxed equally lyrical about meeting her off stage.

On the stage the resemblance to du Maurier's heroine had been perfect. Form and features alike suggested the ministering angel of 'Les trois Angliches at the Place St. Anatole des Arts' but would the resemblance hold good in real life? Trilby herself came downstairs to meet me with parted lips and out-stretched hands wistful and sweet. This was Trilby in the flesh, with a difference though, the singularly level brows were not thick and dark but finely pencilled as if drawn with a camel hair brush in a tone that exactly matched her beautiful golden brown hair which hung down far below her waist and clung in delicious little curves round her broad, low brow.

She was the perfect untouched girl of the period with that added dash of spice which the Left Bank supplied. Nothing was more calculated to arouse the enthusiasm of the dress circle and stalls full of ladies and gentlemen who preferred to keep their ideals unsullied, at least when watching the play.

The play was produced in Manchester in the autumn of 1895 during Tree's autumn tour. Lionel Brough played Taffy, Edmund Maurice the Laird and H. V. Esmond Little Billee, and du Maurier's son Gerald played Zouzou at the large salary of £4 a week. As an entertainment of the period *Trilby* had gay *grisettes*, tuneful melodies and above all Tree playing the best of all his sinister foreigners.

'Svengali, the marvellous Svengali—a weird, spectral Satanic figure which literally took away our breath.' Maud felt that it was a creation that had the sheer force of genius, with its wealth, its unfathomable depths of fantastic, unpremeditated art—the creation was so rich, so rare, so subtle that she said it was beyond estimation and beyond praise. It was also making money.

Shaw was at the first night, but on 2nd November chose to review *The New Magdalen*, by Wilkie Collins, instead. He ended his article: *'Trilby*—no. I have neither time nor space this week for *Trilby*. Trilby can wait—for six months if necessary—though I shall not keep her waiting longer than next Saturday.'

Having paused for breath Shaw was then able to slice into *Trilby* with a great deal of insight and fun. He noted that Trilby was every man's dream, that in the play she had been washed white, her lovers eliminated for the sake of making a correct young English girl of her. Best of all there was Svengali, 'taken seriously at his own foolish valuation, blazed upon with lime-lights, spreading himself intolerably over the whole play with nothing fresh to add to the first five minutes of him'.

Shaw picked out for his utmost scorn the scene where Svengali defies heaven, declares that he is his own God and then topples over with a nasty touch of heart disease—and is restored by reviving draughts of brandy.

Unfortunately, this was one of the splendid scenes which Tree himself had written into the play. Shaw remarked that he got a great deal of amusement out of the absurd scene. And then added that the public deserved nothing better from Mr. Tree. 'It has after all done its silly best to teach him that it wants none of his repeated and honourable attempts to cater for people with some brains.' Shaw was tipping his hat to the man who had produced Ibsen.

The play was, according to Shaw, bright and pleasant, it did not need much acting for all the public wanted was du Maurier's pictures brought to life and this is what the public had been given. He concluded that he would not congratulate Mr. Tree on his Svengali any more than he would dream of congratulating Irving on his doddering old Hero of Waterloo supping his pare-goric.

But if to be successful and rich is the lot of the actor-manager, *Trilby* had achieved that happy accident for Tree. Another bonus for Tree was that he did not seem to tire of acting Svengali as he did of other parts, and he was never two nights alike in it, and revelled in the melodramatic fun. It was one of his greatest trans- formations and in the part he used the quintessence of all the sinister foreigners he had ever played. Even W. S. Gilbert, not over-generous with praise, was impressed with his make-up which was so good, he said, that sitting in the stalls one could almost smell Svengali. The greasy locks, the curling beard, the sliding walk, the mesmeric eyes, and of course, Tree's Germanic thickness of voice—everything added up to one of Tree's best performances. Yet it took him only a matter of minutes to perfect his make-up. Viola once remarked that it took her mother Maud much longer to make herself beautiful than her father took to make himself ugly.

One incident illustrated Tree's perfection of make-up. At the end of the play Svengali had to appear to put his face in a frame, but this bored Tree and at one of the revivals another actor was made up to resemble him. One evening his understudy neglected to turn up and Douglas Jefferies made himself up to fill the gap. When he met Tree on his way out of the theatre—Tree stopped for a moment, looked with amazement at Jefferies and said: 'Oh My God! The Saviour!'

Other men did not have his capacity to transform the physical man as Tree did. There remains a mirror from Tree's dressing room and on it he has sketched three impressions in make-up— they are Svengali, Falstaff and Fagin. Perhaps Tree felt that they satisfied him as the best of all his impressions. It may be that Tree used his own face as a distorting mirror to produce different men, as Max his half-brother used his pencil to produce distortions of other men as caricatures.

But the production of *Trilby* did not entirely satisfy Tree's restless mind and, in May of 1895, he produced *Henry IV* (Part I) for a series of matinées. For the production, even Shaw gave Tree a pat on the back. There had been cuts, but the chief merit of the production was that the play had been accepted as Shakespeare wrote it. On the other hand he did not like Mr. Tree as Falstaff. He only wanted one thing to make him an excellent Falstaff, 'that is to get born over again as unlike himself as possible'. He added a rider: perhaps Mr. Tree would seize the part better when he knew his lines.

Shaw's criticisms, always funny, were often perverse. He seems
to have been the only critic who preferred Tree as himself. Most
other writers of the period agree that Tree was a quirky eccentric
actor and when he appeared in the more 'drawing-room' of his
plays he seemed to lose a dimension. On the other hand Maud
Tree was considered by most people, especially other actresses,
to be bad and amateurish, but Shaw found her intelligent and
perceptive. Perhaps she not only looked like one of his own
heroines, but he hoped that she might play one. However he did
not like her as Lady Percy; it was, said Shaw, the first time he had
ever seen Maud play unintelligently.

If Shaw did not like Svengali, the public were suitably impressed and proved it with cash in the till. Tree himself was not
deceived. He enjoyed the fun and the success, yet called the play
'Hogwash'. But like the dwarf spinning the straw into gold, the
hogwash was producing the means to build a theatre on the other
side of the road, a theatre which would give shape and form to
Tree's dreams.

The season at the theatre ended, as was the custom, at the same
time as the London season. Stalls and boxes departed for country
estates, to Cowes, or abroad. Maud went off to Spa to recuperate
from all the excitement. She was pregnant with their third child,
hoping for a boy which would be a crowning joy to Herbert's
success, and for herself as a wife.

Herbert stayed in London rushing about collecting finance. The
family legend was that 'some very nice Jews' put up the money,
but like all big enterprises it was a jigsaw of hopes, dreams—and
large and small contributions. Tree managed to raise a great
deal of the capital himself out of the profits of *Trilby*. Maud was
asked to talk Ernest Cassel, the Anglo-German financier and
grandfather of Lady Louis Mountbatten, into helping. Herbert
with his great enthusiasm was getting a thousand here and two
thousand there from friends and well-wishers, and larger sums
from City sources who were more difficult to manage, wishing to
see immediate cash in hand in return for finance.

But all these comings and goings had not exhausted his
energies. He was planning his second American tour. He proposed
to open it with a play from the eulogistic Mr. Gilbert Parker,
adapted from his book, *The Seats of the Mighty*.

It is quite easy to see what had attracted Tree to this book and its adaptation. Doltaire, the part he was to play, is described in great detail.

> There was in him a dispassionateness, a breadth, which seemed most strange in a trifler of the Court. I sometimes thought that his elegance and flippancy were deliberate, lest he should be taking himself or life too seriously. His intelligence charmed me . . . he was never dull and his cynicism had an admirable grace and cordiality. A born intriguer, he was above intrigue, justifying it on the basis that life was all sport. In logic a leveller, praising the moles as he called them, he nevertheless held to what was best, and that it could not be altered.

Then Gilbert Parker added a sentence which leads to the thought that he had Tree in mind when he thought out the character. 'I never repent, I have done after my nature, in the sway and impulse of our time. . . . And so when all is done we shall miss the most interesting thing of all; ourselves dead and the gap and ruin we leave behind us.'

As Doltaire gracefully stepped into his travelling coach with a flick of his lace handkerchief, so Tree could leap into his hansom cab with a touch of his top hat, an easily recognisable top hat. For as Tree said, 'Heads are made different sizes to enable us to *recognise* our hats.'

Tree could recognise his hat, but like most theatrical managers it was not always possible for him to recognise that a part or play which appealed to him might not have the same effect on an audience. Doltaire was a part with splendid possibilities. There is always a pull for an actor to portray a villain in the silks and fur-belows of the eighteenth century. In addition the setting was new, Canada at the time of Wolfe and Montcalm, and the wars with France. There was, of course, the obligatory virginal heroine on whom the cynical Doltaire had designs, and her young and equally virginal lover, flung into durance vile, while putting a brave Anglo-Saxon face on his imprisonment and impending death on the scaffold.

While collecting his finance for the new theatre, Tree worked with a will on the play with Mr. Parker and set off for America in October of 1895. Maud stayed behind, pregnant and disconsolate in Sloane Street.

Maud and Herbert seem to have been closer than they had been since the beginning of their marriage. To comfort Maud and to compensate her a little for his absence, Herbert had asked her to sit on the Committee planning his new theatre. It was a sensible move. Maud had many talents—she was clever, practical, artistic and good at managing people. Herbert knew her capabilities and relied on them. She, on the other hand, could only think of how closely loving Herbert had been of late and how their lives, at last, seemed to be so firmly knit together in a bond not only of love, but of a marriage of true minds.

Maud was a very good public relations woman and her determination to gloss over her usefulness was simply the necessity to play the 'little woman'. Perhaps at this stage of their life together she felt that she was the little woman, the dutiful wife fulfilling her natural function to produce a son.

But there were squalls physical and metaphorical ahead in the blue sky of Maud's summer of content. Herbert, never an intrepid traveller by sea, had struck a bad storm on his journey out. The ship was driven off course for three days. The company and the ship were battened down. Herbert in his deck cabin was seasick all through this ordeal. Lionel Brough, one of those hearty travellers who plague the seasick, arrived at Tree's cabin door, knocked and announced, 'Get up, all danger is past—you must pull yourself together—I say it respectfully—but be a *man*.'

In response to this admirably British sentiment, Herbert crawled out of his bunk and a sudden lurch of the ship felled him to the ground.

'When I looked around I saw an object lying there—it was labelled "Life Saving Apparatus".'

The lurching of the ship had detached the life-saving gear from the cabin wall. Herbert remarked that having escaped from the perils of the storm it was just *like* a life-saving apparatus to knock him unconscious.

There was another squall ahead. During his absence someone had written to tell Maud of one of Herbert's affairs. Possibly the knowledge of his two sons had come to light, but it is difficult to piece this together because both Max and Maud later went through his diaries and his letters with the utmost care, burning, tearing out, and throwing away. It was perfectly all right to hint at little aberrations, but the existence of a long and continuing relationship with another woman was something quite different and would have reflected on Maud's image of herself and of Herbert.

Maud's loud complaints arrived during the final run through of *The Seats of the Mighty* which was produced at the Lafayette Square Opera House in Washington. It was one thing to play a suave cynic on-stage, but quite a different kettle of fish to cope with a pregnant and jealous wife at a distance of three thousand miles. Herbert did his best. He promised to be worthy of her beautiful love for him—if only a little worthy. He wrote on the eve of the production. They still had to rehearse Act V. Her letters had made him both happy and sad. 'Don't worry sweet one about that horrid letter.' It was presumably an anonymous letter because he added: 'It was evidently written by some enemy of ours—for who but a cruel and depraved wretch could send such a letter knowing your condition.'

He advised her not to give it another thought but to rely entirely on his love and loyalty to her. But it was not only anonymous letters which were circulating about Herbert. There were also pieces of spicy news. For on the 1st December 1897, some months after the birth of Iris Tree, George Edwardes (of the Gaiety Theatre) wrote to Tree.

I understand that, like me, you have been the victim of attacks in an American paper called the *Telegraph* written by a man called Stanley Jones and signed S. J. Can you give me any information as to this person as if I am able to discover his personality I shall most certainly proceed against him. I shall be obliged if you can assist me.

American papers, as now, were less afraid of libel and the letter was marked *Private*. Possibly attacks had been made against George Edwardes, or maybe suggestions that all was not pure in the purlieus of the West End. There is no record of Herbert's reply. Even those who purveyed curly girlies for stage door Johnnies had to keep a pure front and the ranks of the West End theatre managers closed fast on a purity ticket. But that was in the future. Love and loyalty held firm in 1896.

Herbert was touched by Maud's sending him violets—he was calm. He realised it was to be an important night for him—much was at stake. He promised to wire her after the performance. He ended that he would be encouraged by the knowledge of her great love—for he was her loving but lonely Herbert.

Washington was quite kind to the play, but the New York critics tore it to shreds and gave neither the author nor the actor any hope that anything could be saved from the shipwreck.

Tree decided to bolster up his finances by relying on his old successes, a plan of campaign which never suited his volatile temperament. A month before their child was born he wrote to Maud telling her that they had revived *The Dancing Girl* with great success and it would be followed by *Trilby*. Of course these two old successes would draw money, especially *Trilby*. He thought *The Seats of the Mighty* was too subtle for them. But it is always cold comfort to a manager to produce a play, however intelligent he may think it, if the stalls and boxes are empty.

But Herbert, like the strong swimmer he was, plunged strongly against the seas of adversity. He was not despondent, in fact he was bearing it all with a fortitude which filled him with admiration. But Maud was inclined to believe in ill-luck and the possibility of failure, she lacked Herbert's supreme confidence. Poor old Parker was crumpling under the disappointment, but Herbert bore up, even if he had to do all the fighting. In today's battle the defeat of yesterday was forgotten.

Maud must take care of herself—she must not mope or be unhappy. He added a sentimental touch to make her feel they were always as one; he had taken her picture with that of Felicity and Viola to bed with him. He had prayed for all his darlings.

But amidst the stress of the failure of his play Herbert had not forgotten the building of his dream—Her Majesty's. Maud must keep Sir Algernon West and Wernher interested. It was essential to have people of substance at his back. They might not put money into the building, they would perhaps come in later into the whole project. It had all been difficult and worrying, but now the sky was blue and the way ahead was clear.

Both Gilbert Parker, perhaps like most playwrights easily given to despondency, and Elizabeth Marbury, Tree's American agent, found Tree's fortitude in the face of failure admirable. Herbert ignored his difficulties when writing to Maud. The work was hard, but he was well and the climate was so invigorating that he never felt tired.

In spite of all the discouragement he refused to vacate *The Seats of the Mighty* and played it alternately with *Trilby* and *The Dancing Girl*. Herbert put the failure of the play down to the fact that the American public were anti-Colonialist and *The Seats of the Mighty* being concerned with a colonial war which the British had won was not popular. But the anti-British feeling seemed to disappear as soon as he played *Trilby* or *The Dancing Girl*. There is a sheen which covers successful plays. It is often difficult to see years afterwards why certain plays succeeded and drew the plaudits of the public, later to become either unreadable or incomprehensible. *Trilby* and *The Dancing Girl* had arrived in America with the glow of success. *The Seats of the Mighty* had not.

Herbert seemed to be more concerned about Maud and their coming child than he was about his own success or failure. So many things could go wrong with a birth. By the time she got his letter, all would be over, happily over, he hoped. If only his sweet Maud did not have to suffer. He would be thinking of her at every minute and wishing with all his soul that he could be beside her holding her hand and easing her pain. Sometimes, he wrote, he felt like dropping everything and taking the first steamer back to his darling Maud.

And then he referred again to their difficulties. She must not make herself sad or unhappy about him. She must know how their love was strong and sure. The distance between them distressed him, he could not bring happiness to her face, or even feel her pain himself.

It was a sentiment which came straight from the heart of her loving Herbert and, even in his distress, he was tactful enough to remember her career. When he wrote from the Stenton Hotel in Philadelphia he remarked that although Kate Rorke had played Ophelia well enough, her performance was a mere shadow of Maud's.

But Maud, although distressed, had not been idle. She had been in correspondence with Elizabeth Marbury and suggested that it should be announced that the American tour had been a success. Miss Marbury replied that a great number of people might know differently, but in the event, like so many American tours, it was neither brilliantly successful nor a total failure, in fact it showed a small profit. *Trilby* and *The Dancing Girl* had balanced *The Seats of the Mighty*. Other suggestions were crossing the Atlantic from Miss Marbury. She felt that the thing which Mr. Tree lacked above all was a manager and Tree felt the need of this himself.

Miss Marbury wrote that he must have a man 'who is able, honest, sober and tactful, a man full of energy and invention. He *must* be protected.' Herbert had found in Miss Marbury someone who was to help to solve his problems. She counselled Maud to find Herbert someone before he came back to England, it was vitally necessary that a man should take the business side of the theatre from his hands.

The man was found. He was Henry Dana. It is not clear whether it was Maud or Herbert who had found him.

A photograph of Dana shows a typical Edwardian with a large moustache which hides any evidence which might give a clue to his character. He was photographed in a thoughtful pose which no doubt reflected his state of mind in having to cope with Tree's flights of fancy, which were, as a rule unconnected with references to money.

Dana was a man after Tree's own heart. He had come to his profession by accident and had, as a contemporary interviewer put it, 'tried his hand at cattle ranching for five or six years before he began to learn the rudiments of the profession with which he is now connected. From 1879 to 1884 his home was in America out in the Far West amidst the cattle punchers of Colorado and New Mexico.' Dana's ranching was not a success, men who knew more about it reaped the money and he came back to London much poorer than when he left. America for Dana had hardly been the land of promise, or opportunity. But he had acquired one asset—the ability to speak English with an American accent. He decided to go on the stage.

Like Herbert, Dana was lucky—the part of Horace Bream the American in *Sweet Lavender* came up and he played it for a year. But this brilliant start to his acting career did not last and soon Dana dwindled into management; when Penley produced *Charley's Aunt* he became his manager and then gradually drifted into management on his own account, going from one project to another until Maud (or Tree) thought of him for Her Majesty's, and he had a job for life. 'Tell Dana', or 'ask Dana' became the foundation stone of business with Tree at Her Majesty's Theatre.

Dana having been an actor for eight years himself could understand actors, and having been a manager could also protect Tree

against actors. His American connexions gave him added usefulness. He had all the advantages. He was engaged.

*

Maud and Herbert's third and last child was born at the end of
January 1896. They both longed for a boy. It had been quite
decided that the new baby was to be Herbert's heir. Besides, as
Herbert well knew, he was capable of fathering sons.

The child was another daughter, whom they called Iris. It was a
disappointment, but Maud's sentimental heart was melted by the
sight of the new little baby, so dependent on her. How could any
woman not welcome this ray of sunshine?

Herbert was forty-four. His greatest days were in front of him
and his greatest project was beginning to take shape. He had
always been his own man, undeterred by either critics or dis-
appointments. He would now have his own theatre which would
be the most beautiful in London.

Chapter 6

Her Majesty's—
The Handsomest Theatre
in London

The site Herbert had chosen for his theatre had a history stretching back for nearly two hundred years. When Vanbrugh opened his Queen's Theatre (or New Opera House) in the spring of 1705, his grandiose edifice had been surrounded by farms, and the acoustics were so bad that the actors' voices could not be heard except as echoes.

Since that unlucky opening there had been two other theatres on the site. The last theatre, which had been pulled down, had been built in 1869. Tree's dream building was the fourth.

While he had been in America the theatre had been rising behind the scaffolding. Maud had been busy not only with collecting finance for the project, but also consulting with painters, decorators and upholsterers. For a lady so dedicated to moving it was a happy occupation. It had been decided that inside the theatre the style of Louis XV should prevail. This was in the right Monsieur Ritz spirit of the age.

When Tree got back from America the theatre was not finished and he went on a provincial tour. Neither his American tour nor the English provincial tour had made money to help the exchequer. Maud mentions that the 'new theatre was a monster whose devouring jaws opened wider and wider every day'. And yet when everything was finished and the balance drawn the theatre had cost £55,000 and the costs had exceeded the estimate by only £300. It was a miracle of organisation brought from chaos and somehow typical of Tree's disorganised organising.

It still remains a beautiful theatre with its intricate blue and scarlet picked out in gilt, the foyers and bars mahogany and gilt, and the royal retiring room a circular room in cream and gold with blue classical plaques followed out the same classical theme. From the staircase Tree as King John still looks down on the audience making its way to the circle. The stage itself is sixty feet wide and nearly sixty feet deep, and the acoustics are so good that no mechanical equipment is needed to allow the actors' voices to be heard in any part of the house. The seating is very wide and shallow and the circle stretches out in a gentle curve. On that first night when the theatre was filled with beautifully dressed women, their sparkling jewellery reflected from the overhead chandeliers, it must have had the effect of a *corbeille* of the most expensive flowers in Europe.

The dressing-rooms were on the dress circle level to give the actors more space. Tree's own dressing-room was like an hotel suite, with a small drawing-room, a make-up room and a bathroom with white tiles like an old fashioned Continental hotel. No expense had been spared and all was dedicated to cheerfulness and comfort. Tree's palace of acting was a friendly and welcoming place reflecting the tastes and character of its owner. Yet it was not without its innovations. For Tree had introduced for the first time in England the flat stage in order to simplify the use of stage mechanisms. It excited a certain amount of ridicule in stage circles, although it had been used to good effect in Europe and America. Even Shaw, usually the first person to welcome new ideas to kill the stuffy old traditions of the past, was not on Tree's side when it came to using a flat stage, although he had to admit that most playgoers had laughed at the way a pencil, stick, or log of firewood suddenly took off on its own accord and rolled down towards the footlights. His main objection to the flat stage was that the cultured working men (avid for Ibsen no doubt) would not have a good view from the gallery.

Maud, occupied as she was with the meetings with financiers, or in close consultation with Mr. Phipps the architect and Mr. Romaine Walker, the interior decorator, still had time to be worried about Herbert's first presentation. He was determined in spite of all the storm warnings to cling to his idea of Gilbert Parker's *The Seats of the Mighty*—if it had not 'gone' in the United States it would be quite different in London. It had been too subtle for the Americans.

Publicly Maud stoutly defended the play. Someone had written to her suggesting that Herbert had apologised for Mr. Parker's play. What an idea! It was Mr. Parker who had admitted the crudities of his play in a speech to the audience. Her husband had the highest opinion of Gilbert Parker's work and there was absolutely no question at all but that *The Seats of the Mighty* would open at Her Majesty's Theatre.

She was battling gamely for Herbert, but privately she had the gravest misgivings about the play and was making contingency plans in case Herbert's sanguine hopes should be disappointed. She wrote to Henry Arthur Jones asking how his new play was coming along. She was afraid about *The Seats of the Mighty*, although in fairness to Gilbert Parker, she was trying to seem hopeful.

She not only remained hopeful but she remained steadfast, while keeping a stern eye on the front of the house decorations, and studying her part. Her dedication to interior decoration conflicted with her duties as an actress, for at the last minute on the opening night she was greatly upset when she discovered that some enterprising china manufacturer had sent in 'hundreds of huge vessels, crude and shiny in shades of yellow, peacock blue, and crushed strawberry'. She condemned them as in the worst contemporary style and hardly in keeping with the rich good taste she was envisaging for Herbert's theatre.

Her Majesty's Theatre opened appropriately in the year of the Queen's Diamond Jubilee 1897 on 28th April.

The opening was a gala—a feast of fashion and beauty. Even Shaw had to admit that it was quite the handsomest theatre in London. It was not full of mirrors, it neither gave the feeling of a first class saloon in a P & O liner, nor the window of a furniture store in the Tottenham Court Road. It was a place where you might feel that high scenes were to be enacted and dignified things done.

Mrs. Kate Terry Gielgud, then aged twenty-nine, and an ardent playgoer since childhood, was present at the first night in the fine new theatre. The proceedings opened with Mrs. Tree reciting, gorgeously gowned as a Lady of the Court of Louis Quinze, to fit into the setting of the theatre and the setting of the play. Due to her fright over the unexpected delivery of last minute pottery, Maud was nervous. She recited a poem by the Poet Laureate, Alfred Austin, the alleged author of the immortal words: 'Across the wire the electric message came, He is no better he is much the same.'

On this occasion he did a little better, though his words were hardly immortal:

Leaving life's load of dullness at the door
You come to dwell on Fairyland once more . . .
Magical medley, Kings upon their throne
And Queens, though never one to match our own;
Bewildered innocence, taxed with every crime
And heroes entering in the nick of time
Love, scorning rank, wealth, ease for Beauty's sake
And Pity sobbing till its heart must break.

Mr. Austin's poem then went on to bow very low in praise of the theatre, and its Royal name:

Yet there is One, whose venerated name
We humbly borrow, and will never shame
Who needs no tinsel trappings nor disguise
To shine a Monarch in the whole world's eyes, . . .
Long may she linger, loved, upon the scene,
And long resound the prayer, 'God Save our Gracious Queen.'

The heavy red velvet curtains were then drawn up, disclosing a large contingent from the Queen's Hall Choral Society, who sang the National Anthem. Mrs. Terry Gielgud remarked that it was all elaborate and patriotic, but had nothing to do with the theatre. Shaw thought that it indicated a resolute determination to get the last inch out of the Royal Family: 'Not a man in the house but felt that the Jubilee was good for trade.'

Miss Clara Butt was commended as showing that music can be made out of 'God Save the Queen', though Mrs. Terry Gielgud commented that this version 'took a long time'. The choir sang, the audience stood and the Prince of Wales graced the Royal Box (for the money garnered from the proceedings was to go to the Ratepayers Relief Fund).

One of the few criticisms of the theatre, which Shaw made, was to object to the plush seats for plush people, but he commended the elegant humanised decorations of what he called modern anti-Renaissance ideas. The first night was glorious and 'the proceedings terminated with a play'. He had reviewed the theatre, but he did not intend to review the play.

Kate Terry Gielgud gives a good succinct idea of why the play failed. It was tedious, the arm of coincidence stretched too far and the points made were those of a novelist. There were very long waits between the scenes. There were some good things about the acting. Mr. Lewis Waller was dignified and sympathetic, his voice pleasant to hear, but the part never gave him a chance to be other than passively heroic. Mrs. Tree was good in her early scenes, but then dropped out of the play, 'just one of those loose ends'.

Whether it was because of the excitement of the evening, or the natural nervousness of acting in a play which had already failed elsewhere, Tree gave a very artificial performance. Kate Terry Gielgud noted: 'I felt that Mr. Tree's Doltaire was an over-elaborated study. He posed, he worked his efforts till they lost all spontaneity and failed to convey the fascination of the man and the secret of his power over men and women alike.'

Off stage Herbert had the fascination he needed for the part—an elusive combination of charm, good looks and ease. Yet, on stage, Tree, that most complicated of men and easy acquirer of women, could only play villains and eccentrics with shining success. As soon as he set his mind on trying to charm, or play the simple hero, he failed.

Maud described the opening night as a delirium of pride, terror, joy and anxiety. The garish pots were not the only minor disaster. As soon as the Prince of Wales entered the theatre, he took exception to the grand flunkeys—they were dressed in the same royal liveries as those at Buckingham Palace. That was carrying the dignity of the theatre too far and hardly had he entered the foyer than the electric lights failed, plunging him in total darkness.

It was no wonder that Maud recorded that she heard Clara Butt 'as in a dream' singing 'God Save the Queen' and the thunderous applause greeting Herbert as he made his first bow.

The first words spoken in Herbert's theatre were spoken by Maud 'Very well met—and welcome'. She then launched into Mr. Austin's doggerel.

The play went reasonably well. First night audiences are often warm and a great occasion often produces a cheerful response. The audience, having paid large sums to see and be seen are in no mood to indicate failure. At the end of the play Herbert came forward feeling relief and gratitude.

This is a great moment in my little life. I feel very proud as I stand here facing this theatre and this audience here tonight. There is so much I should like to say, so little that I can, yet I must express my thanks to those to whom I owe this beautiful theatre; I hope you are satisfied with it? I am! Fate is blind but I have one great power behind me in that I have your goodwill and that of the Public. And this at least I can promise, in the words my wife spoke tonight, we shall do nothing to shame the name we are honoured in being allowed to use.

Shaw remarked that Tree had the air of a man who *would* have stooped to forgery, arson, or bigamy but was saved from these horrors by recalling that he was the owner of Her Majesty's Theatre.

Tree concluded that he hoped his audience was pleased with the play and added in the words of the tradesmen of the period, 'I hope that it may be given to me to cater for you for many years to come, as I have been proud and happy to do in the past.'

But the public did not take to the play and it only ran for three months, being dubbed 'The Seats of the Mighty Few'. Wigs, fur-belows and quips disappeared never to be seen again, but the theatre was launched. A dream had been realised.

It was Tree's temple of art. Programmes were not charged for, there were no advertisements to spoil them. Cloakrooms were free. The patrons of the theatre were treated as guests by the servants at the theatre. The orchestra was one of the best in London and the music worth listening to. It was not a background to conversation, it was a pleasure in itself. As at a private ball, the musicians themselves were hidden behind palm leaves. Everything was in the best of taste, for Maud had not been a guest in great country houses without learning something about the discretion of understated elegance.

Up in the Dome, Herbert had built himself a huge reception room. It was fifty feet long, in the Tudor taste, with huge nail studded oak doors and round the walls were painted pictures of himself in his various parts. Here over the years he was to give his lavish parties, with Maud presiding and the exquisite food being sent in from the Carlton Hotel next door.

Inside and out, Herbert was proud of his theatre. He would go out of his way to admire its façade of Portland stone and red granite. It was handsome and enduring. He buttonholed fellow actors to view it from all angles. Squire Bancroft was taken to admire this most impressive of all Tree's productions, he looked at it through his monocle and gave his verdict: 'A great many windows to clean.'

After the first night there was the first of Tree's receptions in the Dome—and then he went off with two of his friends to a cabman's shelter and played dominoes with the cabbies until six o'clock in the morning. It was his way of unwinding. What Maud thought of this procedure is not recorded.

Herbert had not only acquired his own beautiful theatre, he had acquired a great and enduring asset in Henry Dana, the ex-cowboy turned manager. Maud remarked that Dana was a slave to Herbert's interests. 'So much so that he was sometimes a little hard on those who were not his Chief, but that is the perfect Lieutenant.'

Dana paints a sympathetic portrait of his 'Chief'.

We went through strenuous times together and the run of success was not by any means unbroken. At times we differed as to the policy of the theatre, when heated arguments followed, but that never made any difference to our mutual esteem, and a good understanding was soon arrived at. I recall one occasion when tempers ran high. I left the room. He called me back, and I refused to return. Within a few minutes he followed me up to my office, and held out his hand, frankly admitting that he had been in the wrong, and needless to say a complete reconciliation followed. It takes a big man to do that to an employee.

Another fine point in his character was his accessibility to the smallest member of his company or the most humble member of his staff. He treated all with equal courtesy, the result being esteem and loyalty from all who served under his banner.

Dana wrote that he had an exceptional gift of bringing out any talent in others, and many of the leading actors and actresses of his day owed their rise to his training and encouragement. He was an optimist and an opportunist. 'The former trait often led to trouble, but the latter served him well.'

There was one point which Dana felt was unique in his association with Tree. Neither of them had felt it necessary to sign a contract. 'We each knew the other's word was sufficient.' This seemed to Dana to be extraordinary as they were both hot-tempered and impulsive men, but the real affection and appreciation that they had for one another always tided them over any temporary difficulties they might have had.

If Dana appreciated Tree, then Tree appreciated Dana and between them they were able to ride over the stresses and storms of running a theatre.

A few weeks after the opening of Her Majesty's, Tree added a play without words, '*Chand d'Habits* (presumably colloquial for *Marchand d'Habits*), as a prologue to *The Seats of the Mighty*. Shaw wrote that he could not understand what possessed Tree to offer this trifle to such a hoggish audience. 'These plays without words only exist for people who are highly sensitive to music, colour and the complex art of physical expression.' For his own part Shaw had enjoyed it immensely. But Tree was always trying out things which amused or interested him but which did not always please his audience. It was a facet of his changeable nature.

Maud wrote that originally Herbert had intended to open Her Majesty's with *Julius Caesar*, but he could not find the cast he wanted at that time. But he still had the project in mind, although he spent the rest of the year filling in with *Katharine and Petruchio*, Garrick's version of *The Taming of the Shrew*, which did not please the critics, and *The Silver Key* which pleased the public.

The Silver Key was an adaptation by the inevitable Sydney Grundy from *Mademoiselle de Belle Isle* by Dumas, with Tree playing the Duc de Richelieu, yet another eighteenth-century seducer of ladies, but even Shaw could not but applaud Tree's eighteenth-century manners: 'The lapse of a century has left Richelieu (described by Macaulay as "an old fop who had passed his life from sixteen to sixty in seducing women for whom he cared not one straw") still alive and familiar.'

Shaw remarked that 'vice' as he called it was always alive—and familiar. It is possible with hindsight to reflect that if Tree could play the eighteenth-century seducer so well it was perhaps because he was playing one facet of his own nineteenth-century character.

Maud loved *Mademoiselle de Belle Isle*—it had a good comedy part for her and the play was immensely successful being, she said, a witty, dainty and bewitching trifle. Shaw had advised Mr. Grundy to leave the novels of Dumas alone. He had put in pruderies of his own not calculated to improve the plot—Dumas and water was no fare for the discerning critic.

But *The Silver Key* was destined for Tree's autumn tour and it was successful in its genre. Possibly the public wanted Dumas and water—and Grundy's pruderies.

Tree had engaged Evelyn Millard to play the virginal heroine of *The Silver Key*, but not without difficulties from his former Trilby.

On 25th August, before the tour began, he wrote to Dorothea Baird a letter which shows a firm hand with difficult actresses. He had no desire either to treat her with unfairness, or to damage the friendly relations which existed between them. He then set out his case. He had been reminded, presumably by Dana, that it was time to settle his option of renewal with her. He found that there were no important parts for her either in *The Silver Key*, or in *Julius Caesar*. He had offered that she should understudy Evelyn Millard, which Miss Baird had haughtily refused. Tree wrote that he had no recollection of having told her that her engagement would be automatically renewed, but should he have done so, his word would be binding.

Dana would vouch for that statement. Tree went on to say that he had told her he would not want her for the autumn tour and she had replied that she was going to tour on her own account. He admitted that he *may* have spoken in vague terms of possible parts in the future. He was sorry if anything which he had said had interfered with any arrangements which she had made. One point he must stress—he could have put it to her simply that if she refused to understudy Evelyn Millard her contract would be at an end. He regretted his lack of firmness.

In spite of all the difficulties she was making, he made it plain that he would pay her so long as she would hold herself available to him should he want her. He hoped that she would find this fair. He had arrived at this decision after her *first* letter, but had taken some time to reply. As to her second letter, it was a pity she had written it. He concluded quite cheerfully and genially that he hoped they would remain friends and that he would always be mindful of her past services to him and all her kindness.

This letter was written two years after the production of *Trilby* and seems a model of how to reply to a prevaricating actress. It is always hard for an actress who has played in a brilliant first success to dwindle into an understudy. Why Tree did not engage her for Miss Millard's part is not clear; perhaps with his quick perception he did not see her as an eighteenth-century heroine. He always liked a balanced production.

Tree's character seems to shine out from his hastily written letters. His life may have been convoluted, yet when it came to his dealings with actors and actresses, he was the dead straight 'English gentleman'; of foreign origin, but typical of his period.

Having completed his autumn tour Tree returned to plan his greatest Shakespeare production, *Julius Caesar*. He had been busy brooding about it for some time and had decided for the scholar Brutus, for the actor Cassius and for the public, Antony.

Maud had wisely persuaded him to play Antony. Her views had been reinforced by Louis Calvert, an outstanding actor of the day, who had a long career from the 1880s to the 1920s. He had played with all the leading managements from Irving to Reinhardt and was an outstanding exponent of Shakespeare and Shaw. Tree not only knew how to pick his actors, but he would often listen to their advice. Louis Calvert and Maud, did their best to instil into Tree that for this, the first of his large-scale Shakespearean productions, he should follow the road of tradition. But it all ended in Herbert going his own way and as usual his way was the best. Maud remarked that Herbert had really *studied* the play, as if this were a new departure for him. But his notebooks reveal that when it came to Shakespeare he was apt to think out production and performance in depth, as if he were talking to himself. His hurried notes and jottings often show two totally different types of handwriting, as if the two sides of his character were revealed in his writing. His notes on Caesar are of this proverbially scrappy variety, interspersed by total irrelevancies. He asked himself what on earth had happened to the light at the top of the theatre? and what about Viola's £50? His quick mind then darted to the scenery—the women must have a balcony, Caesar should stand at the top of a flight of steps—or would it be better if he were framed by an arch, or a porch for shelter from rain?

The costumes—there was the Germanicus picture, or perhaps it would be better to follow *Imperial Caesar* published by Vertue & Co. That emphasised that hats were not worn.

He added a rider that he *must* keep the absolute production to £2,000. He burned incense to the idea of economy, but whether he ever followed his own advice is in doubt.

When studying his productions and his own part, his mind presented him with a series of pictures which he wrote down. When Caesar's statue was lying on the floor, the populace must first spit at it and then kiss it reverently.

His own part he was considering in depth. When Antony faces Brutus they are like two animals full of nervous energy, who yet refrain from attacking one another.

Antony must speak the names of the conspirators very quietly, pause and then begin the speech 'O Mighty Caesar'. At the words 'fulfil your pleasure' he will open his toga baring his breast.

Every picture presented itself to Tree. Antony was down stage, Brutus and Cassius are unaware of his expression when they are making their proposals to him. But after the words 'good thoughts and reverence' Antony still remains silent and from the silence Cassius speaks. Tree added that as Brutus speaks Antony shivers and then, after taking Cassius' hand, he spits.

All the rest of the speeches are carefully considered and, as he thought, the pictures of the actors who are to bring them to life, spring to the mind as they did to Tree's.

Antony is jerked into action by the entrance of a servant. Suddenly his attitude changes—he sees a kneeling figure, he will kill the man, no, his mind jumps aside and then in the speech 'Thy heart is big—get thee apart and weep—Passion I see is catching for mine eyes seeing those tears of sorrow stand in them—begin to water' he quickly recovers. Possibly, thought Tree, Antony might be playing the hypocrite here. He may be ashamed to acknowledge his grief and transfers his tears and his weakness to the slave. Several of Bret Harte's poems had suggested this idea to him.

This is a curious analogy of Tree's—from considering the character of Antony in Rome, he suddenly compares him to men of action in America, as if men of action and their attitudes towards death and grief were always the same, and always recognisable.

He concluded by sketching in his idea of the Forum scene. Antony addresses the populace from the broken plinth of Caesar's statue. Caesar's image, broken by them, lies below him. He must speak 'Mischief thou art afoot' looking down on the statue as the scene ends. He had thought of this by reading Baring Gould's *Tragedy of Caesar*.

This might seem odd for a man who purported never to read and to find his ideas by a sudden inspiration; it was hardly a part studied without reflections, or reflections made without study.

As soon as Shaw heard of the forthcoming production of *Julius Caesar* he was already attacking the idea of Tree producing it. How could a man who had had the audacity to put on Garrick's garbled version of *The Taming of the Shrew* dare to lay his hands on Caesar? He was just as likely as not to cut it to ribbons. 'If Mr. Tree had suffered as much as I have from seeing Shakespeare butchered to make a Cockney's holiday, he would sympathize with my nervousness on the subject.'

Shaw was keeping a very sharp eye on the production and had even blocked out how he would rearrange the play in three acts, yet, when it came to the first night, his ideas on the act sequence coincided exactly with Tree's.

Tree may have advised himself to keep his production expenses to £2,000, but once the gorgeous palaces began to rise from their designs it was not so simple to keep costs within bounds.

The production was to be noble and grand, the stage was to be filled with splendid pictures bringing the ancient world to life, crowded with senators in togas, busy with hundreds of plebs. When menacing arms were raised, they were to be raised in hundreds—and all this was to take place against the lush background of Alma-Tadema's Rome, glittering with gold, thick with pillars, palaces, balconies, classical statues and archways against the cerulean blue of Roman skies.

Backstage things were not so easily achieved. Scene shifters contended with crowds and crowds with scenery. In the midst of all the chaos Tree's stage manager was rushing about yelling with more despairing gestures than Antony over the death of Caesar. Tree offered up a silent prayer to the Almighty, 'Dear Lord, do look at Bertie Shelton *now*!'

Tree's rehearsals seem to have taken on the character of a civil war, but like the American Civil War the eagle rose triumphant from it—*e pluribus unum*. In some strange way, he always managed to stretch everyone to their peak and in the end order prevailed and, to everyone's intense surprise, the curtain finally went up. Although on this occasion there were many instances of under-rehearsal (huge pageants are ever fraught with pitfalls or, indeed, pratfalls), most critics hailed the play as a triumph. It was more than fifty years since London had seen it, so it had the glow of novelty. The press responded with a paean of praise.

> What Mr. Tree has accomplished in this revival of *Julius Caesar* must give every student pause. With loving labour and at in-finite cost he has resurrected ancient Rome in all its unimagined glory, and paid to the genius of our national poet a tribute unequalled in our time.

It was, wrote another critic, 'an immortal page from the world's history that was unrolled in a series of gorgeous Tadema pictures and it was more than an honourable page that we then saw added to the history of our English stage'.

A month after the ending of Queen Victoria's jubilee the British were conscious of the analogy of their Empire with that of the Roman world and many of them equated those virtues of the stoic father and the Roman matron with those of their own race. If the Roman mother saw her sons leaving for the frontiers of Gaul or Britain, the British matron saw her sons leaving for the North-West Frontier, or darkest Africa. Tree had chosen well.

One dissentient voice was raised almost for the last time in print against Tree—Shaw wrote that while Alma-Tadema was the hero of the evening the stage carpenters seemed intent on spoiling his pictures. 'Every carpenter seems to make it a point of honor to set the cloths swinging in a way that makes Rome reel and the audience seasick. In Brutus's house, the door is on the spectators' left; the knocks on it come from the right. The Roman soldiers take the field each man with his two javelins neatly packed up— like a fishing rod.' And the javelins were still as undisturbed when he came back from fighting a bloody battle 'in perfect trim for a walk-out with the nursery maids of Philippi'.

Shaw noted other points of which he did not approve. Mrs. Tree playing the boy Lucius—and singing a song by Sullivan. Maud had chosen the small part of Lucius herself—a part in which she cast off her shoes and skimmed barefoot all over the stage. But the critics were right to commend Alma-Tadema, for he not only designed and draped every dress in the play, but made phalerians, shields, armour and insignia himself. He worked in the property room binding the faggots borne by the lictors to show how it should be done and drawing the letters SPQR on the insignia of the Roman guards.

For Maud, *Julius Caesar* was more of a triumph than the opening of Her Majesty's Theatre. Shaw might sneer but the public flocked to the play. And Maud remembered every scene. There stood Mark Antony among the murderers, and when Casca smirched with blood the arm of the butchered Caesar's friend, the careless, light-hearted Antony changed. One saw a new soul grow in him as he towered above the cringing conspirators like an angel of revenge. But on second thoughts Maud felt that perhaps there was more of Lucifer the fallen angel than the angel of light, Gabriel, in Herbert's performance.

Maud's head was full of the happy auspicious spring and summer of *Julius Caesar* when on stage she played Lucius barefooted, and when at other times she and Herbert gloried in his triumph. They knew everybody and went everywhere. Herbert in his own theatre was at last recognised as great. Troops of new friends floated in on the tide of success, amongst them Lord Rosebery, who had even made a speech about Herbert at a London County Council meeting. Glory indeed.

Lord Rosebery had placed Herbert on an historic pinnacle, as Herbert had placed Antony on the plinth of Caesar's statue. 'The Roman', said Lord Rosebery to the London County Council, 'was proud of Rome. He should be prouder still of London. Why, gentlemen, within a stone's throw of this Hall, you can see put upon the stage with all the splendour and all the art that taste and expenditure can afford, the sublime tragedy of Julius Caesar.'

Between the flowery sentiments of Maud and the patronising words of Shaw that Tree as Antony was 'not stupid, inane nor Bard of Avon ridden', perhaps Desmond MacCarthy gives the fairest picture of Tree as Antony. 'His genius for representing one who takes advantage of a gush of spontaneous emotion to heighten it for his own ends made his Antony in *Julius Caesar* a performance of the highest excellence. For the same reason he triumphed, though his elocution was seldom perfect, in the delivery of the stage harangue; that over-stippling of his effects which sometimes spoilt them at other junctures, on these occasions added the grace of spontaneity to what he uttered. He understood the orator, the actor, the artist, whose emotions are his own material, and the half-sincere advocate.'

Perhaps he was one of the first of the actors to realise that the way to bring Shakespeare to life was to regard him as a writer trying to say something. In an age when the verse was all and melodious voices mouthing the famous speeches lent somnolent solemnity to Shakespeare—Tree treated him like a man—and a contemporary.

And as a spectacle it had paid off. It ran for over five months and made a nice round profit of £11,000. It had been a profit with honour.

Chapter 7

Keen on Waller

If Maud and Herbert shared a triumph on stage and in society in the second year of Her Majesty's—the year of *Julius Caesar*—off stage and in private, things were not so successful. Herbert's roving eye and possibly Herbert's second family gave Maud's endemic jealousy plenty of fuel.

And now there were possibilities for Maud to seek a revenge. Lewis Waller had triumphed in *Julius Caesar* as Brutus. His melodious voice and good looks added to Tree's success. Waller was on the verge of becoming a matinée idol. The troops of Waller fans wearing their badges marked K.O.W. (Keen on Waller) were in the future, but meanwhile he himself had fallen in love with Maud. Maud was not a strictly pretty woman. Her face in photographs taken about this time shows a woman who is controlled and sure of herself, but there is no hint of impulsiveness in the face. It has a curious sense of being enclosed, as if she were always thinking her own thoughts, and that when she posed for the photographs she did not intend to reveal herself, or her character. But while she was skimming about the stage barefoot playing Lucius to Waller's Brutus, Brutus's eye had fallen on her.

This did not please Tree. It was all perfectly in order for men to stray, they had strong sexual natures and women, in general, could respond to this. But wives, in particular, were not expected to do so. To err was the man's privilege, to forgive was the woman's.

There was never any suggestion that Maud was unfaithful to Herbert. She had already acted with Waller in *A Woman's Reason* at the Shaftesbury, playing the Hon. Nina Keith, a lady who married a Jew, Stephen D'Acosta, for money and subsequently betrayed him. Critics were severe about the author's morality. It had left an unpleasant taste in the mouth of the times. Maud was no doubt fully aware that ladies could sin on stage (beautifully

gowned) but off stage there were more severe penalties than a
curtain call and a wigging from *The Times*. But there is always a
delicate savour to an *amitié amoureuse* which lends a fillip to the
life of a jealous wife. Nor had Maud made the least of Herbert's
own infidelities. She had made scenes, over-acting and over-
reacting in the part of the betrayed wife. He was not prepared to
pass through, as he wrote, a kind of *auto-da-fé*—through which
ordeal a woman will demand a man shall pass with love unscathed.
Herbert preferred to walk out and send for the fire brigade.

On this occasion Herbert seems, in the magnanimous way of
errant husbands, to have forgiven her and she had written him a
loving letter no doubt putting his mind at ease on one important
point.

From Marienbad he wrote to Maud that her too loving words
made him both happy and sad. He had to admit that he had not
understood her for some time. Possibly it was his fault. But just
before he went away, he felt differently. Maud had been so loving
to him. When he thought about it he felt his nature must be back
to front.

Clashes and reconciliations had been the story of their marriage.
To read of their difficulties is to reach the conclusion that they
certainly did not understand either their own, or each other's
temperaments. She could neither condone his infidelities, nor
accept them, and he who was so easy and amusing with others
regarded her reproaches as unreasonable. Yet she was an essential
part of his life and his work—like Henry Dana. Why could she not
be content with that—and her extravagances? As Herbert once
remarked 'Which is the victim? She was—he is.'

It was impossible for them to do without one another and yet
living together was as difficult as living apart. Where their houses,
social life, constant moving expenses and children were concerned Maud had a free hand. But Herbert was determined to
keep his private life his own. He began to spend more and more
time at the theatre.

But although their personal difficulties over Waller had been
temporarily patched up there were also professional rivalries.
Waller had asked Henry Hamilton to write a dramatised version
of Dumas' *The Three Musketeers*, while Tree had engaged Sydney
Grundy to do the same. There were now not *Three Musketeers*,
but Six.

The story of the clash is told rather differently by Mrs. Clement Scott. Clement Scott had often been at loggerheads with Tree and given him some very bad notices in the *Daily Telegraph*. When it came to *Trilby*, Tree had not sent Scott any first night tickets and so the Scotts went off and bought some from Keith Prowse. The quarrel ended with apologies all round. Clement Scott had awarded himself the palm of being the first critic in the land and cultivated his appearance accordingly. He affected a natty man-about-town image—combined with a touch of Bohemianism—the thinning hair, large moustache, carefully reflective eyes, hand placed thoughtfully under the chin, striped suit and spotted bow tie and large carnation buttonhole (with accompanying foliage) all indicated the doyen of critics. According to his enemies he was an eager Duchess spotter. He had watched and commended the rise of Irving and now he charted the overtaking star of Tree with prejudiced eyes. He admitted to having been a dramatic radical in the sixties, and now in 1899 he was a dramatic Unionist. 'I absolutely deny that the subject of Ibsen's *Ghosts* is fit for any stage . . . unless drastic measures are taken at once—the theatre will be as empty in the future as the variety houses will be crowded.'

Mrs. Scott's version of the Six Musketeers was that the unsuspecting and innocent Lewis Waller was in Simpson's in the Strand, tucked into a cosy cubicle with Henry Hamilton discussing steaks, scenes and situations. In a corner, eating an undercover chop, sat Tree—listening to every word. The fact remained, said Mrs. Scott, that a few days after Hamilton had completed his version, Tree sent round a message to Clement Scott giving the news that Sydney Grundy was preparing a new edition of *The Three Musketeers* to be called *His Majesty's Musketeers*.

Waller rushed ahead with his version and managed to get it on in the suburbs by the middle of September 1898. But like some old-time melodrama, complications followed thick and fast. Florence, Waller's wife (playing Miladi), dashed off and found a West End theatre for the play. Waller was under contract to another manager. The manager claimed him. Waller defied the manager—and played. Applause, queues outside the theatre. Success! Success! Just when author Hamilton, Miladi, and Mrs. Scott were ready to sink their teeth into a celebratory luncheon in walked Waller. They at once sensed something was very wrong.

'In one short hour the triumph of his life had been turned into tragedy.'

Tree had given Waller a three-year contract at a huge salary—and he had taken it. That was the story, according to the Scott version, and why Lewis Waller, more popular than any man on the English stage, did not run in the race for Irving's crown. Crown, sceptre and orb went to Tree, that cloak and dagger eater of chops.

There are a few holes in this dramatic story of Tree as under-cover playwright. Firstly it does not fit in with Tree's generous reaction towards Irving when he had hurt his knee after the first night of *Richard III*. (Tree had sent him a sympathetic cable.) And secondly, it was Tree who had given Waller his first chance as Hotspur in *Henry IV*. It may be that the highly coloured views of Mrs. Scott and Mrs. Waller, left out one thing—Tree was a gambler and Waller was not. Possibly Mrs. Waller and Mrs. Scott were not unaware of Waller's penchant for Maud and were anxious to get him away from the pernicious influence of Herbert, and of Maud. The Trees were a worldly couple. Mrs. Pat described the atmosphere in Tree's theatre as a disturbing mixture of domesticity and art, of Society and Bohemia, of conventionality and vagary. It was in fact the vinegar and oil mixture of Maud and Herbert.

But it was not an atmosphere which was uncongenial to Waller and actors must, of necessity, attach themselves to the current focus of success. Possibly Mr. Waller himself felt that a three-year contract in his pocket would have two advantages, it would save him from the trouble of management—and give him an excuse to be near Maud.

Waller's *Three Musketeers* was taken off when playing to full houses and Tree's version was put on at Her Majesty's with great splendour. Waller was given the part of the Duke of Buckingham with a very grand costume in green velvet with pink slashings. Louis XIII wore cloth of silver, with satin brocade in white and silver for his suit. Even the pages were adorned in silks. The designs for these costumes still exist and the thick silk patterns are as bright and charming as the day they were attached to the designs for the approval of Mr. Tree.

Florence Waller lost the part of Miladi which was given to Mrs. Brown Potter, a beautiful American actress, and Maud, feeling slighted, was given the small part of the Queen. To mollify her, she was given lovely dresses and jewels to wear and a chance to sing, 'Enfant, si j'étais roi' to a charming setting, but otherwise her part amounted to very little. It was all the more galling when the beautiful Mrs. Potter left the cast just before the end of the season, that the part of Miladi was not given to Maud. Lewis Waller supported her, and felt that it was an insult that the beautiful Maud should be passed over—in any case, Waller felt that Herbert had never helped Maud's career as an actress. It was a soothing theory to which Maud, in her more angry moments, was only too willing to lend an ear. But the fact that she herself describes how she sat in the wings, crying, when Herbert had given a part she coveted to someone else, gives an idea of the domestic and thespian troubles with which Herbert had to contend. In many ways he was an objective man and possibly he regarded Maud as any other actor whom he might engage. For some parts she was suitable and for others totally wrong. It was this detached attitude which Maud could not accept. *The Three Musketeers* ran successfully for five months and, according to Maud, the theatre was always full to overflowing, filled with joy and excitement—which possibly also included Mr. Waller dressed so splendidly in green velvet with pink slashings.

Herbert's next offering was Henry Arthur Jones's *Carnac Sahib* —adultery, native uprisings and regimental stiff upper lips at Dilghaut and Fyzapore ('India at the present time') with Tree as the Sahib Carnac dicing with love and duty.

'Was ever such rotten luck! To be sent to that hole tonight! To be dished out of all the fighting and nearly all the love making!'

And then saving the day.

'They've broken out, sir—we can't hold them any longer. They demand the gates shall be opened to the Nawab . . . it's all over, sir—can we save the ladies?'

Carnac: 'There's no powder, Dicky—do as I tell you. One false step and we're done for.'

Having had a mull over his attempted fornication Carnac, cornered by the Nawab, admits: 'I daresay if we get out of this I shall be the same worthless fellow I was a month ago—no it's not possible—if I were to get out of this I could never be quite the same man I have been.'

In spite of grand settings of ruined Hindoo temples, the bazaar and exterior of the Ghu-i-noor at Dilghaut and the Jewelled Palace at night, Mr. Jones's play was a failure.

In the autumn of 1899 Tree turned his back on the modern drama and put on *King John*. The critics found Herbert's portrayal panther-like and full of nice ironic touches. After inciting Hubert to kill Arthur, he cut off the heads of the flowers in the garden as he mused on his plotting, and then at the end of the scene fell on his knees—lost in prayer at his prie-dieu before a stained glass window.

The production was voted a page of English history set in glorious motion, of which 'we may be proud and never tire'. There were other results of *King John*—Waller as the Bastard carried the acting laurels, and Maud—annoyed at not being found a part—decided to make some money for the wounded of the Boer War, and to do it alone. She was given to reciting at charity concerts—it was a form of dramatic art which combined her gifts of being actress and social success.

Scanning the paper one morning Maud noticed that Kipling's poem, 'The Absent Minded Beggar' was going to be published in the *Daily Mail*—she telegraphed the Editor and asked if she could recite it at St. James's Hall. When Herbert had already left for the theatre, a copy, sanctioned and corrected by Kipling, arrived at Sloane Street. Maud got into a hansom and went straight round to the Palace Theatre, a music-hall, and offered to recite the poem every night for a large salary—half to be given to war charities.

> When you've shouted 'Rule Britannia', when you've
> sung 'God Save The Queen',
> When you've finished killing Kruger with your mouth
> Will you kindly drop a shilling in my little
> tambourine
> For a gentleman in khaki ordered South?

Maud could see herself asking people to pass the hat for your credit's sake and pay—pay—pay. She fixed up the contract with the Palace Theatre there and then.

Suddenly the idea occurred to her—what would Herbert think? He was not devoted to the music halls, they were considered by him to be a cheap rival to his beloved theatre. She went round to Her Majesty's Theatre where he was acting in *King John*.

As Herbert swept off the stage in his golden robes, Maud was waiting in the wings to confess all. He was very angry with her, but the contract was signed and he had to allow her to stand by it. He made one stipulation 'Give all—give all. Half is half-hearted.'

Maud triumphed with her recitation. Gold and silver were thrown at her feet, ladies even tore their brooches from their gowns and added diamonds to the pile of gold. Maud was praised for her generosity and her talent, but the nicest compliment of all came from Harry Cust who told her with tears in his eyes that she seemed a little bit of England. Herbert did not agree. Maud seemed to him to be a little bit of a nuisance. Acting in a music hall was an insult to the theatre in general and a threat to the success of his own theatre in particular.

He remained unforgiving. After ten weeks of triumphing with her recitation, Herbert claimed Maud for Titania in *A Midsummer Night's Dream*. Maud later wondered to herself how she came to be chosen as the fairy queen. She might well have pondered this, for one of the critics wrote that Mrs. Tree's Titania seemed as if she had come straight from Kensington Gore into Hyde Park.

A Midsummer Night's Dream was to be one of Herbert's most lavish productions, for he had already overtaken Irving as a purveyor of fanciful grandeur. But the rehearsals proved to be more of a nightmare than a dream. Added to complicated scenery were numbers of lively children and even livelier rabbits. The dancing of the sprites did not always satisfy him. 'Children, do try to remember you are fairies, elves, sprites—for goodness sake don't shuffle! Trip! Trip!'

At midnight the fairies, exhausted with tripping, were fed with cake and sandwiches and sent home in a cab. But the rest of the cast toiled on, a raggle-taggle army of despondent actors trying to bring charm to life. In the grey dawn everyone was tired and angry—except Herbert. He called the cast to his office around 4.0 a.m. and gave them a cheery talk. The first night was going to be a triumph—and it was.

Lo, said Maud, the first night brought a performance without a hitch—such fairies, such lighting as were never seen on stage before—loveliness and magic. Only one thing marred the magic for Maud. Herbert had decided to play Bottom and she hated to see him demean himself in that way. But Henry Arthur Jones, who had had many a running skirmish with Tree at rehearsals, found Tree's Bottom especially intuitive. He portrayed the weaver with a blank wall of vanity which was impassable, conveying the utter stolidity of the character. His Bottom was unsurprised that a Fairy Queen should have fallen in love with him—it was his due. Some critics guessed that with Bottom Tree was perhaps making fun of himself—the actor-manager who knew better than anyone. He said that an actor never knew what a damned fool he was till he saw someone copying his performance. In this instance Tree was indeed having a joke with himself. Maud was witty and her wit had a cutting edge, but Tree had a fund of sheer humour and fun in his character and just occasionally he liked to let it bubble over on the stage.

The critics found that the production breathed the very air of poesy and fantasy. Miss Julia Neilson's Oberon shone against the enchanted wood, and nothing gave greater delight than her singing of, 'I know a bank'. If the sets of the forest charmed, the grandeur of Theseus's Palace was equally impressive with its huge classical pillars and swags of flowery garlands. Herbert had proved that Shakespeare could be a commercial success. The 120th performance of *The Dream* fell on the third anniversary of the opening of the theatre and Herbert made his usual speech.

I feel tonight as one who, having scaled a steep ascent finds a moment in which to breathe and gaze back at the perilous road he climbed. My managerial pilgrimage has lasted exactly three years tonight and although on my journey I may at times have had to pause for a brief fight with fortune, I am bound to confess that the progress for the most part has been comparatively easy. If my pride tells me that the result has been largely due to enthusiasm and hard work, my conscience also whispers me that my path has been strewn with the petals of that little flower which is culled in fairyland, and which mortals call 'good luck'. Over dark uneven ways, Puck has with the aid of this magic blossom led me into the light of day.

Herbert gave himself a modest pat on the back for not taking advice and for putting on *Julius Caesar, King John*—and *The Dream*. He paid fulsome tribute to his actors and helpers, bowed gratefully, and accepted his audience's congratulations with a full heart. He bowed not only to his audience, and his fellow actors, but to his lady wife, Maud, the Fairy Queen.

If in public Herbert was inclined to smile on the Fairy Queen, in private he was not so well disposed. Although he had seemed to gloss over Maud's 'Absent Minded Beggar' and her short disaffection to the music hall—it had created a rift. She herself says that Herbert was not disposed to forgive her 'or not for many years'.

In 1901 the old Queen died. Herbert had moved to his splendid new theatre in the year of her Diamond Jubilee, and now, four years later, it was a new reign with which he was much more in tune. He was a link from the theatre of Irving to the theatre of Shaw. From the beginning of his career he had always tried experiments and not always to his financial advantage. But Shakespeare had proved profitable and the year of a Royal funeral and a Coronation was no time for experiments. He had decided to put on *Twelfth Night* with himself as Malvolio. Not only did the play give him scope to be outrageous, but it also gave rein to his romantic side. He loved to bring woods, streams, forests and mountains on to the stage. In *Twelfth Night* he brought to the public dreams of English gardens—terraces, thick hedges, marble benches, statues hidden amongst the greenery. Olivia's gardens and terraces were taken from some pictures which Herbert had seen in *Country Life*.

Although the charm of terraces and gardens were easily brought to the stage, the cast was more difficult. Maud was, as usual, a stumbling block. She had decided that she wanted to play Viola. Tree had decided that he wanted the beautiful Lily Brayton to have the part. Oscar Asche, Miss Brayton's husband, remarked carefully, 'an effort was made in a certain quarter to supplant her, but wiser counsels prevailed, and she made a tremendous success'.

Maud was offered the part of Olivia which she turned down. Olivia! Olivia was dull! She decided that she wanted to do a little more flitting and dancing about the stage and plumped for the comedy part of Maria. Besides, Paul Rubens, a writer of musical comedy numbers, had written a sweet song for Maria 'Roses, their sharp spines being gone'.

The love-lorn Olivia went to another Maud, the actress Maud Jeffries. Maud Tree started to do her flitting at rehearsals. It was not a success. Herbert sent Henry Dana in to administer the blow. With the brutal frankness of the ex-cow puncher roping cattle

Dana spoke out. Maria was a *soubrette*. Maud could spend the rest of her life on the part but she could never be a *soubrette*. It was a bitter blow to her pride, made sharper by the rift in her marriage.

Maud wept and Herbert took her away down to Sussex where they had rented a house by the sea, but here, although she filled yellow vases with daffodils, nothing could ease her pain or her disappointment. There was no doubt that Maud hankering for parts which did not suit her was a cross which Herbert had to bear.

But *Twelfth Night* was a success. Everyone remembered Herbert's Malvolio, 'fantastic, dignified, abundantly absurd, and yet as undeniably pathetic'. The production was full of delights and W. L. Courtney wrote: 'There never was a more beautiful stage picture than Olivia's pleasaunce in *Twelfth Night*. We talk of the hanging gardens of Babylon as of something legendary and rare—here before our eyes were to be seen Olivia's hanging gardens, a dream of exquisite beauty which seemed to bring out the more clearly by contrast the vulgarity and coarseness of Sir Toby Belch and Sir Andrew Aguecheek, which enhanced the delicacy of Viola—and Olivia herself.'

But Maud was not there to enhance that delicacy, the pleasaunce had another tenant.

Maud always remembered that holiday at Aldwick in Sussex— it was a strange, vivid, fervid little holiday and the house had a gate, a faulty gate which would close while one was examining the lock. She was right when she wrote that it was the mistake of her career to refuse the part of Olivia. Maud began to act less and less in Herbert's theatre, and when she was given parts they were often very small ones.

In 1901 he produced *The Last of the Dandies*, a play about the Count d'Orsay, lover of Lady Blessington. There still remains an album of beautiful water-colours of the costumes for all the characters in the play. From the principals to the servants, they all resemble illustrations from *La Belle Assemblée*. Tree's comments are scrawled across the costume designs, and a costume for 'Peters' bears the words, 'Mr. Tree says too rich'. The costumier had suggested that the professional musicians should be dressed as Italian peasants—these designs are marked 'Not wanted'. All Tree's various costumes are marked with prices: 'Bright blue satin cloak for entrance at Crockfords £6 16. 0. Evening dress £20 0. 0. and pair of black trousers.' Lord Ascot's cricket gear

came a little cheaper at only five guineas. The designs for Lady
Blessington had all the charm of the period for which Tree unlike
his contemporaries had a great fondness, as if it were a time during
which he would have preferred to live.

Maud Tree started off in this play acting Lady Summershire,
but seems to have left it after only a week. Had she wanted to
play Lady Blessington and been refused? Having closed at His
Majesty's, she opened in *The Likeness of the Night* by Mrs. W. K.
Clifford only a few days later. Maud played Mary, the mistress of a
man who had married for money but strayed for love. His wife
goes off on a voyage and conveniently drowns herself and he
marries his mistress. A year later the inevitable letter arrives after
her death and the guilty pair are left to a lifetime of remorse.
Some critics thought Mrs. Tree very good and sensitive in her
acting, but others condemned the play on the grounds that
'British audiences—as a rule—do not care for plays in which
marital infidelity is held up to anything but scorn and loathing.'

It is possible that Maud was drawn to this play because she
knew a good deal about marital infidelity, and also knew that
those who practised it were not always held up to scorn and
loathing—and that included Edward VII and Herbert. Another
attraction for her was that in modern plays Maud, as a rule, had a
splendid wardrobe. There was a constant emphasis on what were
called 'frocks' in contemporary criticisms. In describing *The
Likeness of the Night* one paper gives the full splendour of the
creation Maud wore in the last act.

A gown typical of sunshine and happiness, and right well does
Mrs. Tree look in it. White satin, hand painted in floral sprays
form the groundwork, and this is almost completely veiled by
a long-trained coat of lace, powdered with glittering paillettes
and edged with bouillonées of chiffon, the sleeves—which
reach the elbow—being of chiffon.

Maud had become a leader of fashion. When interviewed,
although she admitted to being luxurious in her tastes, she often,
she said, sought inspiration for her gowns from poets and poems.
She understands, said her lady interviewer, the charm of simplicity
and allows her sense of beauty to inspire her costumes.

What the gushing interviewer does not add was that Maud Tree
was very extravagant and she paid her bills very slowly indeed.

It may be that, like many deceived wives, she took her revenge by being fashionable and chic and admired by other people—both men and women—without being untrue to the marriage bed, which would entail great social risks.

In some senses Maud's refusal of Olivia was a watershed. The gate had closed behind her while she was examining the lock. When a husband is the owner of a great theatre there are always eager feminine hands ready to open it.

Chapter 8

Herbert at Dome

Gradually Herbert came to live more and more away from his family. Up in the Dome of his theatre he had planned a flat for himself. Here he had a bed concealed in a wall. When he was planning his flat, he wrote down the things he would need. A bed, bookshelves, books. It would be a dome from home.

There were always excuses—rehearsals, urgent meetings, difficulties with scenery or lighting—which could keep an actor-manager in his theatre. The Dome was becoming Herbert's home. Maud, noting his more frequent absences, remarked crisply that he should have cards printed: 'Herbert at Dome'.

Possibly by the early 1900s she had become accustomed to Herbert's mysterious comings and goings. But her jealousies of parts given to other actresses, or suspicions of her husband's life away from home had not abated. Her remarks became more disillusioned, which was understandable. She felt that in life nothing came off except buttons, and when Herbert recommended a doctor saying that he attended some of the most famous men living, she countered with: 'Dead—you mean.'

Yet when he was at home, he would still walk into her bedroom brandishing the newspapers: 'Have you seen this in *The Referee*?' or 'What did you think of *The Times* today?' She would counsel him on matters of publicity and in many fields she remained his link with the great world outside the theatre. He relied on her sharp intelligence and her judgment.

But due to her jealousies and justified suspicions she was difficult. It was typical that she had left her part in *The Last of the Dandies* after only a week to triumph with her dazzling toilettes in *The Likeness of the Night*.

Herbert's next production was to be *Ulysses*, a verse–drama by Stephen Phillips, author of *Herod* (and other forgotten classics).

The curtain rises disclosing the summit of Olympus an amphi-
theatre of marble hills in the glimmering light of dawn . . . as
the scene progresses the morning light grows clearer, descending gradually from the mountain summit over the figures of the
assembled Gods.

On the summit of Mount Olympus, thought Maud, she would
sit as the Goddess Pallas Athene. Maud visualised the Goddess
(herself) as totally divine and she had already given her costume
some thought. She saw herself (the Goddess) as clothed entirely
in gold, with her slim figure shrouded in a golden veil so that
every time she appeared a misty golden light would be shed upon
her and she would appear more than mortal.

To Herbert, Maud appeared much less than mortal. Stage
goddesses propose and men dispose. Stephen Phillips, the author,
Percy Anderson, the designer, and Herbert had decided that—as a
tribute to the imminent coronation of King Edward VII—it
would be appropriate that the Goddess should appear, not bathed
in a golden light, but as Britannia. Maud was slight and blonde
and no Britannia either in face or figure.

Herbert had already set eyes on his Goddess. It was Miss
Constance Collier, tall, statuesque, dark and handsome. She had
had a hard childhood—much like that of the Terry children—as
the daughter of touring players. Although she was poor and
unknown, she was hardworking and she was ambitious. She had
been in the chorus at George Edwardes's Gaiety Theatre, at a time
when Gaiety girls were the show pieces of London. But Miss
Collier had the intelligence to realise that beauty is a wasting
asset. Her ambition was fired by a small discourtesy. George
Grossmith had asked her out to supper and forgotten about it. He
left her sitting in a restaurant at a time when ladies, who *were*
ladies, did not sit in restaurants by themselves.

She confronted him later: 'How dare you treat me like
that!'

Mr. Grossmith looked at her. She was handsome certainly, but
he was a star. 'You are only a chorus girl', he said.

Miss Collier's dark eyes flashed. 'At that moment', she remembered, 'I thought to myself, I may be only a chorus girl now, but
I *will* be something a damned sight better.'

So she set herself to become a serious actress and to this end she had fixed her eyes on Mr. Tree and His Majesty's Theatre. Meanwhile, she left the Gaiety Theatre. There was a time for sitting on a crescent moon and a time to leave the moon behind. She relinquished her regular salary in the chorus line and she began to act in straight plays. It was a precarious time, for she had to keep her mother as well as herself. Then at last she was sent for by Mr. Tree. She had had many rebuffs from him, but persever-ance finally succeeded.

Her description of Herbert at work brings him to vivid life. She was taken up in the lift to his eyrie in the Dome where there was a bright fire burning and a tall fender with a leather seat round it, with the firelight flickering through the bars.

She waited.

He came in—tall, fair, slender, with intensely blue eyes and a manner of extreme, vague eccentricity. Constance Collier later wrote that she afterwards discovered that this manner was totally assumed and was merely the armour in which he clothed himself. She had often seen him put it on and take it off in the years she worked with him.

On this occasion she was its victim, a young actress terrified at meeting the great man. She had put on her best hat which featured a large green bird and, as he talked to her, he stroked the feathers of the bird continuously. This made her forget everything she was going to say to further her career as an actress. She went off and joined another company acting at the Comedy Theatre, the very theatre where Herbert had first gone into management. It was barely five minutes' walk from her Mecca—His Majesty's. But it could have been a million miles away. She had seemingly failed.

But one night Herbert sent round a note to the Comedy asking her to come and see him the following morning. She went up in the lift, the same fire was burning in the same grate. Herbert sat at his desk. But there was one difference. A whole year had gone by.

Herbert stared at her as she came in, did not speak for some seconds and then asked suddenly: 'Where's that bird?'

Taken aback she did not answer and he stood looking at her for some time saying 'Yes', very thoughtfully. And finally he asked her if she had ever spoken blank verse. She had to admit that she had not.

'Oh, then it's impossible. Good morning, Miss Collier.'

A week later he sent for her again, with the same procedure and the same result.

'It's a pity you have never played in blank verse—because it's impossible.'

Finally, goaded with nervousness and impatience she asked, 'Why?'

Herbert looked at her again and replied: 'I've been thinking of you for one of the parts in my new production of Stephen Phillips's *Ulysses*, but if you have never played blank verse, it's impossible. Good evening, Miss Collier.'

On the third occasion she begged him to let her read one scene, tears were in her eyes. Miss Collier was twenty-four, a tall, beautiful, half Portuguese girl with large black eyes and a wonderful presence. When the velvety eyes were wet they, no doubt, had an extra appeal.

Herbert asked her to wait until the end of the play that day. 'They'll give you a seat—come round at the finish.'

He was acting in *The Last of the Dandies*. At the close of the play he swept into his reception room. When Constance had finally found her way round there it was crowded with people. She waited in a corner, she heard him accept an invitation to supper. Henry Dana took him off to discuss some business and they disappeared from his sitting-room into his make-up room. Through the open door she heard him talking to his friends, jokes, quips, trivialities and laughter echoed from the dressing-room. She was in despair. It was going to be George Grossmith all over again. She had been forgotten.

Then suddenly Tree emerged, spick and span in his street clothes.

'Come along, Miss Collier.'

He ignored his friends waiting to take him to supper and bore her off into the dark theatre. He called to the electricians to turn on the lights, put a script in her hand and in the dim light she began to read.

> 'Father, whose oath in hollow hell is heard;
> Whose act is lightning after thunder-word;
> A boon! a boon! that I compassion find
> For one, the most unhappy of mankind.'

The words seemed to her to be more than appropriate and her voice was squeaky with nerves.

She went on.

'For the wind and the wave have driven him evermore
Mocked by the green of some receding shore;
Yet over wind and wave he had his will,
Blistered and buffeted, unbaffled still.
Ever the snare was set, ever in vain;
The Lotus Island and the Siren strain;
Through Scylla and Charybdis had he run
Sleeplessly plunging to the setting sun.'

The lines were difficult and full of unfamiliar Greek names. The dressing-rooms of decaying variety theatres were not places where a child could pick up a knowledge of the classics.

She peered into the dark stalls. Herbert Tree spoke. 'That will do.' He stated at her for a long time and then repeated the ominous phrase, 'It's a pity you haven't played blank verse before. Good evening, Miss Collier.'

Just as she was turning away trying to control her tears of disappointment, he spoke again. 'Come to rehearsal tomorrow afternoon. Be in the dress circle.'

She went home and her mother helped her to smarten up her clothes. They sewed a fur collar on to an old brown dress—the dress would not look too shabby in the theatre and it had a little train to give it importance.

Miss Collier, full of dread, sat in the dark dress circle watching the stars and the author. There were about a hundred people on the stage, for it was to be a lavish production. When lunchtime came, Tree had his egg brought to him as usual. (Some actors sent for chops, others for buns and milk.) Lunchtime went by and Miss Collier was still sitting there—forgotten.

Then Herbert turned and spoke into the empty theatre. 'Is a Miss Collier up in the circle? Will she kindly come down upon the stage?'

She climbed up the steps on to the stage and was introduced to Stephen Phillips, Lily Hanbury and the beautiful Mrs. Brown Potter.

She began to read once again and this time more nervously than the first time.

'Calypso this long while
Detains him in her languorous ocean-isle
Ogygia, green on the transparent deep.
There did she hush his spirit into sleep,
And all this wisdom swoons beneath the charm
Of her deep bosom and her glimmering arm.
Release him, sire, from soft Calypso's wile,
And dreamy bondage on the Witching Isle.'

Somewhere in the back of her mind she thought she heard people laughing at her. Those Greek names again!

Then the author, like Zeus, spoke. 'Well, at least she has the profile for it!'

Herbert had been considering this aspect of Miss Collier for some time. She was engaged. But at rehearsals no one seemed to take much notice of her. She was simply, as she had been at the Gaiety, a beautiful face and a beautiful body to add to the attractions of the production. She was not rehearsed.

But at the first dress rehearsal she had to walk up a long flight of stairs in her Grecian dress, with spear and helmet. Herbert's voice pulled her up short:

'Isn't it possible to go up those stairs more gracefully than that?'

Beauty was one thing, but a woman had to have the ability to use it. Herbert was going to give her that chance. The bird in Miss Collier's hat had been but a prelude to a long and lasting friendship. Herbert had collected another admiring lady.

When Constance Collier walked into His Majesty's Theatre for the first time she admitted to being twenty, she was in fact twenty-four and seems, according to her own delicately veiled autobiography, to have had some experience of the ways of the world. Herbert Tree was forty-eight, but he could hardly be said to be at a dangerous age, for all ages were dangerous for Herbert. Constance described him with all the delicacy and meticulous observation of a woman who had been in love with him.

The first night of *Ulysses* was etched firmly into her memory. She had a new dress and went to Herbert's glittering first night party. The long trestle tables had been set on the stage and the food was from the Carlton Hotel next door. There were critics, actors, aristocrats, politicians—it was an initiation into the great world outside the theatre.

1a Herbert Tree about 1885

1b Maud Tree

2a The Rev. Robert Spalding in *The Private Secretary*. 'I beg your pardon. I thought I met a petticoat on the stairs'

2b Falstaff in *The Merry Wives of Windsor*. 'Without using any extra padding, he would paint the lines so accurately for Falstaff that it was the face of a fat man'

3a Trilby. *Salut mes Enfants*. Form and features suggested the ministering angel at the Place St. Anatole des Arts

3b Svengali. Maud felt that it was a creation that had the sheer force of genius

4a Her Majesty's, the handsomest theatre in London

4b *Julius Caesar*. The stage was to be filled with splendid pictures bringing the ancient world to life

5 *Oliver Twist*. Tree said that the three parts should be played as one entity:
a Fagin the Brain
b Bill the Body
c Nancy the Heart

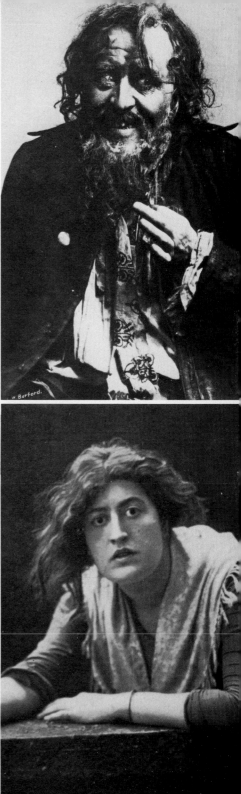

6a Nero and the burning of Rome. 'He continued to paw the air and to recite'

6b Nero and Poppaea. 'Miss Collier showed alluring witchery as the subtle Poppaea'

7 Herod. He was absolutely
dominating

8 Constance freely admitted that she looked very beautiful as Cleopatra

When the notices came out Constance Collier was compared to a young Sarah Siddons. It was a wonderful time for her—at last she was tasting the real joys of success. She would be able to move her mother from the slum they were living in to a better address. She had only to stretch out her hands and the fruits of being a young Sarah Siddons would fall into them.

Above all she was getting to know Herbert. What a sense of fun he had! Unlike other less talented people, he had all three kinds of humour: wit, fun, and satire, but the greatest of all his gifts was his sense of fun and fantasy. He was an eternal schoolboy, known to ring doorbells and run away. Sometimes Herbert could be severe in the theatre, but afterwards he would drop his managerial attitude and become a boy again. He would call to his actors to come with him for a spin in the car.

'Oh that car! Cars were a great luxury in those days and people weren't used to motoring.' It was an open tourer with a door at the back. In they would hop, and how delicious it was if there was no performance in the evening to drive for hours Herbert had no sense of time. They would stop for food. How happy, laughing and irresponsible they were as the soft twilight descended and the roads began to grow mysterious in the dark. Occasionally the car went wrong and they would sit on the roadside until it was mended. They never ate till they were hungry and then they would knock at some inn door, and would get the innkeeper to give them ham and eggs, or bread and cheese. Oh, those were laughing carefree days, when she was first in Tree's company at His Majesty's Theatre!

Constance gives the impression that they were always chaperoned by some other actress or actor, yet it is to be presumed that those happy days would not have remained so vividly in her memory if she and Herbert had not shared them *à deux*. Herbert's was hardly a nature to look for platonic relationships.

But all this was as discreetly veiled as the Greek costumes of the ladies in *Ulysses*, for the pictures of Mrs. Brown Potter and Miss Ruth Maitland depict them in what seem like Edwardian afternoon or evening dresses with the addition of the odd bangle, helmet or metal brassière.

During the run of *Ulysses* came the fifth anniversary of Tree's Theatre. He gave a dinner and, as was the custom on really distinguished occasions, women were excluded.

Tree's male guests included the Lord Chief Justice, the Lord Mayor, the Greek Minister (representing Greek culture), Mr. Pinero, Mr. Forbes Robertson, Mr. Coleridge Taylor, the composer, a sprinkling of earls, lords and baronets and, above all, Sir Henry Irving.

In 1899 Irving had lost control of his own theatre and in the year of Tree's celebratory dinner, 1902, he played for the last time with Ellen Terry in his beloved Lyceum. The King of the Theatre was not dead yet, but the Heir to the Throne was already being honoured.

Tree spelt out his philosophy of theatre management:

> In presenting these works, I have always given the best I could give—for to my mind nothing is too good for the public to accept. It is the *public* to whom alone I have ever looked and to whom I owe what success I have obtained as actor and manager.
>
> I believe that when a man reviews his career he will find that his failures are more often due to taking too mean rather than too lofty an estimate of the public taste. For myself I have always maintained that the public taste is on an infinitely higher plane than is dreamed of in the philosophy of most professional critics. I trust that in saying this I shall not be accused of too gross a self-flattery. Anyhow I shall continue to endeavour to act up to that ideal—always remembering that the first commandment for the manager is:
>
>   *'Thou shalt not bore'*.
>
> Tonight we will pour out libations to all the Gods at Olympus and drink to the good friends of Her Majesty's Theatre.

Tree was being correct, King Edward had not yet been crowned and it was not until that event that he would by special permission be able to change the name of his theatre to His Majesty's.

Sir Henry Irving, King of the Theatre, had been deposed and looked on, unwilling to believe that this joker in the pack could inherit the crown for which he had worked so hard, and so long. Although Irving was unwilling to admit it, times had changed. The old Queen was dead and now under Edward all was ease and luxury, and Tree reflected the age. He understood its capacity for being easily bored, he understood its capacity for self-deception and he understood, and lived, according to its tenets. Its tenets included the appreciation of beauty, especially the beauty of youth, and from the time of the production of *Ulysses* that appreciation was embodied in Miss Collier. Like Ulysses, Herbert was always susceptible to the charm of a deep bosom and a glimmering arm, but unlike Ulysses he did not pray to be released from soft Calypso's wile.

Herbert's next production was to feature Constance as his leading lady, Roma, in Hall Caine's *The Eternal City*. Hall Caine, a long neglected novelist, was a best-seller in his day and Herbert had chosen the dramatisation for two reasons. Caine's books sold in hundreds of thousands and the book gave possibilities for magnificent settings—processions of priests, Cardinals and even the Pope himself. He was to play the Baron Bonelli, a caddish seducer, in evening dress worn with medals and stars and the broad sash of the Order of the Annunciation across his snowy shirt front.

The relations between Roma and the wicked Baron were ambiguous—they even puzzled the critics. But Herbert was never one to wish to outrage public opinion and Miss Collier, with a three-year contract as leading lady in her reticule, was *en grande beauté*. She put it quite simply: 'I am certain that success is the most beautifying thing in the world. Self-confidence and knowledge of power seems to point one's looks amazingly.' She had, she said, almost forgotten that she was a beauty and now that feeling came back to her. Herbert's appreciation may have been a contributory cause though he remarked on some lack of response on Miss Collier's part: 'You don't expect a sense of humour in a passion flower.'

There were subtle tributes to her beauty, she noted crisply, in the smiles of the company. There were no subtle tributes from the critics for Constance's performance as Roma. She admitted frankly that she had not sufficient technique to 'light up' a banal, long-winded heroine, always changing her dresses and spouting platitudes. The platitudes were Hall Caine's. Nor can the book be described as other than a farrago, which contains the immortal lines:

> '*The Pope rose from the stove—he was aroused at last.*'

It came as no surprise that the hero, one Rossi né Leone, turns out to be Pius X's illegitimate son; Miss Collier, as Roma, having been branded as Bonelli's mistress decides to shoot him. But Rossi (the high-minded revolutionary) beats her to it and, with a felicitous aim, drives the Order of the Annunciation straight through Bonelli's evening shirt into his heart. There are several long death scenes, which probably caused Herbert's remark that the suffragettes should be banished to the Isle of Man—and subjected to forcible reading of Hall Caine.

But *The Eternal City* made a great deal of money, and was, as Herbert put it, 'obstinately successful'. He would, said Constance, go around the theatre with a long gloomy face and when she asked him what was the matter he replied: 'The business is up tonight.' At heart he hated long runs. They bored him. Other managers tolerated them with equanimity.

A strange incident marred the run of the play. One of Constance's toilettes was enhanced by a stole made from Russian sables costing thousands of pounds. The furs had been lent to the theatre purely for the advertisement value to the furrier. But Constance began to receive anonymous letters saying she should sell them and give the money to the poor. She was threatened with kidnapping, and the letters became more and more frequent. They arrived at her home and even at restaurants where she was lunching or dining. Terrified she went to Herbert for his help. He reassured her, but the letters continued to arrive ever more frequently. Finally she was threatened that unless she sold the furs immediately—she would be shot. A bodyguard was engaged. The theatre was alive with detectives, and Constance became so nervous and worried that she could hardly act. She made arrangements to give up the part. Herbert was even more concerned than Constance. He read the letters over and over again, and reflected on them.

Suddenly he said to her: 'I feel these letters come from someone quite near us.'

Everyone in the theatre was questioned. A close watch was kept, even on the actors, and the front of the house kept its quota of plain clothes policemen.

The most spectacular scene in *The Eternal City* was when Constance, as Roma, was received in audience by the Pope. She knelt before him as he sat enthroned surrounded by Cardinals in their scarlet robes and to her terrified mind it seemed as if the stage were a sea of blood.

Just as the search for the anonymous letter writer was being given up, it was reported to Herbert that one of the supers was behaving in a very odd manner. Twice the other actors had caught him on his knees praying fervently (a habit not usual in dressing-rooms) and it had also been discovered that he wore nothing but sacking under his suit and no shoes or stockings—although it was deep winter. He was a young, thin, pale young man with a gentle smile who played one of the Cardinals, standing within two yards of Constance Collier. As he was going on stage one night he was seized and underneath his Cardinal's robes they found a long butcher's knife and a manuscript giving his reasons for killing Constance. She must be a sacrifice to the poor. He was taken off to an asylum and the play settled down to be an obstinate success.

As time went on Constance became used to being Tree's leading lady and she paints a vivid picture of the splendid days when the theatre was still exciting and glamour was not a thread-bare word. 'There were gala nights when the King and Queen would command a performance, for the entertainment of some foreign royalty. The men were magnificent in full court dress, with black velvet knee-breeches and decorations, and the women with their magnificent tiaras. No one can imagine the splendour of those nights as you looked from the stage into the auditorium ablaze with jewels. The dress circle was turned into a huge box, decorated with flowers for their Majesties, their royal guests and their retinues. The theatre literally glistened and shone with colour.'

And what more perfect setting for so much splendour could there have been than the scarlet, white and gold of His Majesty's Theatre? At the centre of it was Herbert, living, as Constance said, like a prince, but without money. The expenses of the theatre were on a lavish scale, but Herbert himself never bothered about money and would borrow half-a-crown from the box office for a hansom cab. Because of his lavish and luxurious way of living everyone imagined that he was as rich as the aristocrats who sat in the stalls on his gala nights. He had two gifts, the gift of being able to throw off responsibility in a matter of minutes and the gift of decision.

Yet he himself was careless of grandeur. There was nothing he liked better than to be alone up in his Dome. When everybody had gone home, he would take the lift up there, and rake the fire into life; the great building was empty except for Herbert and the night watchman. Constance said that she did not like to be alone there, it was eerie, but to Herbert the theatre was his home. And with the people who worked in it he had an instinctive understanding. Harry Furniss remarked that of all his clever friends, Tree was the least altered by success. In spite of his position he always had the greatest sympathy with the unfortunate, a fact illustrated by a story told by Constance.

She described, very vividly, how when she was first playing as leading lady at His Majesty's she went home to her flat after having supper out with her mother and when she opened the sitting-room door she found Dan Leno, whom she did not even know, sitting on her sofa. Constance realised that there was something seriously wrong with him by the look in his eyes. Gripping her arm he told her the long story of his life and struggles, and then said he had saved up enough money to give her a contract for five years to play in Shakespeare with him.

'The gas was unlit, the moonlight was shining on his face, his body was trembling and his hands were icy cold.'

Miss Collier, in spite of her immediate fear at this strange tragic face, was aware of other dangers. Suppose he went down to the newspapers and announced that she was to play in Shakespeare with him for five years. She was at the beginning of her career and it would have been fatal to have been made a laughing stock. She calmed him down and told him to come down to the Theatre and see Mr. Tree in the morning.

Dan Leno drove off. 'I felt a traitor', wrote Constance. 'He was so content, so radiantly happy that he was to play the great roles— Richard III and Hamlet. I think I was the first person to whom he ever really told that secret ambition—the innermost hope of his heart.'

When she got to rehearsal the following morning Dan Leno was already there making everyone laugh, signing up small part actors for long term contracts and giving money away.

At last Herbert came and took Dan Leno down to the stalls to talk things over. Dan Leno and Herbert sat in the half light talking and staring into one another's eyes. Constance described how Tree's red hair was standing on end and his blue eyes blazing with excitement. 'It was an odd picture, those two white faces—those geniuses of the theatre—down there in the dimness.'

Then the manager came in with two men—and they took Dan Leno away.

Herbert beckoned Constance to him and said that he feared something was seriously wrong. To Constance, Tree seemed pale and his eyes were sunken—the fading light of inspiration was on his face, as if he had seen a vision that was past. For a long moment he was silent and then he said:

'If this is madness, what is the use of being sane? If he ever plays Richard III it will be the greatest performance of the part we have seen—let's get back to work. How dull normal people are!'

For a few fleeting moments Herbert had touched and understood the soul of a man verging on madness and had not rejected him, but tried to understand. It was no wonder that so many people found Tree's character, in spite of its infuriating vagaries, very endearing. Nor was it surprising that Constance found him a fascinating companion and during her first years at His Majesty's she went everywhere with him. Except on official occasions, Maud did not go about with him.

One of his intimate friends was Byam Shaw, the artist, who had a house in Addison Road where he lived with his young family of five children. Byam Shaw had designed costumes for some of Tree's productions, and they had become friends. In December of 1904 Mrs. Byam Shaw had given birth to her youngest child, Glen—later to become the theatre director, Glen Byam Shaw. Two or three weeks after the birth, Herbert took Constance round to see them. Mrs. Byam Shaw was tired after her recent confinement and went to bed leaving her husband to entertain Constance and Tree. Suddenly the silence of the night was broken by the chauffeur blowing the horn of Herbert's splendid motor car. Mrs. Byam Shaw rang the bell for the maid, and sent her out to the street to find out what was going on. The maid came back with the news that Mr. Tree had ordered the chauffeur to sound the horn every fifteen minutes in honour of the new baby, a salute not appreciated by the tired new mother, or presumably the neighbours.

During all the time that Herbert visited the Byam Shaws' house in Kensington, his companion was always Constance and they never met Maud Tree. It seemed to the Byam Shaws as if the Trees lived entirely separate lives.

Maud presided at the grand first night parties, at the top of one of the long tables and Herbert at the other. There was always a great deal of laughter from Maud's table for she was full of life and wit. Officially the Trees were a brilliant couple. Their private life was their own—but not each other's.

Tree's close friends were discreet. His way of life was his personal secret. It was not to be subjected to public scandal.

Neither Constance Collier, enjoying the euphoria of her first successes and Herbert's company, nor Maud, with her human jealousy, knew that their main and enduring rival was an unknown quiet little mouse with a cosy nest far from the Dome.

Chapter 9

King Herbert and Queen Maud

About 1903 Maud decided to sell their house, 77 Sloane Street, in what was, and still remains, one of the most fashionable parts of London. The ostensible reason was that the family had outgrown it. Viola had grown up to become a talented young woman—she sang, she painted, she acted and she had a literary bent. All options were open to Tree's daughter. She was already, while still in her teens, providing food for the gossip columns:

> Miss Viola Tree is the eldest daughter of Mr. and Mrs. Beerbohm Tree. At present she does not wish to adopt the stage as a profession—but then she is only 17, and has time to change her mind. Dancing is her dear delight, and for music she has some talent, singing, after her fashion, as blithely as any thrush. The fair Viola is nearly six feet tall, and promises to become a very statuesque lady indeed.

For all Viola's various activities Maud felt a studio was needed, presumably away from the younger children. There was a ten-year gap between Viola and Felicity, the next child. The younger sisters respected Viola both for her sharp brain and the fact that she was closer to their godlike father than they were.

Constance described Viola at this time as young, and tenderly springlike. At the theatre she was called 'The Twig'. But she was as witty as her mother, though some guests at the Dome suspected that Viola and her father planned witty sallies to ricochet from one to the other. But Viola had always been precocious and her father had always encouraged her to be amusing.

So Maud had decided that Viola needed space for all her talents, and was determined on moving. She talks about being 'beguiled' into giving up her little house in Sloane Street. But adds regretfully that they left behind more than the white front door and the lattice windows of Mr. Tree's tastefully appointed and decorated dwelling. They moved to a furnished house in what Herbert described as a Westminster slum. Finally, Maud fell in love with a house near the river at Chiswick which had belonged to one of Charles II's mistresses, Barbara Villiers.

Walpole House had an immediate appeal for Maud. It was, and still is, a large house mostly of the Wren period, built in a simple style of red brick with long sash windows facing over a willowy islet, with views to Kew and Fulham along the Thames. There is no garden in the front, but the tall pillars and intricate iron gates add elegance to the façade and in Maud's day the house stood in nearly two acres of a formal eighteenth-century garden with old trees and flagged walks. There was a tennis court and behind the grounds of the house a market garden stretched out to the old high road. The house could have been a gentleman's mansion in the country. Inside there were more than twenty rooms—a dozen bedrooms and dressing-rooms; an elegant carved oak staircase led up to a huge drawing-room with a view of the river; a formal dining-room, a breakfast room, a study for Herbert flanked the entrance hall and there were nurseries, kitchens and pantries and attics ready to be converted into a studio for Viola.

Herbert dutifully signed a twenty-one year lease in 1903. Maud was ready to give rein to her passion for interior decorating. She restored the house in 'a judicious, tasteful and correct fashion'. She then romanticised the garden, filling it with roses and lush flower borders.

To Maud it seemed a perfect setting for her family.

It is to be suspected that this was not a very sensible move of Maud's. Once removed from Sloane Street, she was no longer in a position to join in any of Herbert's intimate supper parties. Except for grand occasions she was away from the social centre. But a woman in those days, if she had children, was also burdened with a staff—cook, maids, governesses and all the myriad duties entailed in running such a household. The Tree family were not, as they said, 'grand enough for a butler', but they had a staff of six besides a governess. The principal parlourmaid did a little valeting for Herbert, but as he spent more and more time in his Dome, his dresser became his valet.

Maud ran a household with constantly changing staff, especially governesses. If Herbert objected to formal schooling for his girls, Maud also hated the idea of schools at all. The result was that her daughters had twenty-five governesses, all of whom, whether originally permanent, turned out to be temporary. Some left because they could not deal with the children, some because they could not deal with Maud. Some were English, some were French, some were disapproved of because of their accents, others because of their manners. This insistence of Maud's on manners and accents was not surprising because the family frequently went to very grand houses indeed, spending many Christmasses at Belvoir Castle, the home of the Dukes of Rutland and the Manners family. While Maud's leanings towards grandeur appealed to Herbert on the level of filling his theatre with sparkling tiaras on first nights and spreading the good news of art amongst the uneducated aristocracy, for himself he liked amusing companions whoever they were. Dominoes with a cab driver amused him as much as, or more than, dining with a Duke.

Little by little Herbert did not seem to have a great deal of time to spend with his children at Chiswick. Over Sunday lunch he would amuse them with his parlour tricks—a short-sighted man looking for the salt cellar, a drunken man, an epileptic man, or copying himself reading a bad play, dropping off to sleep, his head in his hand, with his elbow suddenly slipping off the edge of the table. Even in the streets he would continue to act. He would embarrass his children by handing round his hat begging—for the 'rich of Chiswick'—or suddenly turning into Fagin in the Park, frightening other children with his changed voice and face. It was as if at every moment of the day he needed an audience.

Maud remembered those days as being full of the wine of life. But children, more perceptive than grown-ups give them credit for, remembered him as always slightly distrait. He was not interested in the education of his children, and interrupted their lessons on one occasion to tell the current governess that she was wasting her time, education was useless.

He always seemed to Felicity and Iris to be distant, like a king, and when he was being funny, doing his tricks to amuse them, it was like a king being funny, not like a clown being funny. The clowns in the circus took the children into their confidence, they were funny and familiar, Herbert was funny and distant. Their mother Maud was constantly with them and they adored her. She was pretty, amusing, cared about them and was part of their lives. Their father was different, he was not an integral pivot of the family like their mother. When he was at home it seemed to them as if their father and mother were not cosy and affectionate, but rather that they treated each other like kings and queens, admiring each other at a dignified distance.

Walpole House was a long way from Her Majesty's Theatre in the Haymarket in those days. There were no passing cabs as there had been in Sloane Street and so Maud and Herbert had separate cars and chauffeurs. The break was becoming more complete.

At the theatre was the beautiful Miss Collier, and in Chiswick was Queen Maud.

In the same year when Maud, ill-advisedly, moved from Sloane Street, Tree produced Tolstoy's *Resurrection*, dramatised by Henri Bataille and 'Englished' by Michael Morton. Tree played the Prince Nehludof whose betrayal of the peasant girl Katushka sets the tragedy in motion. The action moved against the rich background of nineteenth-century Russia—a Moscow palace (a set much resembling a Grand Hotel of the period), singing peasants welcoming the Great Prince back to his estates with a rousing chorus of 'Christ is Risen' and a kiss of peace, and a final scene where, against a background lit by camp fires amidst the gold glitter of stars and snow, the erstwhile lovers part forever.

Unlike the Prince in the play, Herbert was hardly prepared to expiate a small peccadillo by trudging all, or even part, of the way to Siberia. Art was one thing, life was quite another.

There was no part for Miss Collier in *Resurrection*, the betrayed Katushka was played by Lena Ashwell. Contemporary photographs give the two aspects of her portrayal. 'Innocence' (long braids and much peasant embroidery) and 'Corruption' (overcoat made from a blanket, headscarf and decadent cigarette hanging from the mouth).

Possibly Miss Collier's passion-flower good looks gave her more of the air of a survivor and counted her out as far as noble suffering was concerned. Or maybe Herbert felt that her expression was hardly in keeping with the peasant in plaits.

In the summer of 1903 Constance went to Dieppe, then a fashionable seaside resort with all the artistic glamour attached to la Belle France and the Impressionists. The company was charming. Painting, the stage, writing and every aspect of art had its representatives—Walter Sickert, Nicholson, Marie Tempest, the young John Barrymore and Maurice Maeterlinck. Herbert dropped in for a day or two, presumably on his way to his beloved Marienbad, only to find his brother Julius gambling away his last louis at the tables.

There in the sun-dappled walks Constance suddenly became engaged to Max Beerbohm. Was this an attempt on her part to get away from the possible scandal of her relations with Herbert? Or on Max's part simply a passing flirtation born of summer sunshine and her enchanting face under a parasol, as they strolled in the sharp sea air?

From the time of this engagement Constance began to join Max's family for their Sunday luncheons which were also gatherings of the artistic young. Here she met all the friends of Max and her own generation, among them Rothenstein and that aspiring, if shabby, young playwright Somerset Maugham. Herbert was, after all, more than twenty years older than she. It was pleasant to be in the swim with younger people. Constance had a friendly outgoing nature and plenty of temperament. Max's fastidious attitudes towards the fair sex and his dilettante attitude towards life were hardly likely to satisfy Constance who was used to stronger meat. Max had according to his friends evaded the Scylla of the actress Grace Conover to become drawn by the Charybdis of Miss Collier. Nor did Max's family approve of Miss Collier. In the days when culture and a family background meant so much—she had neither. She might be a good actress, but that was as far as it went with the Beerbohm family, who were not disposed to appreciate ex-Gaiety girls.

Constance describes Herbert's stepmother, Eliza, as small and keen-eyed in her lace cap and black silk dress, sitting at the head of the table. Her keen eyes were not approving of the beautiful Constance. Perhaps Mrs. Beerbohm suspected her relations with Herbert. Whatever his public image may have been, his stepmother was possibly not unaware of his frailty where the fair sex was concerned. Maud had been received by the Beerbohm family with open arms, but Constance in the family was something quite different. Miss Collier not only looked like a passion-flower but she had the temperament for it. Hardly the wife for the cherished Max.

The vagaries of Miss Collier's love life are discreetly veiled in her autobiography. Hers was not an age for telling all. She seems to have developed a vague *tendresse* for an actor called Julian

L'Estrange. Photographs of Mr. L'Estrange show a man who had missed being good looking by a very small margin. Constance had met him for the first time during the run of *Ulysses* when he had played Hermes (Mercury) wearing 'winged sandals and Cadaceus'. His first speech was strangely appropriate as a description of his own actor-manager: 'Sire, remember we are gods, yet we from human frailties were not *ever* free.'

Miss Collier wrote that during the long run of *The Eternal City*, while she was suffering (in exquisite gowns) she heard that 'Mercury' was not doing very well in America, being both in debt and out of work. She added that it worried her for she felt that it was on her account that he had been sent out of England. She does not specify who sent him, but presumably it may have been Herbert who did not want a rival. But when Tree heard of Julian being in dire straits in New York, he immediately cabled money to the impresario Charles Frohman not only to pay L'Estrange's debts but also his passage home. Tree was always a master of the grand gesture.

His grand gestures off stage were translated into grander gestures on stage.

In Edwardian days, the East was not only mysterious but romantic and dramatic. During 1903 Herbert commissioned Kinsey Peile to dramatise Kipling's short story *The Man Who Was*. It is hard to see why he did this, except that the story gave Herbert a chance to stagger about the stage covered in long hair and whiskers portraying a man who had been wrongfully imprisoned by evil Russians for many years, like some latter day Man in the Iron Mask. Having returned to the Regiment, the scarlet and gold clad White Hussars, the Colonel questioned 'the dingy heap in the chair'.

'How did you come here?' The dingy heap laughed weakly.

A look into the Regimental Rolls had revealed that he was Limmason of the White Hussars, who answered, as of old, to the toast of The Queen, only to be buried three days later with regimental honours.

Pictures of the production show the handsome, well set-up and splendidly dressed White Hussars, and in the centre the wreck of a man, who was the owner of His Majesty's Theatre giving an excellent performance of somebody who had spent thirty years growing hair in Siberia. Close-up pictures of Tree in the part throw more sharply into relief his light eyes than any others.

Having wrung the withers of his audience by this sad wreck, Tree returned to Shakespeare, to Richard II. This was considered by many critics, except Shaw, to have been one of his most successful classical parts. *The Times* wrote:

This is a character which suits Mr. Tree to perfection. The curious blend of the man of shrinking effeminacy and philosophic irony, the dreamy languor interrupted by bouts of half-crazy speculation—all these things the actor brings out with completeness as to make his Richard probably the most haunting figure he has yet given us. The great scene of abdication in Westminster Hall, culminating in that wonderful passage of the broken mirror, was given a quite beautiful ending of the actor's own invention in his silent, pathetic leave-taking of his few faithful friends. His parting with his Queen too was unspeakably touching.

The *Telegraph* found that Mr. Tree was among the very princes of producers of plays. His instinct for effect was little short of the marvellous. The settings were a dream of beauty—scene after scene of mounting magnificence. The *Telegraph* rather blasphemously thanked Heaven that there was a manager who was so obviously indifferent to money that he could present such a striking picture of the times.

From mediaeval England Tree returned to the mysterious East, in *The Darling of the Gods*. He capitalised on the current fondness for old Japan. The *Daily Telegraph* was as carried away by the spectacle of old Japan as it had been by old England.

'A feast of light, colour, and music, a lavish display of beautiful dresses, picturesque scenes, and quaint characteristic types. Gaily dancing Geishas move like a flock of startled doves, or chattering magpies . . . great bronze Gods, cherry and almond blossom'; while the *Daily Graphic* found that the brightly-armed Samurai, and the artistically dressed singing and dancing girls gave wonderful local colour to one of the 'quaintest and most original entertainments that London has ever seen'.

Tree's Sakkuri, the War Minister, a part after his own heart, was a malevolent tyrant with a grim sense of humour which only made his cruelty the more refined.

The play opened with the charming Yo San (played by Lena Ashwell) trying to catch butterflies which rose in swarms from the ever-flowering bushes. From butterflies, to execution and death, the play was a triumph and much to the taste of Tree's public. To modern eyes the stage pictures have much the air of a Japanese tea room.

On the hundredth performance of the play, 23rd March 1904, Tree produced a beautiful souvenir programme. The cover shows a single sword dripping blood on which is perched a frail butterfly. The programme then opens out, like a fan, to reveal scenes from the play in the Japanese style: the heroine amid rocks and cherry blossom, Japanese musicians painted like characters on a vase and the heroine again, dreaming under the moon with only a waterfall and irises for company.

This tale of old Japan had been written for the American actress Blanche Bates, who needed a success to follow her Cho-Cho-San in *Madame Butterfly*. Blood, butterflies and doomed youth had an equal success at His Majesty's as they had in New York.

The play was produced on New Year's Day of 1904 and ran for the whole season. But one project was hardly enough to occupy Herbert's time and in the same year he decided to start an Academy of Dramatic Art. He took over two old houses in Gower Street, furnished them, and set up a school with George Bancroft as his administrator.

It was a curious project for Herbert, because he had always stoutly maintained that acting could not be taught. Acting was an instinctive thing, a kind of *feu sacré* which might descend like the tongues of flame on the apostles at Whitsun. Yet suddenly, perhaps having been impeded by lack of technique on the part of other actors and actresses, he decided that it was imperative for actors to have some stage training. And to prove his confidence in the project he enrolled Viola, his eldest daughter, amongst the first of the pupils. This was not entirely to Maud's satisfaction. She felt that not in the life of an actress was happiness to be found. A curious point of view for a lady who often suffered jealous vapours over having been refused some leading part. Maud warned that acting was a poison, a drug; once a girl had drunk deep of that divine anguish, it would be very difficult for her to become accustomed to a humdrum life. But she pleaded in vain for Viola to be kept apart from the stage. Herbert had decided that he wanted his daughter to act, and she would act.

But having once established the Academy of Dramatic Art, Herbert, in his usual way, lost interest in it. He had had the idea and now, having cracked a bottle of champagne over its bows, the ship could sail on piloted by others. It had been started and from time to time funds were provided by public performances of students at His Majesty's. Tree had been carrying all the financial burdens of his project, but by the spring of 1906, he decided that 'a corporate body' should carry the burdens both financial and administrative. The President was Squire Bancroft and the Council included George Alexander, John Hare, Cyril Maude, Arthur Bourchier and J. M. Barrie. Tree gradually, like the Cheshire Cat, faded out, although years later the Committee were still writing him letters complaining of his lack of interest in R.A.D.A. For Tree, the idea was the main thing, the details were for people who liked details.

When the season of *The Darling of the Gods* ended, off went Herbert to Marienbad as usual. When on holiday it was his habit to study and make notes on productions and the parts he was to play, and he had decided on *The Tempest*. When thinking of Caliban he felt that his teeth must be specially designed, as must his lips, and the hands should be webbed. He added the words 'freckled welp', which gave him the idea that the skin should be that of a crocodile with a surface full of warts. He made notes for the scenery—the cave should have trees growing from the top of it. Before Caliban came on, a roar should be heard like that of a caged beast and suddenly a bat should fly up—heralding the entrance of the monster.

Maud did not approve of Herbert playing Caliban. But she was won over to Viola's stage career. For she remarked that a lovelier or more fairy-like Ariel could not have been found. Viola was just twenty.

When the play was produced in London *The Times* gave Mr. Tree a condescending pat on the head, like the good theatrical dog he was. 'Mr. Tree is getting along with Shakespeare. He is doing, in fact with Shakespeare just what Mr. Wegg failed to do for Gibbon.

'Mr. Wegg—it will be remembered, admitted to Mr. Boffin that he had not been "right slap through Gibbon very lately, having been otherwise engaged, Mr. Boffin". Mr. Tree, too has frequently been otherwise engaged—engaged with queer Eternal Cities and other trifles—yet he is finding time to go right slap through Shakespeare by degrees.'

Tree had produced or acted in eight of Shakespeare's plays—if the much despised Garrick version of *The Taming of the Shrew* was included. *The Tempest*, his ninth Shakespearean production, was well received by the critics, though those who were not entirely on Mr. Tree's side remarked that Caliban had become the principal character. *The Times* noted that Caliban was so grand and grotesque that he virtually swamped the Ferdinand/Miranda motif and the lovers had subsided into the tame state of a conventional modern engaged couple, while the magician Prospero had become a mere male chaperone. There was no new fangled nonsense about Mr. Tree's Caliban, no ill-advised attempt to sickly him o'er with the pale cast of unnumerable commentators' thoughts. It was noted that this Caliban seemed more susceptible to music than earlier Calibans, the isle was full of noises, musical noises and as he rejoiced in them his face lighted up, nor was he repulsive—if it had not been for his tusks, he would have been quite good-looking—for a monster.

The play was tricked out with one of Mr. Tree's spectacular shipwrecks and, unlike that in *The Tempter*, this one did not make the audience seasick. The ship duly sank and the mariners were authentically deluged with water. Instead of 'elves and hounds' Tree substituted dozens of antedilvian monsters, slimy, long, lanterned-jawed things out of the Natural History Museum, while troops of children and a delightfully impudent Cupid enlivened the proceedings with a charming ballet. There was an immense amount of scenery from rocky shores and yellow sands to mysterious blossoming woods and Prospero's cave.

Above all there was the debut of Miss Viola Tree playing Ariel —father and daughter, Caliban and Ariel, the duet had an appeal to the sentiment of the audience.

When writing of her father Viola described him as irresistible and absolutely dominating. It is hard not to feel that it was this irresistible force of his which carried Viola into the theatre. He willed her to swim when she was only four years old. She must put her arms round his neck. He swam into deep water. Gradually he disengaged her arms. Looking at her, his imperious gaze told her that the water would bear her. She must float, he told her. Immediately and submissively—she floated. The same thing happened when she began to ride. She mounted, was commanded to trot, and did.

When it came to playing Ariel it was Herbert's dominating will which governed her performance. He had decided on her debut in the character of Ariel. She had a charming voice and was a beautiful girl. She describes how she was told that she must sing while flying on a wire. She discussed with a professional how she was to do it. Which foot should she use to take off? The wire was hooked into her strait waistcoat and then Herbert walked on to the stage. For a second he listened to the discussion. There was no point in argument. She must not argue, she must fly. He gave the order to the mechanic to let go and up she flew dangling high above his head, tingling like a telegraph wire at the sudden vibrations of his actor's voice. She heard him order her to sing and she sang.

Up, up, she soared above the proscenium arch singing, rather shakily at first, the first bars of 'Where the bee sucks'.

The rehearsal over he wanted her to come out—where was immaterial, just out—out into the street to feel the surge of London around him. He hated delays and liked constant activity. He had to be going somewhere out from the theatre, or back to the theatre to see what was going on.

But his judgement on Viola was right, she was described by critics as indeed a divine spirit, a creature of sunshine and golden air, her singing admirable and her movements showing ineffable grace. In Ariel Viola's talents for dancing, singing and acting came together, and she had done her father justice for his confidence in her abilities.

The Tempest was first produced on 15th September 1904 and was an enormous success. The scenes of ravishing beauty and quaint fantasy, the woods with their pendant boughs in a land of summer sunshine, the fairy revels and the dance of the reapers, everything pleased the *Daily Telegraph*—and the general public.

But there were dissenters. Some critics objected to a disconsolate Caliban left repining on a solitary shore, while the ship sailed away with the whole cast including Prospero. No doubt Prospero (Mr. Haviland) felt the same—for his Epilogue had been cut out altogether, in the interests of leaving Caliban to shade his eyes to catch a last glimpse of the ship that was carrying away a civilisation he had humbly worshipped. He stretched out his arms with a pathetic regret. But *The Times* did not object to this. 'We take leave of Caliban in the mood of pity, an entirely right ending.'

To celebrate the fiftieth performance of *The Tempest* Herbert, like Mr. Puff, decided to publish the text, cuts and all, with illustrations from Mr. Charles Buchel's sets. He also took issue with a writer who had castigated him for 'the vulgar use of stage illusion' an unkind cut from an anonymous critic in *Blackwoods Magazine*. The *Stage*, said Mr. Tree stoutly, *was* illusion, and 'this is written of the work of a man who was an actor and a playwright'.

He had been accused of pandering to a vulgar public and being driven to overloading the play with a lavish expenditure of money. As a matter of fact, wrote Tree, *The Tempest* had cost less than many modern plays and he failed to see why Shakespeare should be treated with less care and less reverence or less lavishness of resource than is demanded by modern authors. 'I claim', he continued, 'that an artist works primarily for himself—his first aim is to satisfy his own artistic conscience. His output is the result of the impetus in him to work out his own ideals.' So far from admitting that his public was a vulgar public, he was conscious that their demands upon the art of the manager are too often in excess of his powers to gratify them. After all, he concluded, this version of *The Tempest* had already been witnessed by vast multitudes and if only a portion of these had been given a deeper insight into, and a wider appreciation of this fantasy, his labours to 'give delight and hurt not' would not have been in vain.

His next venture into Shakespeare, with *Much Ado*, was not a success. It may have given him a chance for garden scenery, but although his Benedick looked the part, it was one of his failures and even 'sweet Winifred Emery' as Maud called her, does not seem to have brought zest to the part of Beatrice. As if to compensate himself for failure as Benedick, Tree ignored his critics and sticking to his guns produced the first of his Shakespeare Festivals. Between Monday 24th April and Saturday 29th April 1905 he staged six plays—*Richard II, The Merry Wives, Twelfth Night, Hamlet, Much Ado,* and *Julius Caesar*, playing in all of them himself. *Julius Caesar* and *Richard II*, in which plays he had the best notices, he staged twice.

When the curtain fell on *Julius Caesar*, he made one of his usual speeches. The Shakespeare Festival had come to a close but he found it hard to tell his audience how overjoyed he and his fellow actors were that 'our efforts to honour Shakespeare have met with so enthusiastic an appreciation on the part of the public'.

Then Tree had a side swipe at his critics: 'Spring is upon us once more, and in the spring the joyous note of the cuckoo is heard—so also is the croaking of the raven. It happens that I have been reading tonight a leading article in a great daily journal lamenting the decadence of the drama. Our best answer to these lamentations is that during the present week more than twelve thousand persons have witnessed the plays of Shakespeare at this theatre, and, indeed for many years past there has taken place here a revival of the Shakespearean drama. Never was there a greater love of Shakespeare than there is today, and you who are lovers of him, will, I am sure, be glad to hear that—God willing—we shall give another Shakespeare Festival next year—I hope on an extended scale.'

Herbert bowed to his audience, 'However great and far reaching the decadence of the drama may be, I am glad to know that it has not yet reached that section of the public whom I have the honour to serve, and to whom I tender my loyal thanks.'

Tree's critics could sneer at his over-decoration and denigrate his performances and yet in his heart of hearts he had a genuine love of Shakespeare, both his comedy and his tragedy. Herbert's over-decoration only reflected his age. It could also be said that his Shakespeare Festivals foreshadowed Stratford and the National Theatre. A man who had founded R.A.D.A. and supported Shakespearean revivals on a lavish scale was entitled to feel he had rendered some small service to the art of the theatre.

Having reverenced the classics he turned his eyes to something new. Herbert had always found material which appealed to him in France or Germany. Also in 1905, he produced *Les Affaires Sont Les Affaires* by Octave Mirbeau adapted by Mr. Sydney Grundy as *Business is Business*. His portrayal of Isidore Izard was a detailed study of a cynical and very unsympathetic character. One critic wrote: 'All the details of the man—his coarse humour, the loud self-satisfied laugh, his faith in the power of money, his affection for his caddish son, are touched on by Tree with masterly skill.' This praise was echoed by other critics, but the public, always less willing than the French to see financial considerations as being one of the mainsprings of human behaviour, did not like the play. Possibly an additional reason for the play's failure was that good King Edward, the uncle of Europe, was in pawn to several 'uncles' who were Jewish and the portrayal of a Jewish financier as other than an upright English gentleman did not please.

On the last day of the 1904 season *Oliver Twist* was produced for one night only. Constance Collier's description of the preliminary hazards of this play highlights the knife-edge hazards of any theatre production. Herbert did not like Comyns Carr's adaptation of *Oliver Twist*, but Constance herself believed in it and decided to take an option on it. This made Herbert ponder—he had never seen Constance with her statuesque good looks as other than a Goddess, an Empress or a romantic heroine, but if she were prepared to risk her own money perhaps she could play the cockney prostitute Nancy? Comyns Carr and Constance petitioned Herbert, and won. Herbert, in his grandiose way, decided to put it on as an experiment for one night only. Comyns Carr more or less produced it with a scratch cast, for most of the company had gone on holiday, or to touring engagements. Because of Tree's lack of interest the production was extremely cheap, although he did decide to play Fagin.

Occasionally Herbert drifted in to the rehearsals, and then suddenly was drawn towards the play, and became as usual a hard taskmaster, making Constance rehearse the same little scene up to thirty different times. When he had reduced her to floods of tears he said, 'Now then, now there is no more Constance Collier, let's find out how to act the part.'

The realism of Nancy carried Herbert, the producer, away. Lyn Harding, as Bill Sikes, did not please him and he kept on urging him to hit Nancy as if he really meant it. Finally, when the actors were overtired with rehearsing Harding's foot slipped and he hit Constance full in the face. She fell to the floor half-stunned and then struggled to her feet with blood streaming from her mouth and her teeth nearly knocked out.

'There,' said Tree triumphantly '*that* is the effect we want to get.'

Constance was also shirking the scream at the end of the murder scene. Tree turned everyone out of the theatre, and Constance, with her imagination working, thought of tough Saturday nights off the Kennington Road and let herself go—at last. Tree put his hands over his ears. And one of the theatre cleaners came rushing on to the stage crying out, 'My God, what's 'appened?'

Herbert laughed. 'We've *got* it', he said.

But in spite of his broad dramatic effects, when it came to the murder of Nancy his careful nerve-end instincts came to the fore. The murder must take place off. Once the audience could not see the actor the imagination could be stirred and they would believe anything.

The unearthly scream, the sound of the thuds of Bill Sikes's club as he beat Nancy to death and the white face of Fagin, staring through the open door with the moonlight shining into his eyes conveyed everything.

Fagin blew out the candle and the curtain came down. There was no applause only a stunned silence. Nor would Tree allow Constance to take a curtain call at the end.

Fagin turned out to be one of Tree's triumphs. In the den scene he crushed an imaginary black beetle so effectively that the audience heard it squelch, and his power of suggestion was such that when he saw the glittering green eyes of a rat and shooed it away, the audience were convinced they had seen a real rat scuttling to its hole. People asked Constance if the rat was alive or a mechanical device. But the rat was merely in the imaginative eyes of Tree as Fagin.

Although Tree liked to shine, he never liked an unbalanced production and, as Shaw had said to Ellen Terry, he always surrounded himself with excellent actors and did not mind if they acted him off the stage so long as the play was a success. When planning *Oliver Twist* he remarked that the three parts in it should be played as if they were one entity—Fagin the Brain, Bill the Body, and Nancy the Heart.

Oliver Twist was a triumph and swamped any idea of new productions. It ran for a year, an immense run on the Edwardian stage, and was constantly revived.

It was running in December of 1906 when Carol Reed was born, the fourth son of Herbert and May Pinney—a baby who was to grow up to be knighted like his father and to produce *Oliver!* as a film musical.

Herbert often cheered himself up with practical jokes, presenting Constance as Nancy with bunches of spring onions, or producing anything from dead rabbits, to live kittens, tiaras and even a pair of new patent leather boots out of his sack. These he put on and played the whole scene wearing them. Constance, the dedicated trouper, hated fooling on the stage and Herbert did everything he could to break her determination not to laugh. The audience remained unaware, feeling that kittens, patent boots and tiaras were all part of the scene.

Tree shared with Ellen Terry this lighthearted appreciation of a jolly good jape, and when he was playing Falstaff with Ellen, she once stuck a hatpin into his fat belly and Falstaff began slowly to deflate. Tree had met a fellow and better joker.

During the run of *Oliver Twist*, Constance suddenly went off and married Julian L'Estrange.

She later remarked, 'I don't know to this day how it came about.' Julian had asked her out to lunch and suddenly produced a marriage licence; three weeks later they were married, before the matinée performance, and had then gone back to their respective theatres and their acting.

It was a curious event and nothing in Constance's account of it gives the impression that she was in love with Julian. Her picture of Herbert stands out dominant, compelling, amusing and admired. Julian remains a shadowy figure. Why did she marry? It is an unanswered question, but Herbert had a wife, and perhaps she needed a husband to act as a screen against scandal, as Maud acted as a screen for Herbert. She had still been engaged to Max when she went off on one of Mr. Tree's grand tours, playing Viola in *Twelfth Night*, Trilby and Portia in *Julius Caesar*.

Constance makes it clear that when a Tree company toured they were treated with respect. 'We were very magnificent, with a private train and the Royal Coach attached. I had the Queen's suite.' She thought back to the days of touring with her mother, spending Sundays in cold third class carriages. Now it was different. The company would be met at the station by the Mayor and his minions. There were formal banquets and receptions for all the company to attend in the different towns they visited. Miss Collier made it clear that while all this might sound snobbish

Mr. Tree's position was an official one and great actors were regarded as a very 'serious' part of the establishment.

The *Tatler* devoted a whole page to Miss Collier's tour, but expressed the utmost amazement at the preparations. 'Unless anyone has had actual experience of the preliminary preparations necessary for the organising of a big touring company, no adequate idea can be formed of the labour given to the tour—months before it starts—at His Majesty's Theatre.'

To get three plays out of London and round the provinces and over to Ireland required twelve railway trucks, a special steamer and a pantechnicon looking rather like a covered wagon. Painted on the side of the pantechnicon in large letters was the legend, 'Mr. Tree's Company from His Majesty's Theatre, London'—the big letters, said the *Tatler* perceptively, serving to herald the arrival of the actors from His Majesty's. The company was seventy strong, not including the managers and 'office people' who travelled ahead. It was their business to engage and rehearse the local 'supers' and children required in the performances.

On this grand tour, amongst Mr. Tree's company, was Mr. Julian L'Estrange—out of debt and in looks. He sent Constance flowers with a card 'Journeys End in Lovers Meeting'. This meeting ended with Constance breaking off her engagement to Max. She dismissed the whole thing quite casually, remarking to a friend: 'You know how it is—on tour. Something more exciting turned up.'

To Constance, culture like that of Max and his friends, was a mere trimming to her career as an actress, not a way of life. But she continued to enjoy the life of a leading lady and, more especially, the grandeur of being Tree's leading lady.

What Tree thought of these feminine vagaries is not recorded, but he was hardly a man to repine. Possibly he had enjoyed two years of his passion-flower and now contemplated other pastures and other flowers.

*

But they were not pastures new. It has been said that beautiful and talented wives, or mistresses, do not need, as a rule, to fear other beautiful and talented women. It is the little brown mouse in the corner who can inherit the cheese if not carefully watched. The mysterious Miss Pinney was perhaps that little brown mouse.

Herbert remarked in his journal that he regarded women not as domestics, but as domestic angels. Maud was not, and did not wish to be, a domestic angel. Clever, talented and good-looking she required more consideration than that role. Miss Pinney was possibly that domestic angel which Herbert craved in his quiet reflective moments, when he did not feel disposed to shine.

Miss Pinney was transformed by deed-poll into Mrs. Reed and suddenly re-appeared in Herbert's life. Or possibly she had never left it. By the late summer of 1904 Mrs. Reed, installed in her commodious house Daisyfield on Putney Hill, was happily pregnant and in March of 1904 she presented Herbert with their third son, Vivian Guy.

Herbert with his capacity for insouciance took his growing second family in his stride. If rumours went round in theatre or artistic circles, or if his sudden mysterious journies to Putney had been noted, there was never a breath of open scandal attached to Herbert's name. And presumably Mrs. Reed led a quiet respectable life with her family, walking on Wimbledon Common and bringing the children up to respect their mysterious father.

Some of Herbert's close friends, including the Byam Shaws talked of him having 'a house on Putney Hill'. Did they also know of his growing extra-marital family? Presumably questions were not asked, so answers were not necessary.

If sexual modes and manners change over the centuries so do attitudes to bastardy. From the age of Jane Austen and the spread of gentility, it had been a taboo subject, and children who were born of famous parents on the wrong side of the blanket concealed the fact, but in the ages of chivalry and courtly love, there was no such concealment. Legitimate and illegitimate sons were able to carry the arms of their fathers. It was clearly stated 'A bastard may carry the Arms of his father with a Batton Sinister and take his Sirname from the Lordship from whence his father Titles himself.' The Bastard in *King John*, on hearing from his mother that King Richard Coeur de Lion was his father, takes an enlightened view of the subject. 'Now by this light were I to get again, Madam, I would not wish a better father. Some sins do bear their privilege on earth and so doth yours.'

But at the beginning of the twentieth century, though men's morals did not differ from the ages of chivalry, their attitude towards their children born out of wedlock and their children's attitudes were quite different. They did not gallop into battle with three shields argent on a field gules and a bend sinister indicating the wrong side of the blanket, they kept their suspicions secret. And very often they stayed secret. It was not to the children's advantage for the truth to be known. Sons were called 'cousins' and mothers became 'distant cousins'.

Mrs. Reed's two eldest sons Claude and Robin were now in their teens. Claude was already launched on his acting career about 1914. Perhaps Constance had found out about Herbert's other family or felt that she had been a mere cloak to hide it. This could explain her sudden marriage, not so much a marriage of convenience as a marriage of self-defence. A lover with a wife was one thing, but a lover with two families was a more complicated proposition. No progress seemed likely on a personal basis. But complications did not bother Herbert, whether they were the complications of his vast theatre productions, the intricacies of his intuitive acting of leading roles, or the highways and by-ways of his interwoven and ever increasing families.

In December of 1906 Miss Pinney produced Herbert's fourth son, Carol Reed, who kept his parentage a secret until the day of his death.

By the beginning of 1907 Herbert had four natural sons, three legitimate daughters, a huge theatre to run, a period house in Chiswick, an extravagant wife and a second 'wife' comfortably installed on Putney Hill. The upkeep of two families, seven children, a dozen or so servants and two motor cars (with chauffeurs) seems a great load for one pair of shoulders. No wonder Herbert drew a very careful picture of a man carrying fardels—he had a number to bear himself. But he carried them with insouciance and even gaiety. Four sons is a great many sons to conceal, and yet somehow Herbert carried his responsibilities cheerfully, and continued to run his vast theatre.

Nor was Miss Collier the only diversion in Mr. Tree's life— there were always those little expeditions to the Continent and the annual 'cures' at Marienbad.

But as the Mephisto character played by Herbert remarked in Henry Arthur Jones's *The Tempter*: 'There is moderation in everything, especially in sin. He that sins moderately sins twice as long, twice as much, and twice as pleasantly,' and Herbert's geniality overcame many strayings by the wayside. The age he

lived in helped him. For as Mr. Jones's devil concluded: 'That's
scarce a sin at all that never comes to light—the worst of sin is
that it sets a bad example. When it's strictly covered up and
nothing known there's not much harm in it.'

There was little harm in Herbert, but it was no wonder that
many people, including his family, found him distrait. . . .

Chapter 10

Some Years ago in Marienbad

'The Man says: I will talk to the stars,
and the woman: I won't let you talk to the stars alone.'
HERBERT BEERBOHM TREE

Herbert had been going to Marienbad for many years. It was the summer of *The Dancing Girl*, in 1891, when he took Maud there for the first visit. She describes the town as not being much sought after, or fashionable at that time, although in fact it had been growing in popularity for more than fifty years. Maud was astonished at how much Herbert enjoyed the pine-scented walks, the drinking of the waters and all the ceremonies which went with the 'cure'.

Marienbad suited Herbert. It combined all the attractions of town life with a backdrop of mountains amongst which gaily clad peasants toiled away in their immemorial way, adding a human note to the amenities of the scenery. It was a set from His Majesty's dropped into Bohemia, with the good cooking of the Adler or the Erzherzogin Gisela to mitigate the terrors of *villégiature*.

Herbert had never been an outdoor man. He did not like sports, but he played amateur golf. When fishing, he would give a joking imitation of a man fishing. He was more interested in his observation of a man fishing than actually catching the fish himself. The two sports which he enjoyed were riding, usually in Hyde Park, and swimming. He was a strong swimmer and would brave the cold seas off Norfolk in high waves, and on one occasion saved a man's life. But organised sport he hated. He had, he said, not much sympathy with athletes 'who kick a football when it is down'. But Marienbad was different. The town was built over 2,000 feet up. From the original village it had expanded, until by the 1890s it had become a sophisticated town folded in the pine-clad hills. The air, as the guide book promised, was deliciously light and pure. The walks led from the fashionable promenades straight into the heart of those pine forests where the happy visitor could drink in the health-giving, resinous odour of the trees.

The season began about 1st May and finished on 1st September, giving the London visitor a chance to finish the season and then recover from it amongst the Bohemian hills. What could be more beneficial for the health than to stroll out into the bracing early morning air, to take a glass of water from the spring and listen to the band playing on the Promenade Platz from 6 to 7.30 a.m.? Only perhaps a quick climb to the heights of the Kaiserthurm to drink in the glorious panorama surrounding one, before strolling back to the Bäckerei for coffee, rolls and, if the doctor allowed, butter and honey. A very light lunch would follow about midday, only five courses, soup, fish, a roast joint, vegetables and stewed fruit, washed down with moderate quantities of claret, hock, light German beer, or even better the refreshing light country wines of Bohemia diluted with sparkling Gieshubl or Krondorfer water.

The attractions of Marienbad had been founded on a spring discovered by some astute monks at Tepl, who had begun to exploit the health giving waters about 1870. They seem to have belonged to a very curious order, for they wore black top hats with their white habits; and profiting by the spa mania of the nineteenth century, they grew rich. As Marienbad became bigger and more fashionable, the glasses of water, the steam baths and the health-giving walks became less and less of a medical treatment and more and more of an excuse for a holiday.

By the nineties Marienbad was growing rapidly, and by 1900 it boasted half a dozen good hotels and dozens of boarding houses. Churches catering for all the official religions of the various nationalities who thronged the town had been built. After politely saluting the Almighty the visitors could walk under the trees to the Kreuzbrunnen spring, or to the Ferdinands Brunnen where the water was carried to the Promenade Platz where it flowed into a large vase of alabaster, thus giving the impression that the visitor could, after all, still be in one of M. Ritz's hotels. The spring which was used for bathing was the Marienquelle 'highly charged with carbonic gas'. Gas baths were built and patients were shut up in boxes with only their heads showing.

It is not recorded whether Herbert endured the box treatment, but he revelled in the walks among the pine trees and was always one of the early risers taking his glass of water in the Curhaus. He walked along the shady avenues near the Kreuzbrunnen and listened to the band in the Curgarten. Every night he went to the opera, or to the play and in the day time he could sit amongst the parterres of flowers, watching the comings and goings of the modish cosmopolitans, for in 1899 Marienbad had become a favourite haunt of the Prince of Wales, who disported himself 'en garçon' as it was discreetly put. The town had achieved that rich *mélange* which was so typical of the age. Herbert wrote that the English always imitated their inferiors—the middle classes imitated the upper classes and the upper classes the demi-monde. Marienbad was a porridge of all these elements, and in the centre walked the Prince seemingly unaware of the attention he attracted, yet annoyed if he did not receive better service than others at the Weimar hotel where he stayed, and full of complaints if impeded by sightseers, even to the extent of complaining to the Austrian Emperor. It was seemingly difficult to strike a balance between incognito and the deference due to Royalty.

It was also noted that the Prince had different ways of nodding, smiling, lifting his hat or acknowledging the presence of friends and acquaintances, all these gestures were graduated according to their rank. While perhaps he was prepared to be entertained by Tree in his splendid new theatre, when a Prince of Wales was disporting himself on holiday, there were lines to be drawn. Acquaintance with royalty could not be presumed upon.

Maud admitted freely that she could not enter into the spirit of Marienbad as Herbert did. She contented herself with sitting under the trees reading novels, or driving through the woods. It was naturally easier for Herbert, who spoke fluent German, to join in the social life of the town, than it was for Maud. Her deep knowledge of the classics in Greek and Latin did not help her here. She seems to have found Herbert's good German a source of amusement. At Cologne on their homeward journey they missed all trains, all connexions, lost their luggage, stormed and raved and finally were obliged to alter their route all due to Herbert's perfect German which, said Maud, no one could understand.

Herbert came to realise that Marienbad was not the place for

Maud, and after a time it became his custom to take his 'cure' every year alone, while Maud stayed with friends at their grand houses, or sometimes sent her children off to farms in the country where they could be fed with butter, eggs and cream and lead a healthy outdoor life. Or she rented a house at the sea, or in the country for the summer and arrived with children, governesses, cooks and maids, prepared to lead a simple life of country austerity.

Herbert preferred Marienbad. It gave him time to think. But while thinking, it was natural that he should study his surroundings. At the opera, at the play, under the shady walks, or in the gardens of the Curhaus he watched the ladies. There were ladies about to be divorced, ladies hoping to be divorced and ladies who did not need to be divorced, having never achieved a state of holy wedlock in the first place, though their charms kept them in discreet comfort.

Tree described his feelings about Marienbad, and about himself, in a short story he wrote which was set in 'Kreuzbrunn in the Bohemian Forest'.

His power of unswitching himself at will from any mode of life was one of the accomplishments of this many sided man. To such men as Guy, men who live every moment of their lives, this power of unswitchment is the salvation of the nervous system, and Guy revelled in the luxury of laziness with the same energy which he threw into the active enjoyment of life.

Amongst the pine woods, listening to the birds and hearing the ripple of water on the rocks, Guy/Herbert 'reviewed his past life, made new resolves, and swore a truce to frivolity'. This mood, naturally, did not last for in rescuing a butterfly from the water he saw a rhapsody of red and gold. It was the face of a woman.

In the story the rhapsody promptly dropped a yellow rose on the sward and Guy/Herbert went back to his hotel and three portions of *truite au bleu*. But his interest was aroused. Fortified by the trout he went looking for the woman.

'The wild strains of the Hungarian band were in accord with his mood.' He caught sight of his rhapsody in red and gold, whirling by in the arms of Baron von Steumpel, and he took it as a sign of assent that she was wearing one of her yellow roses, matching that in his own buttonhole.

9 Waller and Maud (caricatures)
Maud. 'A gown typical of sunshine
and happiness and right well does
Mrs. Tree look in it'

Waller. 'First he proposes the
renewal of their old relations'

Mr LEWIS
WALLER

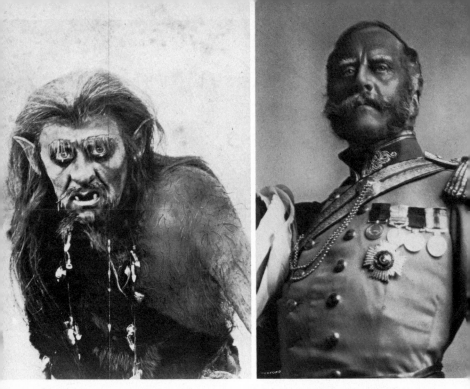

Above: 10a Caliban and 10b Colonel Newcome. *Below:* 10c Demetrius
in *The Red Lamp* and 10d Richard II

Above: 11a Limasson in *The Man Who Was* and 11b Paragot in *The Beloved Vagabond. Below:* 11c Benedick in *Much ado about Nothing* and 11d Beethoven

Above: 12a Tree as Macbeth and Violet Vanbrugh as Lady Macbeth

Below: 12b *Macbeth* ensemble

Left: 13a Wolsey. 'The wily, crafty, strong-hearted Cardinal lives and breathes'
Below: 13b 'The magnificence of costuming and skill in grouping made *Henry VIII* a production of beauty'

14a *The Darling of the Gods*. The *Daily Telegraph* was carried away by the spectacle of old Japan and voted it 'a feast of light and colour'

14b *David Copperfield*. A nostalgic reminder of that ideal England which glimmered in the minds of men at war

15a Queuing for the first night of *Carnac Sahib*, 1899

15b Tree with his Company in Berlin, 1907

| COURTICE POUNDS | CECIL KING | FISHER WHITE | LYN HARDING | BASIL GILL | CHARLES QUARTER-MAINE | JULIAN L'ESTRANGE |

HENRY NEVILLE   CONSTANCE COLLIER   SIR HERBERT TREE   VIOLA TREE

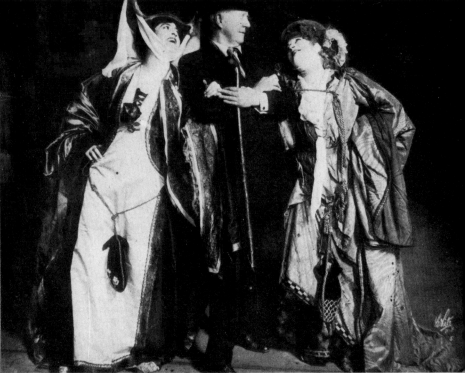

16a Constance Collier and Tree
(in street clothes) rehearsing
The Merry Wives of Windsor

16b Mrs. Patrick Campbell

'Amongst the gay throng of dyspeptics, the curves of her figure made the woman in brown holland the most conspicuous from among the throng.' Further enquiries elicited the welcome information that she was in Kreuzbrunn '*en garçonne*'—though reputed to be most exclusive. But Guy/Herbert was no amateur at these encounters. He told himself: 'It is the clumsy wooer who pays a direct compliment at first sight.' But fortune favoured Guy/Herbert and she immediately gave him a speaking look and dropped her rose.

'There was no secret between them, they understood. For she was the elemental woman—he was just a man.'

Having come to this mathematical realisation they presumably trotted out into the woods, for the next sentence denotes a certain passing of time. 'The perfume of her body mingled with the scent of the roses; their incense intoxicated his being. The music seemed to say: "Let us be wise tomorrow but let us live tonight. It is madness—let us be mad. There is only one moment—that is the present. The moment is worth the pain of repentance".'

Then in Herbert's story, a handy nightingale trilled, 'and they were lovers as in Eden'.

It was impossible to imagine that in that soft relaxing, yet invigorating air, with so many available ladies, Herbert should not find some companion to help him drink in the heady scent of the pines. But Herbert's short story gives an idealised version of an encounter. There are no recriminations. Real life women did not end an affair by saying cheerfully 'Bye-bye Butterfly'. They were more difficult to shake off.

There remains, amongst Herbert's papers, a book of German poems to trace the progress of a real life encounter at Marienbad. It is headed simply: 'His Book'.

It must be admitted that the lady who wrote the poems showed more emotion than talent. She seems to have seen Tree first while strolling along carrying a posy, which he took from her hand, while darting her a look of deep admiration—the look of the true artist, as she described it. Then he spoke. His voice was so beautiful that her heart was immediately captured. It seemed that she showed her intentions or perhaps her acceptance too soon, because he said nothing and sloped off in silence.

'Is he going in silence? His voice to sound again only in my dreams?' She wonders whether *she* should speak, but that would be breaking the bonds of propriety, so instead she confided her thoughts to her journal. When the night folds the woods in its arms, she wrote, she would like to stray in the silver moonlight, when all the flowers are quiet. Then she could speak of things which in the daylight she must hide. In the dark garden she would sink down in front of the flowers to try to push away the idea of him, and the flowers would dry her tears, and the cool earth would soothe her burning cheeks.

He still remained cautious, even aloof. Perhaps he had something on his mind? But deep hopes thronged her breast, although her lips had not yet formed her thought, her silent mouth did not need to speak of what was in the inner depths of her soul. On the other hand, she had a quick wonder whether she would see him today and finally she achieved the ultimate joy—a rendezvous.

She was early, but it was a nicely chosen spot. 'A little rivulet runs over the small stones in the green woods, on a small twig a small bird is singing. Come soon, the gold of the sun glows on the mountain. I am happy to be here—the breath flies from my lips as a greeting to you.'

But gradually the healthy regime and the sharp scent of the pines seem to have helped the lady to a happy conclusion of her dearest aspirations. She felt that she was tamed, like a woman in the ancient sagas, as they wandered through the tempest tossed trees. Dreams drew them along, far nothingness was their goal and her senses were overcome. His blood called to hers and so she sank down. . . .

Having achieved the fulfilment of her love, she began to have more enlarged ideas. She now felt like journeying with him to places where no foot had trodden before. She also had the idea of hearing songs no voice had sung and wished to sink (together with him) in a flaming kiss through everlasting night into one single soul. She saw *his* soul as an endless sea which breaks in the morning light on the shore uncovering the pearls in its depths. Joyfully she sank into the bosom of this sea.

Encounters at Marienbad were one thing. Eternal commitments were another. There is nothing the casual lover desires less than journeying into places where no foot has trodden before. A little light flirtation in the Curhaus listening to the band, or a moonlight stroll had uncovered unsuspected depths.

Herbert had once remarked that it was possible for a woman to have 'virtuousness but not virtue'. From the hidden depths, with a little light fishing, he had caught such a one. But as he also remarked, it is not pace but boredom that kills, and overflowing sentimentality could very well cause boredom—a thing devoutly to be avoided.

He may, as he wrote of Guy/Herbert, have felt himself to be an aeolian harp upon which the winds of love played, but on this occasion the aeolian harp seemed to be playing a discordant tune. Something would have to be done.

While she was trembling, and hurrying to the spot of their encounters, she found him 'like a shadow hurrying away—silently and rapidly like a marsh light'. This was not to be wondered at. A man cannot be blamed for taking cover. After all, she had taken to raging about his wife, threatening to break the trees with her knuckles and destroy the municipal flower beds. There were, thought Herbert, amenities to be preserved. The air at Marienbad could perhaps be too bracing. How soon, Herbert remarked to his diary, the day after tomorrow becomes the day before yesterday, for 'our whole civilisation is one long battle against the forces of nature'. And some ladies who began an encounter with soft glances and succumbed to easy passion rapidly degenerated into being one of those forces of nature.

A year or so later he wrote in a notebook a suggestion for a 'gag' in *The Vandyke*—'a mad chaos of sea, drowned mermaids on a shrieking shore'. It was perhaps an echo of the lady from the woods of Marienbad and the book of poems she had given him. 'Take thy book—it is thine with all its moans and memories of love.' One last pressed flower from the only gift he had given her told of the death of that love.

The marriage law, wrote Tree, was the most immoral of all, not excepting that relating to income tax, for 'it is productive of more subterfuge, lying and hypocrisy than any that governs us'. But on the other hand it had its advantages. Marriage could—when used with discretion—provide a refuge from other women and creditors, like a man's club.

A man is allowed to think, wrote Herbert, but not aloud, adding a page or two later: 'It is no use beating your head against the brick wall of convention, a lifetime makes little impression on the wall.' He noted down another thought: 'Mens sana in corpore sano—but there are after all men's and women's sana.' They were totally different, sometimes he felt like giving women back a little of the wisdom they had inflicted on him. The lady in Marienbad did not have the one quality which he admired, the reticence of passion. Love was a battered instinct and needed to be used with discretion. The function of women was to forgive and not to cling.

However fervent the wooing, a man must turn back to the world of ideas. The great maxim in life was to be able to be entirely oneself. For Herbert this was not an easy task. He was, as he himself wrote, everything by turns and everything sincerely. Iris, his daughter, once asked him whether he was like any of the characters he played. He replied: 'I am like nearly all of them— Hamlet, Falstaff, Dr. Stockman, Svengali, Gringoire, Paragot, Antony, Othello, Nero, Macbeth, and Micawber. I have lived them all.'

It was not an accident that acting had chosen him as a profession. It was one of the few professions where a man, without jeopardising his reputation, could be a villain or a hero on alternate days, a sneering cynic at a matinée, or a passionately sincere lover at the 8.30 performance. He was a square peg in a square hole and he fitted comfortably into his setting. It was for others to arrange themselves around him.

When at Marienbad Herbert used much of his leisure for thinking. He jotted down random thoughts, epigrams, plots of plays, ideas for quick dramatic curtains.

His German education had given him a distaste for the learned life. He preferred to believe that he had been born educated, having that inherited knowledge which is called instinct. The result was a strange amalgam of lightning strokes of imagination —as if several different teachers were writing on a blackboard on different subjects. There was a theatrical situation in a flash of lightning which suddenly revealed a third person in the room. Humour was more important in tragedy than in comedy. How did a man come by a philosophy of life—by commonsense out of misfortune.

Herbert liked to give the impression that he never read, but when he was free of responsibilities at Marienbad, he had time to read and did. Many of the jottings in his notebooks make this plain. But the age of Bertie, Prince of Wales, was not an age that admired erudition. Both Herbert and Maud preferred to give the impression that they were not clever. Maud covered her sharp brain with a layer of chiffon and topped it with a fashionable hat, and Herbert liked to pretend that everything he did was produced by the light of nature. He wished to appear a conjuror who could produce a wriggling rabbit out of his top hat, with no effort and no thought.

As early as 1893 he gave a lecture on the imaginative faculty at the Royal Institution and began by expressing his deepest feelings.

When the gift of the imagination was conferred upon mankind, a double-edged sword covered with flowers was thrust into its baby hands. Just as the highest joys which are known to us are those of the imagination, so also are our deepest sorrows—the sorrows of our fantasy.

Love, ambition, heroism, the sense of beauty, virtue itself, become intensified by the imagination, until they reach that acute and passionate expression which renders them potent factors for good or evil in individuals. Even so has the imagination ever been the strongest power in fostering the aspirations, in shaping the destinations of nations. It is the vision through whose lens we see the realities of life, either in the convex or in the concave, diabolically distorted or divinely out of drawing.

Then, as if he felt that the audience did not expect such a serious theme from himself, the actor, the wit, the man about the Haymarket, the image which he liked to represent, he changed the tone. He felt vaguely, he said, that much wiser and profounder things had been written on the subject than could possibly come from him. 'But valour is the better part of indiscretion, and no plagiarist is so prolific as he who does not read. Happily, or unhappily, I happen to be one of those whose valour has not been blunted by too much speculative reading, whose imagination has not been cramped by research, or warped by scientific knowledge.'

He had, he went on, at first thought of calling his lecture, 'The Imaginative Faculty, together with some reflections on the pernicious habit of reading books'. He was speaking with the voice of the Edwardian house party where 'larks' were the thing. But looking at his distinguished audience at the Royal Institution he felt that perhaps the sub-title smacked of levity. It was an honour to be asked to address the assembly, and even more so since he was the first member of his calling to be so honoured.

Because he had never been able to annexe the thoughts of others from books he was able to explore the giddy heights of the imagination. 'But just as each eye will catch a different reflection of a landscape, just as a musical instrument possessing but a limited number of notes will yet admit of an infinite variety of combinations, so I may be so fortunate as to give some variations of the eternal melody whose leit-motif poets and thinkers have sung to mankind.'

He proposed, he said, to talk about his own profession—at least, he went on, modestly, he would be able to speak from personal observation and, in that sense, with the authority of experience. Then he asked himself and his audience the question 'Can acting be taught?' He answered himself in the negative, saying that the actor was the 'passion-winged minister of thought'.

Other actors had a different view of acting, and critics often had a different view of Tree. Playwrights, once they were incarcerated with him at rehearsal, reacted in various ways, from sending round their solicitors, to leaving the theatre, directing the play them-selves, or refusing to sell their plays to him in the first place. Pinero said: 'I like him so much that nothing would induce me to write a play for him.'

But there were no playwrights to break the calm of the Royal Institution, so Tree ended with a hymn to the imagination. 'Its loftiest mission is to preserve for us, amid the din and clash of life, those illusions which are its better part—to epitomise for us the aspirations of mankind, to stifle its sobs, to nurse its wounds, to requite its unrequited love, to sing its lullaby of death. It is the unwept tear of the criminal, it is the ode of the agnostic, it is the toy of childhood, the fairyland of the mature, and gilds old age with the afterglow of youth.'

No doubt he sat down to thunderous applause. It was an excellent curtain speech, sincerely meant and sincerely delivered. The actor had reflected his audience.

At Marienbad, he was able to let his own imagination go free. Unhampered by the everyday running of his theatre, or the compli-cations of his two families he was able to reflect. To conjure up in his imagination the characters he was to play and to note his feelings about them in tranquillity.

Before he played Nero, he had studied the character in depth.

He had read several books about the Emperor and his period. He felt that flattery was the root cause of the evil in Nero. The seed of cruelty may have been there, but flattery fed and tended it. Flattery made the great little, never the little great. A philosopher should be detached from the world. Although Nero may have begun as an idealist he was drawn into politics, where politicians were mere 'daughters of the game'.

Sometimes even fair ends are brought about by foul means, the tyrant is destroyed by a bomb. The populace holds up its hands in horror at the murder, but applauds the result. The strongest emotion in politics was fear—love of mankind ran it a bad second. Ethics were a mere habit. When the first death warrant was placed before Nero he said: 'I would I had never learned to write'. As death warrant followed death warrant, Nero could sign them with an easy conscience. It was so very simple to blur personal conscience by the expedience of politics. A man might shrink from a deed which as a member of a committee he would applaud. Committees were devoid of ethics.

Tree was against committees on principle, and remarked that the perfect committee consisted of four men—three of whom were absent.

He ended his notes on Nero by saying that in losing his ideals, Nero had lost the whole world. Possibly Nero could have said that every man was equal—except himself. Tree put his initials against this thought—H. B. T. He was perfectly honest in his derivations of jokes and epigrams and occasionally would put in brackets 'not my own'.

A few random thoughts from his short stories bring a breath of life to the incident at Marienbad. One of his heroes admits to having a dual nature (while toying with his glass of Château Lafitte). In 'The Fatal Fairy' the hero admits sadly: 'One should never take a fairy to one's bosom lest it should turn into a bald headed vulture; let not the rude hand of humanity seek to meddle with the intangible which is real just so long as it is not touched by the dissolving breath of mortality.'

Herbert's romanticising led him to believe that things towards which one has a tendency, come to one—so the lover comes to love. Love came to Herbert only too easily. It takes two to make a love affair, it only needs one to break it. But if his lady from Marienbad had 'that nameless perfume—that subtle atmosphere

which surrounds some women and hypnotises the soul of man'—
there was a point when the perfume cloyed.

There was nothing for it but to leave by carriage for the railway
station (Two miles from the town: One horse carriage: 1 florin;
two horses 1 fl. 80 kroner).

Some situations needed at least one and a half days of train
journeying between oneself and the fairy which had turned into a
bald headed vulture. Even the Channel crossing (and Herbert was
a very bad sailor) was a welcome relief from the raging of love
sick ladies 'en garçonne'.

Chapter 11

Nero, Newcome
and the Serpent of Old Nile

The spring of 1906 saw the production of *Nero*, in which, much to her surprise, Maud was given the part of Agrippina. She was probably surprised because she felt herself in many senses supplanted. When Maud looked back on her life with Herbert she felt deeply that 'Herbert and I' came to an end when the family moved to Chiswick. She was clear sighted enough to realise that Herbert strode forward alone towards his goal. That moment, at their marriage, when she had felt a strong feeling to protect and cosset him was long past. Herbert walked hand-in-hand with no one. She softened this sharp thought by adding that the family walked beside him—Viola, Felicity and Iris were all made interested in his work. The average woman sees her husband and herself as a team, children are not the be-all and end-all of a marriage. They are adjuncts who join it for a time and then leave to make their own lives. But to a woman whose husband spends his life with other people, and whose interests and suspected loves lie outside the home, children become all important. They are the sole link with the beautiful past and the sole life-line to the future.

So Maud was surprised at being given the part of Agrippina while the beautiful Constance played Poppaea. Maud waxed lyrical about the days of wine and Nero. Nobility and beauty crowned the play, the settings how rich and sumptuous, the music how haunting—the whole excitement and glory of the play brimmed over. She had never lived so intensely for her part and for the theatre. Nothing else filled her mind. It was not only her cup which was brimming, the audience was brimming too. They had never had such a success and this in spite of the fact that it cost more than £200 to ring up the curtain each night.

The first night of *Nero* was on 25th January 1906. The *Illustrated*

London News found that in this play spectacle had reached the limit of its resources. The luxury and decadence of Imperial Rome were brought to vivid life. The play itself seemed a mere libretto for scene painters and Coleridge Taylor's music. Nor was it true to history, Nero's shameful death was perversely omitted. There was remarkable acting by Mrs. Tree who showed a fine frenzy in the part of the scheming, ambitious and passionate Queen Mother Agrippina. Constance Collier was beautiful, showing alluring witchery in the varying moods of the subtle Poppaea. She also had some alluring costumes in peacock blue, pink, or purple with pallium in saffron decorated with heavy gold. Maud as the Queen Mother always appeared in matronly garb heavily covered, while Constance displayed both her talents and her *décolleté*.

In spite of his intricate study of Nero, carried out amongst the pines of Marienbad, Herbert's impersonation of him was found not yet to have received its finishing touches, although it bade fair to be a brilliantly imaginative study in morbid psychology. Pictures of Tree as Nero show him as splendidly decadent with scarlet sensual mouth and pendant lower lip, his red hair crowned with laurels, or plucking madly at his lyre against the background of burning Rome.

This burning was the final scene of Stephen Phillips's play, a grand pyromaniac effect which was to be its climax. The set was a classic loggia with the panorama of Rome in the distance. Gradually little sparks were to appear here and there in the landscape, indicating the increasing menace of the flames. Then the whole city would begin to burn and the flames would rise higher and higher. Poppaea lay dead on her couch and as Nero watched the licking flames he played upon his lyre, reciting verse.

That was the plan.

But when the moment came for the grand climactic fire—nothing happened. Tree began to be nervous. He had his eyes on the effect and his fingers never touched the lyre, he was plucking away in mid-air. No flames appeared. He continued to paw the air and recite. Constance/Poppaea opened her eyes, although she had been 'dead' for some time. The audience tittered. Suddenly there was a loud explosion covering Nero and Poppaea in soot. The curtain came down, but the audience applauded the mishap sympathetically. The stage manager—reacting in the usual way to applause—raised the curtain for the actors to take a bow, revealing Herbert and Constance blacked up like nigger minstrels. Spectacle had culminated in farce.

Constance did not consider that Nero was one of Tree's better performances, but Mr. William Archer found much to praise. 'No one can doubt that Mr. Tree has a very keen—one might almost say—a sympathetic realisation of the character of Nero.'

Tree's detailed study of Nero had not gone unnoticed. He had made notes on his insight into the inner workings of the man's mind. 'Once they—the artist/governors lose their ideals, they lose the world, once they give themselves up to crime, they wade deeper and deeper in blood.' Looking into his own heart Tree added, 'The artist is one to whom only the unrealities of life are important.'

William Archer had noted all these thoughts in Tree's performance. 'He throws himself with infinite gusto into the character of the aesthetic-megalomaniac, the autocrat who is convinced that he has an artistic mission (as others believe in their religious or political calling, or election) and who makes it an excuse for every sort of cruelty and crime. He plays the part with extraordinary picturesqueness and subtlety of detail. The limitations of his performance are the limitations of his voice and method.'

Tree's painstaking study of Nero's character had struck chords but the actor's limitations are often physical—a big, fat, rosy boy could never play Oliver Twist. The unhappy blacking-up on the first night had not helped. An additional burden was that an Edwardian audience, with their philistine optimistic outlook, was unreceptive to a study of pure evil. But the spectacle made the play a draw, as Maud remarked. If the audience, like Constance, tended to ignore Tree's subtle effects, they enjoyed the grandeur that was Rome, and—once the fire was effectively burning on the second night—its eventual destruction. But when writing about the play later it seemed to Maud that never had she been happier and never had Herbert been so successful, as when *Nero* was running in 1906.

Esmé Percy played Britannicus. A story has come down in theatrical circles, presumably through the late Mr. Percy, that Tree was attracted to him. He is supposed to have been having supper with Maud and Herbert, when she got up from the table, wished the two men good night and then turned and said: 'Remember Herbert, it is *adultery* all the same.'

In viewing the progress of Tree's life, it is impossible to believe this story to be true. It is incontestable that Esmé Percy was beautiful in a very feminine way about this time, and in his Roman costume he had great charm. But, in middle age, people, both men and women, are apt to exaggerate both their charms and their conquests. Perhaps it cheers their growing realisation that beauty is ephemeral and has been lost. Esmé Percy was in the first flush of his good looks and his success when playing Britannicus and perhaps, like Ellen Terry when she made her first success, he felt that everyone was in love with him—including the owner of His Majesty's Theatre.

Tree in his usual grand way interrupted the money-making run of *Nero* to put on his second Shakespeare Festival. He gave six plays during the week—acting in every one of them himself. The week culminated in two performances of *The Merry Wives of Windsor* with Ellen herself celebrating her fiftieth year on the stage by acting Mistress Page. On 27th April 1906 Tree took full advantage of the occasion.

The press recorded the proceedings with smiles brimming with sentimental tears.

The dominant note in the performance at His Majesty's on the 27th ult. was struck on the appearance of Miss Ellen Terry, who for that night played Mistress Page in *The Merry Wives of Windsor* in celebration of her Jubilee on the stage. Cheer after cheer rang out when the well-beloved actress, radiant with smiles, appeared before the footlights and the enthusiasm was continued at high pressure throughout the evening. The popular actress was the life of the performance and enraptured the audience by her charm and gaiety. Mr. Beerbohm Tree entered fully into the spirit of the evening playing Falstaff with added zest and contributing in all possible ways to the special significance of the occasion.

Tree had planned a tender climax to the play. Louis N. Parker had written an epilogue to be spoken by him and answered by Miss Terry.

Mr. Tree: Stop, mistress, stop! Our Will has had his way
But now you're in *my* house and I can say
What Shakespeare never thought of in his play.

> Stand here, dear sister-artist, England's pride,
> The Genius of her stage personified,
> Queenlike, pathetic, tragic, tender, merry—
> Oh rare, O sweet, O wondrous Ellen Terry.

Mr. Tree continued for another twenty lines listing the characters she had played, the authors who had benefited from her performances as she made bricks from the playwrights' straw, a sentiment not perhaps so highly appreciated by the playwrights (from Shakespeare to Shaw) as by Miss Terry. Mr. Tree's peroration ended.

'We praise you—we admire you and we love you!' A tucket was sounded, the people cheered. Miss Terry appeared prettily confused and said: 'Oh Mr. Tree I cannot find a word—' On cue a well-trained dove flew down bearing a document which was handed to Ellen by an adjacent fairy.

Fairy: Here, Ellen Terry—from a little bird.

Miss Terry (greatly relieved): Thank you. Can I trust
> > myself to read?
> You know how much indulgence I must need.
> I want to thank you—all of you—I see
> Through tear-dimmed eyes, your loves envelop me,
> Wrap me as 'twere through a shining cloud,
> And I am very humble—very proud,
> I want to say—I want to say—alas.
> These written words are but as sounding brass
> And tinkling cymbals, for at such a time
> Silence were better than a puny rhyme
> > (To Mr. Tree)
> Shake hands! I thank you—phrases I have none.
> I pray you leave me here a while alone.

At which point Tree kissed her hand ceremoniously, as though endeavouring to hide a life-long love, and the scene was left to Ellen—and her audience. Cheers, tears and memories mingled on this sentimental occasion. Ellen was then regaled with a long address from the President of the Playgoers Club which was solemnly put into a silver casket and handed to her as a tribute. The evening ended with 'Auld Lang Syne' sung by Tree's entire company—and the audience.

After sentiment came business and the run of *Nero* was

resumed. But having set the town on fire as Nero, Tree abruptly changed roles. He decided to play Colonel Newcome in the dramatisation of Thackeray's book.

For some reason, now obscure, people had become heated about the idea of Tree playing that beloved old soldier Colonel Newcome. The *Daily Mail* printed an article with the banner headline 'Should Mr. Tree be *allowed* to play Colonel Newcome?' Whether the *Daily Mail* proposed that their readers should storm Mr. Tree's theatre, or whether the Guards should be called out to stop him by force of arms was not made clear.

Tree's own comments on the affairs were detached. He said the article was a '*somewhat* brilliant attack'.

On the first night the play was a huge success, a success which was greatly enhanced by the discussion that had taken place, although it had had the effect of hindering the box office receipts before the play was produced. The enthusiasm at the end of the performance was very great on the first night.

Tree was called on to make a speech. It was brief. He came forward and said: 'Ladies and Gentlemen—I think we win.'

Later on Herbert met Lord Northcliffe at the Beefsteak Club. Northcliffe unwisely remarked: 'By the by, where *is* His Majesty's Theatre?' 'Oh, within a stone's throw of the *Daily Mail*', said Tree. The two men parted quite amicably and subsequently he came round to see Tree play.

But if Tree had his attackers, his defenders were equally passionate. H. A. Milton, the writer of the *Daily Mail* article, had written that Colonel Newcome was too sweet a character to be portrayed on any stage. An anonymous defender replying to the newspaper called in all the forces of God, Shakespeare and Goethe to make his points. At Oberammergau they had portrayed Jesus Christ himself, was Colonel Newcome more sacred, he demanded.

'Mr. Tree has never been known to handle his roles with aught but love and devotion. Is not his whole life dedicated as perhaps no other actor's now on our stage to the advancement, not of his own ambition as this virtuous gentleman so basely hints, but that of his Art? The Glory of Our Drama and his ambition are synonymous and must such a man sit down quietly whilst this little bully treats him as some performing dog paid by him to cut such capers as he thinks fit?'

Mr. Tree's defender then went into a panegyric on the different roles he had played over the years. He was a master of comedy, tragedy and pathos. If Mr. Milton thought Mr. Tree's acting had deteriorated, as he said, it was nothing but blind prejudice and jealousy! Mr. Tree's stalwart friend had not yet had time to see him as Colonel Newcome, but he had high hopes after his Hamlet and Richard II.

Tree paid no attention to his attackers but took advantage of his disadvantages, while Colonel Newcome marched on to success.

Constance remarked that Herbert had determination, and he had luck. Herbert did not believe in luck, as he had said, he always knew why men failed and he was determined not to be of their company. He believed in acting with celerity and courage.

During the run of one of his plays he arrived at His Majesty's to find that there was a crack in the proscenium arch above the stage and that the L.C.C. had condemned the theatre until it was mended. It was only at the beginning of the play's run.

Tree commented: 'It is always well to make capital out of one's misfortune. I at once determined that we should open on the following night at another theatre. Such a dramatic coup I felt would save the situation and turn the sow's ear of misfortune into the silk purse of opportunity. I sent out to six different theatres. Among these I secured the Strand, where we opened. At His Majesty's I announced the fact to the audience saying: "Just above the place where I stand there is a crack in the proscenium arch which is a source of danger."'

He added with pardonable pride: 'Ladies and Gentlemen we shall open tomorrow night at the Strand Theatre.'

This architectural *coup de théâtre* produced a tremendous house, and the play ran for some weeks until the crack was repaired and Tree was able to return to His Majesty's.

Tree was essentially a man of his time—he admired action— virtue was for the woman, valour for the man.

If Tree valued virtue in women it was on a purely academic level, valour he certainly had. Constance always admired his ability to make decisions, he dismissed this quality lightly, remarking that men who were always afraid of making mistakes achieved nothing. He was never afraid of making a mistake and those who hoped he would were often sorely disappointed.

He had studied Colonel Newcome's character with his usual meticulousness. Even his small effects came from life. He had noted two old people who each confided to a third that the other one was very frail. Then they helped each other out of the room. He commented, 'I used this in Colonel Newcome.'

But in spite of all the controversy, W. L. Courtney, a contemporary critic, considered that Tree could, and did, express tenderness and sentiment extremely well. It was a trait of his own character and came out clearly in his relations with his eldest daughter, Viola. Perhaps that was part of the reason for the rift between himself and Maud—she was clever and worldly, tender with her children, but unable either to accept, or to forgive Herbert's curious view of a man's life. It is hard for some women to express their sentiments, and Edwardian women, although often absurdly sentimental in their letters and writing, were sometimes inhibited in their relationships with their husbands.

In Colonel Newcome, Tree was able to give full play to the tender side of his nature and succeeded with the critics, the public and with Maud. She wrote that Colonel Newcome was a thing of beauty. Tender, lovable, gay, gallant, infinitely dignified, infinitely touching, with all its sweet weaknesses and sweet sublimities. 'There is everything in Colonel Newcome that Herbert most admired and revered. This was perceptible in every instant of his acting.'

But although the critic W. L. Courtney admitted that Tree had succeeded as Newcome he held to the general view that Tree was at his best in the representation of fantastic bizarre characters with a twist in them which made them peculiarly original.

Perhaps the best criticism of Tree's acting was written by Desmond MacCarthy, whose life spanned several generations and styles of acting.

He was essentially a romantic actor, perhaps the last descendant of Romanticism flowering on the English stage . . . the next thing to note about him is that he was a character actor . . . he excelled in building up before our eyes a definite human being. Of all his contemporaries he had the largest share of this authors' gift. His gift of conceiving character outran his power of representing it to the eye and ear. His power of understanding character was far wider than his power of representing it and his extraordinary skill in making-up, in which he was unmatched, often tempted him to play characters which were outside his temperamental and physical range.

Then MacCarthy added a contradictory phrase: 'He had not the animal vigour which is necessary to great excellence in violent tragedy or in robust comedy.'

This contradiction was odd because when the character of Tree is studied with attention and his life fitted into his character, it might have been thought that animal vigour was one thing which he possessed and that his love of comedy, on and off the stage, in all its forms should have made him a superb comedy actor. But many of his critics missed his more subtle effects, and others found his more broad strokes too obvious. Perhaps his denial of the intellect in his life and his clinging to the fact that everything in art should be done by the light of nature, made him transfer his more complicated thoughts into tiny strokes of characterisation which were too miniature for the stage. Because of German and Russian blood, he was often drawn to foreign plays where he could display the talents he knew he had, and yet many of these attempts failed. He also lived in an age which admired men of action and his chameleon character adapted itself accordingly. Above all one must never bore. Boredom was something to defend oneself against.

Having succeeded against all the odds as Colonel Newcome, Herbert returned to Shakespeare. He produced *The Winter's Tale* for Ellen, but did not act in it himself. Maud appeared as Paulina and was found to be eloquently impressive. 'Indeed,' said the *Daily Telegraph*, 'this was a performance in which she acted throughout with a sincerity and strength, voicing as she does our natural indignation against the frantic intemperance of Leontes.'

But the superlatives went to Ellen as Hermione. 'She came before us a woman clothed in white samite, mystic wonderful—pleading with proud dignity for her innocence and the blamelessness of her life.' She stood above criticism, added the *Telegraph*, because her personality admits of no challenge. 'Her Hermione was an extremely gracious and impressive piece of work.'

Viola Tree's Perdita merited nearly as much praise. She was found to be truly the Queen of Curds and Cream and captured all eyes with her bewitching dance, charming in her youthfulness and grace. Miss Tree was felt to have several delightful moments, particularly her *dainty* flight from her lover across the rustic bridge over the stream.

Maud was very proud of her daughter and wrote that she seemed like one of the 'daffodils that come before the swallow dares and take the winds of March with beauty'. Viola had pleased her parents and her critics both as Ariel, and as Perdita. She was in the words of the music hall song 'following in father's footsteps', content to be, for the time being, part of the family team at His Majesty's Theatre. One wonders if the trouper Miss Collier, who had seen the hard side of the stage, sometimes envied the easy way in which the gifts of the theatre fell into the young hands of Miss Tree. Constance always writes with kindness of the springlike quality which Viola had, and of her witty amusing tongue. But sometimes the contrast must indeed have seemed sharp between the struggles she herself had had, and the daughter of Mr. Tree for whom the red carpet had led straight into star parts.

It was while Maud was appearing in *The Winter's Tale* that she had a motor accident. 'Out for a spin', as it was then called, with Lewis Waller, the car crashed and Maud's jaw was broken.

She spoke of this in a roundabout way when she mentions the family move to Walpole House, which was said to be haunted by the ghost of Barbara Villiers. It was a legend that the sad lady was to be seen in the great drawing-room of Walpole House looking out of the long windows towards the river, lamenting the loss of her beauty, and sometimes the sharp tap of her heels could be heard on the polished stairs as she hurried past the mirrors afraid to confirm her fears.

Maud remembered that before she took the house she had met a woman in the garden who had asked her if she was quite determined on living in Walpole House. Maud said that she was quite determined, and the unknown woman replied that she could say nothing more. Had she felt an echo of Barbara Villiers' unease? Maud never found out. The woman simply walked away and left the new tenant wondering.

Later Maud remembered the woman as she stood at the windows looking over the grey river bewailing the loss of her own looks. Herbert took her away, and with his kindness tried to restore her spirit. It was a quiet interlude in their married life when a disaster for a space brought them together.

While Viola continued to charm her audiences with her virginal performance as the Queen of Curds and Cream, Constance was in the provinces on one of Mr. Tree's grand tours. This tour which went out after the production of *Nero* was, said Constance, by way of being her honeymoon. 'Julian and I would get up early, and breakfast at the strawberry beds just outside Dublin.'

When Constance got back from the strawberry beds she went into immediate rehearsals for the great production of the autumn season *Antony and Cleopatra*. The idea of producing the play had come to Herbert when he had seen Constance as Poppaea and he suddenly visualised her as Cleopatra. Pictures of Constance in the part show her beauty at its peak, her dark good looks and velvety black eyes were enhanced by the lavish clothes and settings which Herbert had planned.

The stage had been cut to pieces for the entrance of Cleopatra's barge. Each setting was more magnificent than the last. The atrium of Caesar's house in Rome was dominated by enormous marbled pillars, surrounding a pool and fountain flanked by massive flowering trees, while overhead the cerulean sky and slim cypress trees gave promise of gardens beyond. Cleopatra's Palace was equally grand with lotiform pillars and statues of barbaric gods, while the market-place at Alexandria rivalled the palace in splendour. To modern eyes the market-place has a feeling of an Odeon cinema of the thirties.

The splendour was there and the acting and actors had to be placed in these settings. Constance, determined to get slim for the part, was eating very little and becoming very strained. The rehearsals seemed to her to go on for ever, lasting till five or six o'clock in the morning. The company slept in the boxes and had to be awakened for their cues, while the limelight men and scene shifters dropped to sleep at their posts. Constance herself slept in the dress circle, so exhausted that if anyone trod on her in the dark she was too tired to mind. She opened an eye—and then fell asleep again.

Herbert remained as fresh as a daisy. Constance remarked that his vitality never wavered and his voice, giving directions and supervising the smallest detail, could be heard unceasingly throughout the night. There never had been anyone with so much will power, or capacity for work. 'He was like Napoleon or Edison, he didn't seem to need to sleep at all.'

When the dawn came up, as Herbert once wrote, 'with an inflamed eye', he went up to his Dome to sleep. Constance took a 'growler' and spent an hour trotting home to Sheffield Terrace in Kensington. She arrived with the milkman to find that her husband Julian had tried to wait up for her. But when his Queen arrived, the fire was out and Pompey was asleep.

Finally the day of the dress rehearsal was reached, not without the usual displays of temper and temperament. The most spectacular scene in the play was when Cleopatra appeared as the Goddess Isis. There is only one mention of this in *Antony and Cleopatra* but Tree had turned it into the richest scene of all. Cleopatra robed in silver, crowned in silver, carrying a golden sceptre, with the symbol of the sacred golden calf in her hand went in procession through the streets of Alexandria while the populace screamed at her, half in hate and half in superstitious fear and joy.

Constance admitted freely that she herself looked very beautiful in this scene, and photographs prove it. The contrast of the silver robe and her dusky brown skin made a wonderful picture. It was a picture which bade fair to be spoiled by Herbert. He had discovered that the Egyptian Queen had five children. Constance Collier quarrelled bitterly with Herbert over this. 'The splendid passionate queen was ridiculous with a large family. This domestic side of Cleopatra seemed utterly incongruous. I simply could not bear it. I implored him to take them away, but he insisted on all five at the dress rehearsal.'

It was impossible to be romantic under those circumstances, remarked Miss Collier acidly. He had spoiled her glorious entrance with a procession of children getting smaller and smaller until the last one was quite tiny. She refused to play, and finally they compromised on three. Constance played the scene as if they did not belong to her, treating them with great scorn while the two smallest, robed in silver, looking like miniatures of the great Queen, were seemingly bewildered at their mother's harsh attitude. She would willingly have strangled the entire family— given the chance. The children spoiled Constance's enjoyment of the part but for Herbert they were an everlasting joke. She would mount the steps of her throne to find a note saying 'Ptolemy Junior' pinned to it, or she would find dolls on her dressing-table, in her room, or sitting at the side of the stage. One night in the middle of one of the very serious scenes he slipped a little naked doll into her hand. Herbert's spasmodic lack of professionalism irritated a trouper like Constance, but she found it a good lesson in discipline, and in not interfering with Herbert's ideas. In the future she minded her own business and got on with her acting.

Not surprisingly, Constance felt that she had not given of her best on the first night. She blamed it on her dieting, but it must be thought that Herbert's troops of tiny children had not improved her image of herself as the Queen of Love. Mr. Walkley of *The Times* and many other critics praised her, but in her heart of hearts she felt she had lost her opportunity.

Maud considered Antony to have been one of Herbert's failures and few of the critics liked his Antony, though pictures of him in the part give him the right air of the warrior lover. If off stage Herbert seems to have succeeded only too well with the frail sex, on stage he was not accepted as a lover. Although he was always daring, always original, Tree's critics were constantly disconcerted by his abrupt changes of character. He seemed to act superbly when they anticipated a failure, as with *Colonel Newcome*, and badly when they expected him to be outstanding, as in *Antony and Cleopatra*.

1906 had been a crowded year for Tree. He had acted Nero, Newcome and Antony. He had produced six of Shakespeare's plays in a week acting in all of them, crowning the week with celebrating the fiftieth anniversary of Ellen Terry.

Chapter 12

Sir Herbert—At Last

The Kaiser had sent a letter to Tree asking him to go to Berlin and act for ten days at the State Theatre. The Emperor of Germany had a fancy to view a selection of Mr. Tree's pieces—*Hamlet*, *Trilby*, *The Merry Wives of Windsor* and of course, the spectacular *Antony and Cleopatra*.

It was not a request but a command and considered a great honour, although an honour which laid a heavy penalty on the exchequer of Mr. Tree's theatre. The Emperor did not concern himself with freight charges—a few banquets could be laid on for travelling actors, but the prestige which would come to His Majesty's Theatre for the company to act before the Kaiser was considered to be sufficient payment.

The whole company crossed to Holland in April of 1907. The picture taken of the stars shows Herbert in a *flâneur* pose with serious face under his curly brimmed top hat; on one side of him, Constance, her dark beauty shaded by a veil and a hat with flowers; on the other side, Viola, sweetly pretty and vulnerably young, her youthful charm somewhat loaded down by hat, furs and the heavy travelling dress of the period. The clothes of the time did not make the best of young women. They were planned for hostesses of a certain age and both Constance and Viola appear blotted out by their finery.

Constance found Berlin thrilling beyond her wildest dreams. There were banquets lasting for hours, enormous quantities of food and even more enormous quantities of wine in great goblets. The company were fêted and Constance was admired but had to remain dumb. She could not speak a word of German. But the message got through to her by the language of flowers. She was sent quantities of bouquets of 'Bleeding Hearts'.

But there were no bleeding hearts amongst the German stage hands nor amongst the German supers who were not in the mood

to put themselves out for foreigners. However, the week proceeded with packed houses. The reviews were splendid and
Constance felt that her performance as Cleopatra had improved
out of all knowledge. (Perhaps Herbert had left Cleopatra's children in London.) There were small troubles of casting: Constance
wanted to play both Cleopatra and Trilby to show her range. But
Trilby went to the virginal Viola who brought her naturalness and
charm to a part which needed those qualities.

But the stage hands had been getting more aggressive. In
the graveyard scene, Hamlet was short of his skull which was
smashed to pieces. Properties of all kinds disappeared, or were
found broken.

The climax arrived on the great gala night when the Emperor
and Empress were in front in all their glory. There were ten scene
changes in *Antony and Cleopatra* and the scene changes became
slower and slower—which made Herbert excessively nervous. He
gave one of the stage hands a push which spilt his beer. This was
regarded as an international insult and the whole posse of stage
hands walked out. The scenery was stuck at the market-place in
Alexandria. At first the company tried to move the scenery themselves. But it was too solidly built and the muddle became worse
than ever. In front, the Emperor had been waiting for an hour.
Baulked of entertainment Kaiser Wilhelm II sent round to enquire
the reason for the delay. When he was told the reason he had staff
rushed round from other theatres. This made confusion worse
confounded and the rest of the play had to be continued in the
market-place at Alexandria forcing the Queen of Egypt to die in a
commercial setting.

The Emperor sent for the stars but while they were in the ante-
room of the Royal Box the students began breaking up the benches,
and a general riot commenced. The Emperor became very white
and angry. He led Herbert, Viola and Constance to the front of the
Royal Box. The commotion died down. Jeers changed into cheers.

Herbert was presented with what he described as 'a second class
decoration' by the Emperor. Both Viola and Constance were given
bracelets of diamonds and sapphires. Viola, not easily impressed,
described hers as being expensive but in execrable Teutonic taste.
Perhaps Constance, the girl from the other side of the tracks, was
more admiring.

Viola had the artistic taste of her background, and with her mother's connexion with the Duchess of Rutland and the Manners family leaned towards the simplicity of the 'Souls'. Large vulgar pieces of jewellery were not to her liking.

*

In 1908 Tree turned to Dickens and his unfinished novel *Edwin Drood*, another of Comyns Carr's adaptations. The newspapers were polite, but in spite of opium dens and drugs and a melodramatic part for Tree ('Mr. Tree gives a fine study of character in the flamboyant style'), the play failed and was taken off after a month.

Herbert wrote to the editor of *Punch* 'Drood is coming off—after that *The Beloved Vagabond*'. It was a change and a part much more suited to his character.

Maud remarked that as soon as she had read *Trilby* she knew at once that Svengali was the part for Herbert, and in the same way when she read Locke's *Vagabond* she felt the same tingle of anticipation. The picturesque romance of *The Beloved Vagabond* and the sentiments expressed by Paragot coincided with Herbert's own. 'I am going to educate you, my little Asticot, through the imagination. The intellect can look after itself.' Paragot is described as the centre of his little world, adulation was as the breath to his nostrils. Like Herbert, Paragot had to talk to something—if he were alone he would have talked to his shadow, in his coffin he would have apostrophised the worms.

W. J. Locke was delighted to have lured Herbert into playing his hero. Who could have been better chosen to play the fiddle down the dusty roads of France than Tree? On 29th August he wrote to Tree that he was back in London and 'ready to do anything that might be required of him'. This was perhaps mistaken eagerness on the playwright's part because a great deal was required of him. Instead of Paragot departing with his capable *paysanne* Blanquette de Veau, Paragot ended by marrying the distant Joanna, '*pure et ravissante comme une aube d'avril*' and became the proud protector of her '*petits pieds si adorés*'. It was not perhaps what the author intended. Tree's Paragot was considered by some critics to be more like a cheerful Svengali out for larks. Others felt that at His Majesty's playgoers would see the vagabond of their affections, with his Bohemian hatred of respectability, love of café life and comradeship, and his Gascon flow of rhetoric,

'This Paragot gay, sentimental, pensive, cynical, self-absorbed, boisterous—will be a revelation to the playgoer.'

However romantically exaggerated the character might be, there was something about it which touched Tree's performance into life. 'There is nothing in this comical universe I don't laugh at,' said Paragot, 'I am like old Montaigne—I would rather laugh than weep because to laugh is the more dignified.' It was a sentiment heartily endorsed by Herbert.

The play had a difficult beginning in Ireland where it was tried out. Locke wrote to Tree: 'A sense of humour doesn't seem to be a strong point in Cork. Let us hope for Paragot's sake it will be stronger in Dublin.' Perhaps the amoral Paragot had offended the Cork bourgeoisie. The *Daily Express*, maybe sensing a failure, went over to Ireland to report the Dublin first night. But there both critic and audience found the play to its taste. 'Mr. Tree's portrayal of Gaston, the rich exuberant nature, the artist who plans palaces, who can play the fiddle so that it sings a devil into your body, and who can make love in sixteen languages, who can rise to the splendid renunciation of his life, and descend to the wild life of a gipsy tramp to drink and outward degradation, yet who enshrines in the darkened skies of his life and heart the one great star of his love for Joanna. His kindness, bounty and sympathy are universal—he can save, help, and comfort others, but himself he cannot save.'

Herbert must have felt that it was himself to the life. Perhaps he did not make love in sixteen languages. Three seemed to suffice. 'Who but Paragot would have woken you at three in the morning?' asked the author in the book, 'to announce that he had had an inspiration?' No one else but Tree at his final rehearsals at His Majesty's Theatre was the answer.

Maud was delighted with Herbert in the part. It gave him just the chance he revelled in, dreamy, fantastic, poetic, debonair, the book could have been written with Herbert in mind. Perhaps it was. It certainly gave the obliging Mr. Locke's reputation a great boost, although the *Daily Express* did add a puritan rider: 'I do not think the character commands much sympathy or respect—it has too much weakness.'

When the play opened at His Majesty's *The Times*' critic who had re-read the book remarked tersely on the changes. 'The author has made considerable alterations in the story. The boy

Asticot is turned into a hunchback—and Mr. Rushforth (Joanna's father) promoted to the peerage.' The Edwardian audience, as Mr. Maugham once remarked, liked a programme studded with titles. The critics may have preferred Tree in the fantastic rather than the romantic side of Paragot. But London took him to its heart.

Having enjoyed himself as Paragot Herbert returned to the classics. He introduced the forest scene in Humperdinck's *Hansel and Gretel* as a curtain raiser to *The Beloved Vagabond*, with Viola as Hansel and Alice Moffatt as Gretel. Viola, like himself, must have her chance to show her versatility.

Then on 11th April 1908 he played Shylock for the first time. For once Tree does not seem to have backed his Shylock with a strong enough cast except for Basil Gill whose Bassanio was described as 'resonant'. But in Tree's hands *The Merchant of Venice* became an actor-manager's dream.

> Shylock from his entrance dominates the stage, and Mr. Tree's performance dwarfs those of his associates. Compared with Henry Irving this new study is at once far more individualised and far more typical—Jewish through and through. This Shylock epitomises the history of the Jew, dignity under ridicule, patience and suppleness under persecution, isolation among alien races and creeds, faithfulness to his own national and religious traditions, devotion to wealth as a weapon of power.

The critics spoke of his tragic capacity for grief and how he made the house ring with his cries when he found Jessica had fled.

The descriptions of his bewailing with utter abandonment his lost daughter and lost ducats, rending his garments, heaping ashes on his head and then giving ferocious shrieks of joy at Antonio's misfortunes, lead the modern reader to think that Mr. Tree had rather overdone his various passions and the illustrative business with which he kept reminding the audience of Shylock's Jewishness. Miss Alexandra Carlisle was felt to lack Shakespearean training as Portia though she looked charming enough. The run was interrupted for Tree's Shakespearean Festival with Viola playing Viola in *Twelfth Night* and Ophelia to Tree's Hamlet. Some time during the run Viola seems to have taken over the part of Portia, for Ellen Terry wrote to Tree saying that she was so sorry to have missed dear Viola's Portia. But she was down in the country staying with dear Graham Robertson. Ellen had recently, much to everyone's surprise, married James Carew, a man some twenty odd years her junior, and was occupied once more being a married lady.

Suddenly, in the autumn of 1908, Tree decided to do a children's play, *Pinkie and the Fairies*, written by Ellen's friend Graham Robertson. This sudden decision was possibly because Herbert had turned down *Peter Pan*. Barrie read him two acts, whereupon Herbert decided that the author had gone mad and begged to be let off the rest of the play. Tree would have been excellent as the evil Captain Hook, an Etonian Svengali for children and when he was asked why he had not played in it he said: 'God knows—and I have promised to tell no one else!'

Robertson's play (with music by Frederic Norton) had been written nearly ten years before and Pinkie, and her fairy wings, had become somewhat bedraggled during the ten years she had spent wandering from one manager's office to another. The author had given up all hope of a production. Suddenly he was summoned by Herbert to come to His Majesty's to discuss it.

'I did not know that he had it under consideration', said Robertson. He had heard from many different people that reading a play to Herbert was an ordeal. He found Tree in 'his palatial suite of apartments (I can find no better description than this well-worn phrase of the house agent) situated in the dome of his theatre'.

To Robertson's intense surprise he never had a more sympathetic audience. Tree had accepted the play. The rehearsals were to begin at once. Robertson wrote telling Ellen the happy news.

From Smallhythe she wrote back delightedly: 'Blow the trumpets, beat the drums! I am delighted my dear. Did you read it to Tree? I do like Tree, he *does* things. But take care. You must have your say in all of it or—' This was a warning to all authors against all managements from someone who knew all the pitfalls.

The cast delighted the author. 'Charming Iris Hawkins was the obvious Pinkie, Marie Löhr, then at the height of her girlish beauty, was Cinderella, Viola Tree with her stately presence and beautiful voice, was the Sleeping Beauty, Stella Campbell lent her lovely gravity to Molly.'

But the best was yet to come. Ellen wrote again from Small-hythe. 'Do you know I believe I really would like to play Aunt Imogen for I think I might be very funny in that very funny part. I wonder', she wrote modestly, 'Would Tree think it worth while?'

When Tree was shown the letter he complimented the author on being an expert forger, but finally, convinced that it was true, he telegraphed to Ellen clinching the bargain.

Robertson obviously liked Tree whom he described as a born actor, but added acidly that he had known several born actors and they were so absorbed in registering their reactions to every emotion that the shadow outweighed the substance, and they used speech not to express their thoughts but to arrest attention, lacking simplicity and sincerity.

Tree was different. He did himself, according to Robertson, a great injustice by never allowing his warm-hearted generous nature to be seen. Like Constance, Robertson felt that the genuine Herbert Tree was so much nicer than the gallery of assumed characters he played—the man of mystery, the eccentric, or the witty man about town. 'When the real man put in an appearance, as if by accident, it gave one a pleasurable start, like the sudden sight of a friend's face among a crowd of strangers.'

Quite wrongly, Robertson remarked that 'there was nothing mysterious about Tree'. But the mystery about Tree was his double life which his eccentricity carefully cloaked.

In the theatre Tree was understood and liked. Robertson said, 'He had the lovable quality of liking to be liked, he hated enmity and rancour.' Once, after a row at rehearsal in which Tree was entirely in the right, he asked Robertson, 'Do you think I should apologise?'

Robertson, amazed, replied: 'Why should *you* apologise for someone *else's* rudeness?'

'Yes, yes, of course. But it seems a pity', said Tree. He had ceased to be angry and only wanted peace.

His kindness was long remembered by Robertson. 'Tree was an extraordinarily clever man and a kind friend; he gave me my big chance, and I am very grateful to him.' It was a generous tribute. In our age of bubble reputations made by the mouths of media representatives, it is pleasant to read of the generosities of the past.

A curious footnote to the reception of the play was added by Robertson.

Pinkie, intended to interest the Nursery captured—the Military. Night after night the stalls at His Majesty's looked like a parade at Aldershot. I was much puzzled by this phenomenon and asked a soldier of my acquaintance to enquire into it.

Why did the military come so often? 'They say it makes them cry.'

Apparently what they found most devastating was the close of the second Act, when the children's dream ends, and the vision of Fairyland slowly fades, the lights twinkling out, the music dying away until all is darkness and silence save for the murmur of the stream among the shadows. And in the darkness, Aldershot sat weeping for its lost Fairyland.

Herbert had paid himself back for his mistake over *Peter Pan*.

But he had been very shrewd over the preliminary publicity. He gave a pre-dress rehearsal performance for all the County Council children in London, and his own children were made to post the invitations personally to each child. The large numbers of children in the play were supplied by a stage school, who suggested a charming Fairy Queen, with baby blue eyes and long fair ringlets. When she sang she had a thick cockney accent. A murmur of disapproval went round the stalls at the auditioning. But Herbert stuck to his guns, the cockney accent should remain and was the reason for the child's success.

At the command performance for the cockneys of London, Tree's children Felicity and Iris acted as hostesses, dressed in their party frocks they welcomed the children of London. When his children looked back on those days they remembered the grandeur of the theatre. always so well organised, the footmen with their powdered wigs, the sparkling chandeliers, the rich carpets and the excitement of the moment when the house lights were lowered and the curtain went up to reveal the enchantments of their magician father.

Although 1908 may have seemed a time of general success and rejoicing the undercurrents of Maud's marriage presaged storms. Outwardly she was the successful wife of the grand Mr. Tree. When asked by some Society friend why she had no tiara, Maud replied grandly that she needed no jewels—Herbert had presented her with His Majesty's Theatre, which was not strictly true, although a beautiful thought. She bore herself proudly, but privately she was the wife who was left at home. Herbert's children remembered that the first thing he did when he came back from abroad was to go to the theatre. Or possibly to Miss Pinney at Putney?

In July of 1908 a letter came from a solicitor called Russell in Norfolk Street, Strand, London, W.C. addressed to Maud. Writing on that July day Solicitor Russell was reassuring. He wrote, in reply to a letter of Maud's, saying that Mrs. Tree could write to him privately to his home near Hyde Park Square—and no one in the office would see the letter. She could rely on that.

Did Maud by this time know of Tree's four sons, Claude and Robin then teenagers and Guy and Carol aged three and two? Had she decided that she had been affronted enough by Herbert's double life and was she thinking of a divorce, or at best a legal separation? But to a woman in the early years of the century, however much virtue, honour and duty were on her side, when it came to a divorce or a separation, the dice were heavily loaded against her. Society was not to be relied on when it came to a woman on her own, and although a wife might play second or even third fiddle, she was the acknowledged partner, the woman who presided at the head of the table on grand occasions.

Many years later Shaw drew up a balance sheet of debits and credits of Maud's life with Herbert. She was in the thick of everything, courted by interesting people, she had the continually renewed excitement of splendid productions, she was a queen with a coronation every three months. She was the happiest of women. On the other hand she was married to Herbert, who was married to his theatre and to everyone who played on his feelings, or his vanity. Shaw added that Maud was married to a monster— she was the wretchedest of women. Shaw's summing-up might have been made years earlier by Maud herself when she had *not* taken up Solicitor Russell's kind offers to act for her. She decided to remain a queen—if only in name.

Tree was in many ways an eighteenth-century character. He loved to play fops and dandies, and the wit in which he rejoiced usually had a worldly edge to it. But most of his humour was kindly and he did not like bitter satire. He liked everything to

spring from cheerful life. 'Humour is the milk taken from a
mother's breast, satire is that taken from a bottle chemically
prepared', he wrote. He had sentiment without sentimentality
and a great enjoyment of all aspects of life and art, though little
servile respect for the great world, or its dignity. On the other
hand, Maud fitted absolutely into her age, she was of the age and
in the age. Tree was a law unto himself and, if he wished to live
his own life in his own way, Maud had nothing to do but to
submit.

The year 1909 opened with Tree writing a few notes to himself
to celebrate the beginning of a new year. Although he wrote down
the words 'good resolutions' and indeed underlined them, none
occurred to him, and the first month of the year was blank. Having
settled his January bills, February opened with an injunction to
himself to make money for his dear ones. Including Maud and
Miss Pinney, he had nine. By July of 1909 another child by Miss
Pinney would be conceived, making a round ten dependents for
Herbert by the year 1910.

After a few stray thoughts about the necessity of more money,
Herbert had the sensible thought that frugal living was a good
plan. At length he did think of a good resolution, every day he
would try to do someone a kindness. Then—perhaps thinking of
some people to whom he might *have* to do kindnesses—he added
that he must not resent chicanery.

*

He was travelling to Egypt at the beginning of this year with
some idea of using the background for a dramatised version of
Hall Caine's book *The White Prophet*. But having read the book
with attention he was full of misgivings and wrote to Hall Caine
'Egypt is a theme which must appeal above all others at this time,
and the whole atmosphere of the life there is so absorbingly
interesting that I should be disappointed indeed if I were denied
the chance of putting such a play on the boards of His Majesty's,
but it seems there is a very strong similarity between the character
of the Agent General in *The White Prophet* and Lord Cromer
himself who is regarded here with veneration.'

The strong feelings among the English in Egypt of a hero
refusing to carry out the orders of his chief in command might be

of a painful nature. This neither the author nor himself would wish to happen, wrote Tree.

Tree was hardly a fervent admirer of Hall Caine's heavy masterpieces. He constantly wrote jokes against the author, remarking that he was inclined to jot down serious 'immortalisms' in a spare moment. In the end, in spite of all the introductions from Hall Caine to people in Egypt and the charm of the settings proposed, he decided against the project.

For his first production of 1909 he went back to the eighteenth century and played in *The School for Scandal*. This was one of his handsomest productions. Percy Macquoid designed all the costumes and sets, which fell so gently into place in Tree's handsome theatre that Sheridan would have found himself very much at ease had he walked on stage. The charming Marie Löhr played Lady Teazle to Tree's Sir Peter. Congratulatory letters give a very good picture of the way Tree had brought Sheridan's character to life.

The distinguished actress Gertrude Kingston, who had acted with Tree at the Haymarket, wrote:

My dear friend, I did not come round to see you last evening because I saw crowds being personally conducted to your room, and I prefer to see you alone to have your individual attention. But I want to tell you how thoroughly I appreciated your fine characterisation of Sir Peter Teazle. It was a real treat to see the waist line in the right place both mentally and physically.

W. J. Locke also wrote that he did not 'come round' because of the crowds, but said that Tree's Sir Peter had dignity, humour and pathos. 'This is the only time I have ever seen the real *poignancy* of the screen scene on the stage—the only time I have had a real thrill.'

Frederic Harrison went into more detail:

I enjoyed the play greatly last night. It is no doubt a fine presentment of the most brilliant comedy in our language. I would not have missed it on any account. Your idea of making Sir Peter a middle-aged man of spirit and of heart and not an old fool is a great new reading and Lady Teazle is in my opinion both charming and right. I cannot agree with those superfine critics who say that sweet Marie Löhr is 'not equal' to such a part. I thought her quite perfect and looking lovely and fascinating—it is the best thing I have seen her in. Your Sir Peter was quite the hero of the piece as no Sir Peter ever before was. He used always to be the butt of the piece which is quite wrong. The mise en scène was admirable if rather too flamboyant. I have seen the play often before but never *heard* it before and the repartee and the epigrams seemed to me all new and fresh. I never before realised what a masterpiece it is— what a cataract of wit and fun . . . it will run all the season.

F. C. Burnand wrote that he found Tree's Sir Peter perceptively not too old for the genuinely girlish Lady Teazle. He added that he found Sheridan's ending very strange, 'He turns Joseph out of his own rooms and the remaining dramatis personae coolly take possession of the place!' Curiously enough, generations of theatre critics do not seem to have noticed this odd fact.

All his correspondents hoped that his Sir Peter would run the whole season and so it would have done, if Tree had not decided to take it off in order to play his usual Shakespeare season, rather later than usual—and for a very good reason. He had been knighted.

*

It was the crown to Tree's career, and a crown which Maud had tried to get for Herbert for some time. If one was to be only a wife *en titre*, one might as well have a title to give form and substance to one's status. Maud had been working towards Herbert's crown for some time and without his knowledge. In 1902 she had tried to interest the Lord Chamberlain, Lord Clarendon, in the idea with no success. In 1905 she returned to the charge and had approached her close friend the artistic Duchess of Rutland to use her influence with the same end in view. Again with no success. But by 1909 Asquith had become Prime Minister and the Asquiths were close friends of the Tree family. Herbert Asquith was fond of Viola Tree, and wrote to her most affectionately, while Margot Asquith loved the whole family and wrote to them with the familiarity born of genuine liking and understanding.

Maud liked to give the impression that Herbert's knighthood was a great surprise. It was probably only a surprise to Herbert who remarked that he hoped he would not be expected to become genteel. Maud said he could be a very parfait but not a genteel knight. A friend who was writing to congratulate both Maud and Herbert, before Herbert had been 'dubbed', asked Max whether she should address Maud as Lady Tree. The reply was that it seemed to be correct as she was already Lady Tree 'in the sight of God'.

The bestowal of the accolade brought about an immense flood of admiration and congratulations. The carefully preserved letters and telegrams fill two large volumes. Herbert, although at the beginning he had professed to be entirely unmoved by his honour, began to share the general excitement and was genuinely moved by the affection which everyone showed to him and the pleasure they had in his knighthood.

By a careful *coup de théâtre* Tree was acting Malvolio in *Twelfth Night* when his honour was publicly announced. As he reached the lines, 'Some have greatness thrust upon them' the house 'rose' to him.

Holding the hands of Viola and Maud, Herbert made a little speech:

> I have no words to thank you for the kindness you have shown me. This has been a very touching day for me, and in moments of profound emotion one can hardly find expression for one's feelings; but I feel thankful to think that this honour to our art has come at a time when Shakespeare is being honoured here. I only hope I may have health and strength to continue my work and to serve my loyal Public as loyally as I can. From the depths of my heart I thank all my kind friends tonight.

It was an expression of his genuine surprise at the sudden uprush of affection for him which had been shown.

When the accolade was about to be bestowed by King Edward, Herbert and Arthur Pinero were waiting in an ante-room for the touch of the sword. Pinero said to Herbert: 'Do you think we could have it done under gas?'

Maud had become Lady Tree at last. Her place in Society was confirmed. She not only used the title as a social grace, but forever afterwards her name appeared in the programmes of plays and even films as 'Lady Tree'. It was an honour for which she had worked hard and was determined to use.

Herbert, unruffled by his new honours, cheerfully launched himself into unknown pastures. He was, perhaps alone amongst his contemporaries interested in the Continental theatre. He had produced *L'Intruse* by Maeterlinck in 1890 and Ibsen's *An Enemy of the People*, and had even been drawn to Shaw when the rest of the theatre world considered his plays to be Socialistic rubbish. Shaw, although he considered Tree to be tarred with the same actor-manager's brush as the others, could scarce forbear to cheer. He had to admit that Tree's 'notion of feeding the popular drama with ideas and gradually educating the public by classical matinées, financed by the spoils of the popular plays in the evening bill, seems to have been the right one'.

So, after Sheridan, Tree decided to launch into Brieux. He was the controversial author of *Les Avariés* which dealt with venereal disease and had been produced as *Damaged Goods*. The play which Herbert had decided to produce was *La Foi* which was changed to *False Gods*.

There were many false starts to *False Gods*. For once Tree was unperceptive as to the true meaning of the piece which was set in ancient Egypt. The play depended for its impact on the blind faith given to the Goddess Isis and the human sacrifice of the girl Yaouma to the River Nile to save the country by bringing the life-giving floods to the parched land. Although the ostensible theme, and its exotic setting, seemed merely to indicate a touching if melodramatic plot, the real analogy was between the faith of Egypt and her cat-headed gods and the blind faith of Catholics and their belief in miracles. Tree ignored, or perhaps did not notice this. He produced the play in his usual spectacular way, which infuriated Brieux.

The row rumbled on long after the play was off. Herbert had written to Viola in Italy, telling her that he would have to go to France to meet Brieux who was in a bad mood over the production, the actors and the fact that Tree had not called on him on his way to Marienbad. Sadly Herbert thought of his production, how much better he told Viola if *she* had played the Blind Woman in *La Foi*. It would not only have given Viola a touching part, but it would have saved Tree from Mrs. Pat. When Viola wrote her book later, she remembered the production of the play in the spring before she left London for Italy. There had been more ructions than usual in a Tree production. Brieux took the view that Herbert had completely misunderstood his play. Her father had seen it only as a sad and lovely story, not as a reflection on modern life and a harsh commentary on religion and superstition. Her father should have been told the real message of the play, but like many great men he was surrounded by flatterers.

Before the production of the play Brieux had been all sweetness and light when writing to Tree about his knighthood: *'J'apprend la bonne nouvelle et je vous félicite sincèrement pour la haute distinction qui vient de vous être accordée.'* Brieux asks Tree to reply to him but adds: *'Et si vous voulez être tout a fait aimable écrivez-moi en français parceque vous le parlez très bien et que moi je ne puis lire vos lettres en anglais qu'à coups de dictionnaire.'*

The following year, after the production of the play, Brieux was no longer *aimable* and the *coups* were falling on Tree.

Additional plagues of Egypt were the composer of the music, the Frenchman, Saint-Saëns and the German conductor Adolphe Schmidt who, much to Tree's amusement, took to screaming at one another.

'Ze flutes is too loud!' shouted Saint-Saëns.

''Ow shall flutes play more softly as dey can?'

'But zey do!'

Mrs. Patrick Campbell was her usual difficult self. She played the blind woman, Mieris, who fails to be cured by faith alone. Herbert played the High Priest. Mrs. Clement Scott, wife of the critic, was at her scratchy best when she wrote about the dress rehearsal. 'I haven't the faintest recollection of the play, I only remembered that Mrs. Pat babbled of Isis and that Tree appeared as a High Priest of something or other in white robes with blue ribbons in his hair.'

Maud, also at her sharpest, remarked to Mrs. Scott, very audibly, 'Surely *nobody* could say that Herbert looks like *Our Miss Gibbs* could they?' This remark from Maud seems to indicate that she was inclined to tell the truth, not always to Herbert's advantage, and perhaps affords a clue for the existence of that domestic angel about the house, Beatrice May Pinney.

The critics were not deceived by the grandeur of Herbert's production. They pierced to the heart of the author's message.

'A biting and beautiful work', one said, 'a great theme but while we were enthralled, we were repelled and distressed. There is a subtle poison in it. The faith and beliefs and hopes of millions of men and women are attacked ruthlessly and insidiously by this story of Egypt 3,000 years ago. Brieux—let there be no mistake about it—seeks to attack and demolish the Christian faith by his attack on the false Gods of Egypt. He is no hypocrite; he would not be afraid to raise his voice against Christianity—but he is more subtle and more dangerous in the way he has chosen. He would have us say "These were the fetiches of yesterday, wherein do they differ from the fetiches of today?"'

False Gods was first produced in Monte Carlo and was seen in London before the Parisian production. It was considered to be one of Tree's triumphs and combined, said one critic, the atmosphere of dreamlike glamour which the mists of time have cast round one of the world's earliest empires with historical accuracy.

Having played a High Priest in blue ribbons, Tree turned from producing the blind Mieris to playing the deaf Beethoven. The play was another adaptation from the French by Louis N. Parker, but in spite of the wonderful music played by an augmented orchestra, it was a failure with the public. Yet Tree himself was startling as Beethoven. Parker wrote:

> I shall never forget our gasp of surprise when Tree made his entrance at the dress rehearsal—a short, stocky, square-set little man with dark eyes. His head was Beethoven's head. I have two portraits before me—one of Beethoven and one of Tree in the part, it is difficult to tell which is which. . . . The effect of even a wonderful make-up evaporates after the first three minutes; in this instance it was not so. Tree got into the skin of the part and increased the illusion to the very end of the play.

Tree was able to convey Beethoven in his facial expression, and every movement of his body and of his eloquent hands was in perfect agreement with the complicated music. 'We felt', wrote Parker, 'that we had surprised Beethoven in the act of composing.' In the scene where Beethoven realises his deafness Tree was tragically true to nature.

It is possible to wonder whether some of Tree's intuition about music might have been helped by Beatrice May, daughter of the music professor William Pinney. But music while it may have drawn him to May was to divide him from Viola.

In 1910, a year after her father's knighthood, she went away to Italy. She had just played Portia and Trilby with her father at His Majesty's Theatre, but now she had decided to become an opera singer. It is hard to understand why she did this. She was her father's favourite child, the child of his springtime love for Maud. She had stepped, as of right, into principal parts in his grand productions. She was as fond of Herbert as he was of her. To Viola her father was always an adventure, an excitement. On stage, one never knew quite what he would do, but 'it was always the right thing to give inspiration to one's next line'. He always became the part he was playing, this was the reason why he was never the same from one performance to the next. When playing Gringoire, the revolutionary poet, he felt thin and hungry, as Svengali magnetic, dirty and compelling, as Fagin evil and as Beethoven he became and appeared, small and square, with big strong, rather stumpy hands.

But she turned her back on her much loved father, and her prospects in his theatre, and went off to Italy to her studies of singing. She loved acting with her father, but she felt she would never make a great career on the stage because she was too self-conscious. Viola had studied at the Royal College of Music, and sung in two College performances and was earning money singing at concerts. Through her father's influence she knew many of the leading musicians of the day, Sir Charles Stanford, Sir Walter Parratt, Percy Grainger, Quilter, Fauré and Debussy. Everything had come to her so easily up to that moment, there seemed nothing that she could not do. But she left the substance for the shadow.

While she was in Italy she wrote a number of letters to her future husband, later the distinguished theatre critic, Alan Parsons. These letters plot the progress of her ambitions and have a touching sadness about them in the light of hindsight.

On 1st September 1910, before she left she had had a quarrel with the red-haired Felicity. She was angry that she was still surrounded by schoolroom tantrums. Viola's riposte was to say that she was going to Milan. Mademoiselle asked in her prissy governess way *when* she was going. Suddenly Viola announced that she was going the very next week. She felt that settled it. She was free, not so much from her father and mother, whom she loved, as from the toils of the nursery and schoolroom clocks and compulsory glasses of milk and 'be careful how you cross the road, darling'.

Viola was already twenty-six and this childish entry in her

diary gives an idea of how much girls were kept in tutelage until they married. Reading her book one gets the feeling that Italy was more of an escape from the enfolding family life than the pursuit of a career. The Tree family had moved from Viola's much cherished Walpole House, facing the flowing river, and now lived in a wedge-shaped house opposite the Langham Hotel, at the corner of the buildings near the present Broadcasting House, behind All Souls Church. Some of Maud's writing-paper with the All Souls Place address on it still exists. It is white and the envelopes have a flamboyant orange lining and the flap consists of a single Tree with the address in equally flamboyant orange. No one could mistake either Maud's writing—or her writing-paper.

None of the family liked the house, Herbert was sarcastic about it and Viola fled from it. But to dedicated movers any new house is a challenge, and perhaps Maud felt that her wedge-shaped house would drive a wedge to take her back into a more expansive social life.

About Viola's departure Herbert does not seem to have complained, but merely remarked: 'If that is what you want to do dear. . . .' Once she was trained and there were strings to pull, he would pull them.

Viola had been away a month when Herbert wrote to her, giving news of what he was doing. He had been to the Crippen case. A very strange affair—the prisoner in the dock, the shadow of the rope already round his neck, but still struggling and hoping to be free. Herbert knew he was guilty and had no pity for him. But the atmosphere of the court did strike him—with its calm and lack of histrionics. Crippen himself seemed without shame, showing no trace of excitement, he even flashed his false teeth at the Court from time to time.

At the theatre Herbert was happy; he was coining money. For once an obstinate success pleased him. There was to be a Gala performance which the 'dear Prince' had arranged. Herbert hoped that Viola's singing was going well, and then he voiced the thought uppermost in his mind—when was she thinking of coming home? He wanted to see her before the year's end. She ought to be seen soon, singing in opera, time was going by, precious time. He was sure that her teachers in Milan would give her voice the volume that it needed. That was the only thing she lacked.

He was obviously sad that Viola had left him and the theatre. He wanted her back. He missed his favourite.

Viola went to Italy in September of 1910 according to her book and, by a curious coincidence, Herbert's only daughter by 'Mrs.' Reed—Juliet—had been born in April of that year. He had temporarily lost one daughter and fathered another.

He ended his letter with family news, Felicity had grown quite fat. The whole family had been to Sutton Courtney at the weekend. Personally, he thought the small house awful and added, with the resigned tone of someone married to a dedicated 'mover', that perhaps her mother would manage to make something of it.

Maud had bought The Wharf on the Thames at Sutton Courtney. She had transformed it into a country house and then, just as speedily as she had bought it, she sold it to Margot Asquith, the Prime Minister's wife.

By the end of the year Herbert was again questioning Viola about Alan (her fiancé). Perhaps, as money was rolling in from *Henry*, it might be a good idea if Alan became his secretary. Viola was touched by her father's thought, it was just like her father to think up a job for Alan; she was sure that he would have offered Napoleon on St. Helena a secretary's job. In fact she believed that Herbert had once offered a job to Churchill when he was out of office.

Henry was, of course, Shakespeare's *Henry VIII*, one of the grandest of all Herbert's grand productions. All the pageantry fell very appropriately into place, for it ran from 1910 into 1911 when George V was crowned. There could have been no better play for a Coronation Year.

Chapter 13

Grandeur and Good Nature

If *Henry VIII* proved to be one of Herbert's greatest monetary successes, it was not only because of his lavish spending on the production, but of three things which he preferred to hide—time, thought and study.

In the summer of 1910 when he was staying at his beloved Marienbad amongst the pine trees which he loved, he wrote down his thoughts about the characters in the play, these were later published as a small book. Although the edited, corrected version lacks the dash and incoherence of the thoughts he scribbled down, the essence remains the same, showing the spontaneity and intelligence of his writing.

Sheridan's father said of Richard Brinsley that when he wrote of the characters of Charles and Joseph Surface in *The School for Scandal* he 'dipped his pen into his own character', for they were the two sides of himself. On reading Tree's notes for the various characters in *Henry VIII*, the same feeling occurs. Tree was dipping his pen into his own character and examining all aspects of himself and others. *Henry VIII and his Court* was published by Cassell & Co. in 1910. Tree wrote a modest preface to the book saying that it was not meant to be an exhaustive record of events, it was written as a holiday task at Marienbad, in the hope that it would give the playgoer a 'fuller appreciation of the conditions which governed the actions' of Wolsey and Henry.

It might also be thought that Tree was examining his own motives, and those of others, when he glanced back at the past. He jotted down the thought that for a king to have a brilliant reign, he must allow others to become great. It could also be said of an actor-manager.

Tree began his thoughts on *Henry VIII* by stating that he was perhaps the most outstanding figure in English history. The reason was not far to seek. 'The genial adventurer with the sporting tendencies is always popular with the mob and "Bluff King Hal" as he was called, was of the eternal type adored by the people.'

Perhaps Henry VIII had some outward and inward affinities with Nero—he was corpulent, red haired, sang and poetised, he was a lover of horsemanship, a master of the arts and a slave of his passions.

Perhaps as Herbert brooded on Henry, he felt that he shared many of these qualities, but he added a modifying phrase—'If his private vices were great, his public virtues were no less considerable.' He may have taken the Divine Right of Kings to be synonymous with '*le droit de seigneur*', but most people tolerate excesses in the great men of their day which they would deprecate in their inferiors. Possibly Herbert was thinking of himself and his double life.

The King—wrote Tree 'had the ineffable quality called charm, and the appearance of good nature which captivated all who came within the orbit of his radiant personality. He was the '*beau garçon*' endearing himself to all women by his 'compelling and all conquering manhood'.

Did this last phrase describe Tree as he saw himself and his relations with women?

But the King had other and less endearing qualities.

There is above all in the face of Henry as depicted by Holbein that look of impenetrable mystery which was the background of his character. Many royal men have this strange quality; with some it is inborn, with others it is assumed. It is extraordinary that, in spite of Henry's brutality, both Katherine and Anne Boleyn spoke of him as a model of kindness. This cannot be accounted for alone by that divinity which doth hedge a King.

He had charm, thought Tree. There must have been the witchery of charm, which kept women loyal to the edge of the rejection by divorce, or of death by the axe. But there was also 'something baffling and terrifying in the mysterious bonhomie of the King. In spite of Caesar's dictum, it is the fat enemy who is to be feared, the thin villain is more easily seen through'.

Tree then went on to examine the motives of Henry.

The condemnation or non-condemnation of Henry's public life

depends upon our point of view, on which side we take in the
eternal strife between Church and State. In this dilemma we
must then judge by results, for the honest expression of a man is
his work; his greatness or littleness is measured by his output.
Henry produced great results, though he may have been the
unconscious instrument of Fate. The motives which guided him
in his dealings with the Roman Catholic Church may have been
only selfish—they resulted in the emancipation of England
from the tyrannous Popedom.

This sentiment was typical of Tree's age. In our own, we have
seen Marxism elevated to a religion and where once great Popes
and Cardinals bowed before the richness of kings and emperors
and compromised with Mammon, now churchmen speak un-
solicited testimonials to various ideologies perverted in the sacred
name of democracy and social justice, or burn incense to the
closed shop and the Trade Unions. The idols are different, but the
pusillanimity of churchmen remains the same.

Although Tree expressed the true feelings of his age his final
comments remain true of all ages and all hypocrisies. Men may
worship God and serve the devil, but in the end they will always
compromise with God, so that they do not offend Mammon.

He ended his general thoughts on the play:

And thus the injustice of the world is once more triumphantly
vindicated; Wolsey, the devoted servant of the King has crept
into an ignominious sanctuary, Katharine has been driven to a
martyr's doom, the adulterous union has been blessed by the
Court of Bishops, the minor poets have sung their blasphemous
paeans in unison. The offspring of Anne Boleyn over whose
head the shadow of the axe is already hovering has been
christened, amid the acclamations of the mob, the King paces
forth to hold the child up to the gaze of the shouting populace
accompanied by the Court, the Clergy; trumpets blare, drums
roll, the organ thunders, cannons boom, hymns are sung, the
joy bells are pealing.

Tree could see the whole wonderful pageant passing before his
eyes. And then suddenly he added a dark note, something which
was hidden in his own character and which he seldom revealed.

'A lonely figure in black enters, weeping—it is the Fool.'

While at Marienbad Tree had been reading and making notes.

His printed bibliography included Ernest Law's *History of Hampton Court*, Strickland's *Queens of England*, Taunton's *Thomas Wolsey, Legate and Reformer* and Cavendish's *Life of Wolsey*. If Tree's *Henry VIII* was a spectacle, it was a spectacle to which he had given much thought. He made notes on the dances, on the psychological aspects of Henry's marriage with Katharine, on the political motives and moves of the characters in the play. There was something in the brutal age of the Tudors which attracted Tree. He notes that tournaments and disguises appear to have formed part of the amusements of the daily life of the King and his courtiers. Did Tree see an analogy between a great court and a great theatre?

Tree then went on to examine in detail the motives of Wolsey, the part he had decided to play.

> Wolsey, in the first instance, was undoubtedly a party however unwilling to the separation of the King and Queen . . . when Wolsey and Campeggio visited the Queen she was doing her needlework with her maids. It appears (and this is important as showing the inwardness of Wolsey's attitude in the matter of the divorce) that 'from this interview the Queen gained over both legates to her cause, indeed they would never pronounce against her, and this was the head and front of the King's enmity to his former favourite Wolsey'.

He then wrote down a brief life of Wolsey and noted that he had lived at a time when the very atmosphere was charged with intrigue. 'Had he not yielded to a Government by slaughter, he would not have existed. Men murdered in order to live themselves. Wolsey was created Cardinal in spite of the hatred which Leo I bore him.' Possibly there had been some hesitancy which bribery and threats overcame. Whatever one thought about the motives of King, Pope or Cardinal, crime could not be abolished by a few drops of holy water. Blood ran thicker than water and was a more telling argument. But gold conquered blood.

From Taunton's *Thomas Wolsey, Legate and Reformer* Tree reinforced his view, that the Cardinal was a reformer of the church—an aspect of Wolsey which would obviously gain for the actor who played him some contemporary anti-Popish sympathy.

Throughout, Wolsey had dealt as a giant with his gigantic task. Herbert admired the enormous tasks which Henry and Wolsey undertook, perhaps he saw his own wooden O at His Majesty's Theatre as a modern equivalent. He quoted a passage from Taunton: 'Ignorance, he knew, was the root of most of the mischiefs of the day; so by education he endeavoured to give the men the means to know better. Falsehood can only be expelled by truth.'

Tree's family often remarked on his love of the truth, which he constantly recommended to them as a prime virtue. But for a man who loved truth, Herbert lived by many lies and confusions. Possibly a man admires the qualities which he lacks. They can then remain as a shining ideal of the totally unattainable.

Wolsey's idea was to bring the clergy in touch with the thought and conditions of the time. It seemed extraordinary to Tree that one man should have been able to hold the destinies of a kingdom, both the Church and the State in his hands and keep all the complicated threads so clearly in his brain. But in the end he wrote, 'A great man is stronger than a system only while he lives, the system often outlives the man.'

It seemed to Tree that Wolsey could only be inspired by the gigantic things of statecraft. When he was set by Henry to deal with the sordid matter of the divorce he felt restricted and cramped. He was a better patriot than a royal servant. 'A first rate man cannot do second rate things well,' wrote Tree.

Although Henry VIII and Wolsey were like two giants littered in a single day, they had fallen foul of one another on a simple fact: 'His passion for marriage lines in his amours was one of Henry's most distinguishing qualities.'

There was no doubt that Wolsey made several attempts to become Pope, 'but this enterprise was doomed to failure, although in it he was supported by the King. To gain this end much bribery was needed especially to the younger men who are generally the most needy.'

Wolsey was hated, feared, flattered and cajoled. As a man of God he strongly disapproved of the divorce, but as the King's Chancellor, he felt himself bound to urge his case to the best of his ability. One could not imagine a more terrible position for a man of conscience to be placed in, but once embarked on politics the animation of his conscience was temporarily suspended. It was the eternal strife—for a man who embraced politics the ten commandments became a negligible quantity.

Tree found the end of Wolsey inexpressibly moving. He had failed where he had most served. 'To those who regard characters as either black or white, Wolsey's was indeed a contradiction. Charges of a personal character have been brought against the great Prelate, which need not here be referred to, unless it be to say that if they were true, by so much the less he was a priest, by so much more he was a man.'

In his notebook Tree was less circumlocutory. He stated quite baldly that Wolsey was supposed to have had two children. Well, maybe he did have two children, but when it came down to it a saint was a man. He had the vices of a man, and if great sinners make great saints, it could be said that Wolsey was a saint. Not the general view taken by Holy Mother Church.

Tree also quoted Brewer on Henry VIII: 'Few would have thought that under so careless and splendid an exterior, the very ideal of bluff, open-hearted good humour, and frankness, there lay a watchful and secret eye.' Did Tree admire this quality in Henry, and feel that, perhaps, like *Henry VIII*, he had that watchful and secret eye—even if he only used it to create his gallery of characters? Herbert admired Henry as a man, but he certainly was not a gentleman, in which he differed profoundly from Tree.

When Tree was in Marienbad doing his 'holiday tasks' he often broke off to remind himself of things he must do. He must ask Professor Budge (of the British Museum) to the first night of *Henry*, and for good measure Eckstein and Sir Oliver Lodge.

The notes which Tree made for his production of *Henry VIII*, while breathing the invigorating pine-scented air at Marienbad, prove that he took the greatest trouble with his reading. He quoted many different sources and often added a shrewd comment or relevant thought of his own. Remorse, the fatal egg by pleasure laid, could shadow its joy.

It was not perhaps a shadow which troubled Tree himself, but in certain circumstances he could see the validity of the sentiment.

Tree had studied and studied alone, at Marienbad, but when it came to his production, he preferred to pretend that everything came to him by the light of nature. He had very good excuses for cutting much of the narrative of the play and concentrating on two things—the domestic plot, and the conflict between Henry and his Cardinal.

He also needed to cut the play to make way for his lavish

scenery and his even more lavish costumes. These were designed by Percy Macquoid and the designs, nearly a hundred of them, still exist in all their intricate and complicated detail. They were edited in equal detail by Tree. On the elaborate costumes of the morris dancers a note has been written: 'Change tights to one leg blue and one leg orange.' The design shows them to be grey and orange. Lord Abergavenny's rich costume has a pencilled note: 'This costume on *no* account to be worn at Banquet Scene.' Possibly the reason for this was that it would take away the attention of the audience from the principals. Anne Boleyn's crimson coronation dress is richly pearled and trimmed with ermine. Every costume has its separate design, Katharine's ladies are very charming in gold and blue brocade with little Tudor bonnets. Thomas Cromwell wears a much richer dress than when he appears in modern productions—a purple gown, furred, with velvet sleeves, richly trimmed, with a little white pleated veston.

Henry VIII himself is rich in green and gold, with a gold dagger enamelled in green, while Cardinal Wolsey, to indicate the sybaritic side of his character, holds a golden pomander. The executioner appears standing out boldly in a suit of bloody scarlet.

All these designs by Percy Macquoid were to be made by B. & J. Simmons (theatrical costumiers). There were ninety-two numbered designs, some were approved and carried out, but all, down to the Banqueting Ladies, were done with great meticulousness, each design different, and all put into a folder with watered paper to protect them. Dressmakers who waited on theatre managers in those days did not skimp their tasks and were glad to serve the great actors who served the public. It was an honour to be theatrical costumier to Sir Herbert Tree.

Henry VIII was the play which was running when Tree wrote so cheerfully to Viola saying that he was coining money and would it be a good idea for him to take on her young man as a secretary?

Herbert's good nature was widely known, the letters written to him which remain contain little of the sycophancy which can be noted in people who wish to gain some advantage for themselves, but they take his good nature for granted.

I rejoice in your success—so well earned, so nobly borne. The public as they learn more and more of your generous disposition and glad good nature, will feel for you as your friends feel, that the charm of your devotion to art is the frankness and happiness of its dedication.

This from Harold Begbie, a journalist who had no favours to ask. But Herbert's glad good nature was in some senses a great disadvantage to him. He was plagued by friends, relations, bishops, beggars, and even Prime Minister's wives. Margot Asquith, writing from 10 Downing Street (Tel. 2812 Vic):

I cannot thank you enough, dear Sir Herbert, for your kindness. I *wish* you would let Annie Schletter do her single piece which takes *just* 20 mins and is very remarkable. Any day after you shut your theatre morning or afternoon—I should be *so* grateful.

Or Lady Anglesey from Belvoir Castle:

Dear Daddy, If I have to be Anne Boleyn in my step grandmother-in-law's quadrille at the Shakespeare Theatre Fancy Dress Ball at the Albert Hall in June will you lend me a dress? I am at my wits end what to do, but pray you will lend me some sort of Henry VIII dress. My step grandmother is Lady Wemyss—I wonder if Lord Wemyss is going to be King Henry? *I* have no news of Viola and miss her *forever*. Marjorie.

Violet Asquith joined the suppliants wondering whether there was any opening for a protégée of hers. The girl's talent was small, should she think of some other profession?

Tree was also bothered with friends and acquaintances recommending child geniuses. 'A little dancer called Ellaline Mills (nine years old) has been a pupil at the Guildhall School for two years, Mr. Wyndham and Miss Kate Rorke think a *great* deal of her powers.' There is no evidence that Sir Herbert did.

Actors wrote recommending actresses. Irving's son Laurence (on tour with his father's old plays) wrote introducing Miss Dorothy Green. 'She has been on tour with me, playing one of my wife's parts, and as she is really a clever and experienced actress I wanted her to see you.' Scrawled across this letter (in shorthand) and presumably dictated by Tree are the words, 'She called—not very attractive—rather prim'. The latter quality would hardly have appealed to Tree.

Madge Kendal wrote recommending herself, for Lady Macbeth.

The Bishop of London wrote from Fulham Palace about a
Mrs. Blair, the orphan daughter of a clergyman. She and her
family were living actually outside the gates of Fulham Palace.
Her husband was acting with Cyril Maude in *Toddles* but she was
anxious to get something in London—as his money was not
enough to keep them both. If *only* Sir Herbert could see his way to
giving her the smallest of parts. The Bishop ended with a real *cri de
coeur*, 'I have so many poor clergy on my hands that I find it a
handful to have members of another profession as well.' He was
hedging his suppliants on to Sir Herbert.

W. T. Stead wrote recommending his daughter who was in one
of Mr. Benson's smaller companies. She was willing, industrious
and intelligent and anxious to get her foot on the rungs of the London ladder. There was no comment about Miss Stead's ability and
nothing to prove whether she set the ladder on fire, or even
climbed it.

A man called Edmund Grace (alleging he was an old pensioner
of Sir Herbert's) wrote a series of letters which read much like the
second act of a melodrama (the scenes where the hero goes down
and down):

> Darling and Beloved Vagabond,
> Propped up on a rickety couch racked with the pain of a blood
> poisoned ancle [*sic*] I turn my weary eyes towards His Majesty's
> Mecca and Its great and generous High Priest. That this wasted
> life of mine is not worth the preservation is patent—endure this
> bitter cold, this insidious hunger is too terrible too unbearable.
> I know how murders are committed lives wrecked. But that
> 'I am pigeon livered and lack gall' I believe I could attack the
> well formed body of the Secy. of the A.B.T. or F.

He asks if Tree could keep the doubly damned in the slightest
vestige of happiness or comfort. Writing some time later he
brings a Dickensian touch to his begging. 'A fresh lease to an
active life is the wish of yours truly who will never see another
Christmas (if he gets through this). If in the goodness of thy great
heart, thou canst lighten the transitory moment I pray thee!'

Presumably Sir Herbert had sent no money in answer to the
second appeal so it was followed up.

Frozen (for God's sake help)! The exigencies of the weather

added to unparalleled hardship, have laid me low, *very* low
indeed; so much so that I wish it had been my lot to have
departed to that fairer region, far, far away rather than endure
this cold, hunger and misery. If at this season of goodwill
towards men, the ever generous heart of His Majesty's Head
beats responsive I beg you to keep this poor wretch who on
borrowed envelope and stamp, makes a frenzied appeal. Let
half a pound of cheap steak adorn the miserable bench on
which he eats—an occupation which to this poor devil is like
Othello's gone! Gone! The fruit of a prosperous season be
yours and health to enjoy the same.

Starving actors wrote for money to help out with ailing wives,
singers wanted to sing to him, children wished to dance for him,
playwrights wanted to read plays to him and composers wished
him to hear their music. Friends pestered him with invitations to
grand houses for week-ends, luncheons, or dinners and asked him
to give special performances for charity.

But Charity concerts had their pitfalls. Constance Collier wrote
from New York: 'Who is this Mr. H. S. Booth who is giving a
matinée at His Majesty's Theatre on the 30th November? *Do* be
careful I fear he is the man that wrote to me some time ago about
Shakespearean productions. If so, don't let him use His Majesty's
to exploit himself even under the guise of charity. Don't say
anything about it but just look well into it. (It says in the papers
that the matinée is for a tribute to Madame Ristori).'

She signs herself 'Always Constance'. Herbert kept his friends—
and lovers. In spite of their marriages, Constance and Herbert
remained good friends and she was anxious to preserve him from
trouble.

Experts troubled Herbert. Sir Edward Clarke writing from the
Royal Courts of Justice took exception to the fact that Herbert
moved about when he was acting Antony in *Julius Caesar*. 'Would
any orator move about among the crowd he was addressing?' Sir
Edward did not explain his rhetorical question, he took it as read
that he was right. A fussy gentleman called G. Ambrose Lee (of the
Heralds College) was constantly on the watch for historical
inaccuracies. He was advising Sir Herbert about *The Merchant of
Venice*. He had been looking into the archaeology of the play and
it might be advisable to bring it back to the middle of the fifteenth

century instead—as was usually done—setting it 150 years later. Meanwhile he wondered if Tree had forgotten to send him a box for *The Darling of the Gods*, and would he remember that Mr. Lee was very anxious to buy a suit of Japanese armour for his small collection?

A few years later Mr. Lee was still on the watch for difficulties in Tree's Cardinal Wolsey. Shoes and gloves should be put on *before* and, taken off immediately *after* singing High Mass. The episcopal ring should be worn on the third *not* the first finger of the right hand. Incidentally, it is the *ring* which is kissed by the faithful not the *hand*. Mr. Lee could not understand why Tree was not wearing a proper Rochet which, with the Mozetta or chimere was the ordinary dress of prelates in pre-Reformation times and why was the Cappa Magna not worn at the Consistory Court at Blackfriars? *Another helpful point*: 'If your Biretta were made on a foundation of Buckram as is St. Charles at Milan, you could take it off and put it on *quite* easily.' Of course these points had probably been noted by Mr. Tree's experts, said Mr. Lee. He added modestly that perhaps they possessed information unknown to himself?

The most sensible and practical letters with a few exceptions came from successful members of the 'profession'. They merely wrote about business, parts for themselves, or complications of contracts, or the difficulties of fitting in the dates of productions. Sometimes they were even thinking of Herbert himself. Lillah Granville Barker (the actress Lillah McCarthy) wrote asking him could he 'possibly' come and see *The Master Builder*—it was being played for the last time on the Friday matinée 'Solness would be such a wonderful part for you.' This last sentence was underlined by Tree and the lady's telephone number added.

The letters filed under the name of Julia Neilson show the lady in a less sentimental light than the romantic parts she played.

My dear Mr. Tree, From our conversation last night I fear you still think that I accepted the terms of engagement in your letter to me of July 15th. I have thought it over carefully and hope you will see your way to giving me the terms I asked, namely thirty-five pounds (£35) per week for the season 1893/1894 at the Haymarket Theatre as I should be very sorry to quit a theatre associated with so much happiness.

She then wrote another very businesslike letter complaining
that she was *so* unbusinesslike and should have written 1892/1893.
She also made it clear that she was keeping copies of her letters.
Having achieved her point and her contract she wrote an ecstatic
letter: '*My dear*—Thank you for that beautiful letter.'

Gilbert Parker, the playwright, wrote regretting he could not
pay Tree the money he owed him—but he thought he could see
his way to letting him have £800 'next Thursday week'. Parker's
letter bears much resemblance to Sheridan's jokes about how to
refuse charity. Having (to a certain extent) quieted his financial
conscience Parker, writing from an expensive address, Carlton
House Terrace, perhaps feeling that he had pushed his own luck
far enough with Tree, approached him through Dana on behalf of
a Mrs. Froleigh and her daughter, Madeleine. Mrs. Froleigh, like
Mrs. Worthington, wanted to get her daughter on the stage. They
had come all the way from Canada; did Dana think Tree would
advise them? Perhaps he could even give the girl a small part, she
was not good-looking, but had *fire*.

It was perhaps hardly surprising that Herbert looked very
distrait from time to time—so many Mrs. Worthingtons, frozen
pensioners, singers, dancers and playwrights reading to him, were
enough to sink a battleship, let alone tire out an actor-manager.
No wonder he sought refuge in his Dome, away from the
clamour of the petitioners.

Viola described his Dome as being the space where rats and fire
escapes would normally have been kept, but he had made it into a
wonderful place in which to live and work. The high banqueting
hall ended in rafters and something which looked like a belfy.
Then he had a small inner room which she said was very like
himself, it was an ordinary comfortable room with a frieze
running round it painted with scenes from *Twelfth Night*, *The
Tempest* and *The Taming of the Shrew*. Under the frieze were his
bookshelves, a mass of useful illustrated books to help with the
visual presentation of his plays and a mass of what Viola called
'hopeless' presentation copies. 'Shakespeare Through An Old
Stager's Spectacles' or 'Sardanapalus: A Tragedy in 8 Acts.' The
books and papers were piled up with his methodical untidiness on
chairs, sofas and desks and the room had that nice glow of hard
work. It was not stuffy—it was interesting and full of projects. A
creative room—a room where things were going on—and would

always go on. Herbert had the feeling that once he had shut his two great doors he was out of this world and away from the petitioners. He had time to think.

Viola found him absolutely natural and unaffected. He went up to his Dome and although he turned neither to left nor right, his pale eyes showed that his brain was at work. He may have seemed as if he looked right through people and things, but this was no mask to hide his real feelings, it was his way, as he said in his short story, of 'switching himself off'. But if the theatre staff thought that this meant he had not noticed things which were going wrong, they were disappointed. They might say, 'It's all right—the Chief won't notice', but he did notice—and speedily switched himself on again to draw attention to failings and inefficiencies.

He may have seemed superficial and trivial to superficial and trivial people, but the people who loved him, like Viola, found him absolutely sincere, hating artificiality or sham. This perhaps explains his understanding of such a gallery of portraits which he created on the stage. He was always sincere to the character he was playing.

*

He hated the technical terms of the theatre. 'Do you know they call the curtain *the rag*?' he once announced in wonder, and added, 'The rag came down on mud' meant the play was a failure. For this reason he found it difficult to make himself understood where the technicalities of rehearsals were concerned. Most people delight in the inner jargon of their trade but not Tree. Lighting baffled him, 'That one, that one there—it gives no light' was translated as 'Don't check your battens', while 'More mystery' was translated by the stage manager to the limelight man as, 'Biff your Number Threes'.

He knew nothing of music and yet, like Sheridan, he would hum or buzz a tune to a composer and by this means give him exactly the right mood which was needed for the play and the emotions which it portrayed.

Totally uninterested in clothes he would change an old tie or hat for a new one and then walk out of the shop leaving the worn-out one behind. His looks bothered him. He admired good looks both in men and women and once said of a young actor: 'He has the sort of looks *I* ought to have had.' Tree's was an age of handsome actors, both men and women, and perhaps because of his looks he preferred to retreat into disguise to take on a different form and to astonish by his versatility.

His daughter Iris remarked that she had never liked him in ordinary parts—the soldier, or conventional lover. He was not a modern comedy actor. His strength was in the faculty he had of stirring the imagination—Fagin's asthmatic cough before the open window which made the audience feel the fog rolling in from the river, the taste of dust and the smell of damp walls. The clenched, awkward gestures of Beethoven, the thin, slightly affected voice of Richard II which gave a pitiful beauty to his weakness—it was in parts which could conjure up from his inner soul the sinister fancy, the whimsical humour, the nightmares and the dreams, which enabled him to reach his audience leaving them haunted or bewitched.

But in spite of his looks, or his failings, he took things as they came. He regarded the world with a tolerant eye: 'With all the drawbacks of life—I would rather be myself than anybody else—This is a happy instinct of mankind.'

It was also a very happy instinct of Herbert.

Chapter 14

Herbert and Viola

While Viola was in Italy, writing constantly to her young man, she was equally constantly in her father's mind. He had been promising himself the pleasure of writing to her. He wanted to tell her about the world and life from his point of view, but somehow things—perhaps the world itself—held him back. The reason he had sent her the £10 was that he was suddenly afraid that she might stint herself, she must have those little extras that she was used to. He would also like her to have another £2 a week on her allowance. What a pleasure it was to hear of the real progress of her voice. He longed to hear her sing again and, if he was not able to come to Italy, she must come to London. It was noble of his darling to be so dedicated to her work, but she must be *seen*, that was essential for her singing career.

Herbert sent Viola the theatre news, he thought of coming to see her when *Midsummer Night's Dream* was revived. Although it was said to be a bad thing if he was not in it, he felt it would be sufficiently attractive without him. The company had given him eight silver plates and made beautiful speeches, which had left Herbert himself *without* speech. He had missed her so much at the rejoicing dinner on 1st January. Her description of the 'advanced' lighting of the Milan operas amused him. It was all very well for opera singers, their faces did not need to be seen—and in fact if their figures were also in shadow that would be an added benefit. Perhaps it was better to have the lights at the back. But for some plays it could have a dramatic impact, he was going to use the idea in *Macbeth*.

All went well with *Henry VIII*, he told her. All his debts were paid and £10,000 was smiling in his account at the Bank. How wonderful it was that he was temporarily rich! He was anxious for news about Viola's feeling towards Alan Parsons. Were they engaged? He wanted to know the exact attitude he should adopt with regard to the young man, he wanted to help the young people. When the spring came Tree was in Paris, and was proposing to whisk Viola off to Berlin with him, 'on a sort of business', as Viola put it. Viola met him at Turin where he planned to see the International Exhibition, but unfortunately Herbert was two weeks too early. There was nothing to see—or to do, but stay the night in a very large hotel with Viola, who was irritated at the restricting presence of her 'mademoiselle' Maria. Viola remarked on her father's very conventional ideas of chaperonage—even when he was alone with his own daughter.

From the pages of Viola's book *Castles in the Air* comes the perfume of that easy life before 1914 with Daddy as the *Deus ex Machina*, sending money, arriving from Paris, Berlin, Rome, Russia or Marienbad, full of plans and projects. Daddy could arrange anything. He would lease his theatre to Beecham and enable her to sing. He could arrange for her to sing to Strauss, or give her a leading part in an operetta. There was nothing which he could not achieve or cause to be achieved.

Viola remembered her father's visit vividly and with some regrets. Ricordi had been staying in their hotel—it seemed to her to be a wonderful piece of luck—and she managed to get Herbert to a dress rehearsal of Verdi's *Falstaff*. He was bored but tried to look interested for her sake. Herbert was not without a feeling for music. He had employed many of the leading composers of the day but the technique of music bored him as did the routine technique of acting, producing, or lighting. He preferred to have sudden inspirations. Other people could concern themselves with the details.

Viola took him to see *Rosenkavalier*. She had conceived the idea of singing in that opera. Possibly the part of Octavian, she had not made up her mind. Beecham was arranging to take His Majesty's for an opera season. Should this happen Viola saw that her father would be in a very strong position to help her with both Beecham and with Strauss. Viola had it all worked out. She dragged her father round Milan in one horse cabs to meet singers and musicians. She took him back to her house to sing arias at him out of *The Girl of the Golden West*. They did have one or two days on Lake Como but, thinking it over later, Viola felt her father was disappointed that she would not leave her work behind her while he was there.

Herbert was out for a holiday, but Viola was planning her singing career. She wrote to Alan that Daddy was *delighted* by her singing. What a revenge she was going to have on the people who had tried to discourage her! As soon as her father had heard her voice, plans for her future poured from his ever fertile brain. Herbert aimed to please and if his daughter wanted to be an opera singer she would be an opera singer, if he had anything to do with it. He had come abroad to get away from people reading their plays to him or singing at him. But as Viola regretfully remarked later, youth is selfish.

Viola was writing delightedly to Alan about how Daddy's views on her voice had quite changed. Once he was constantly asking her if it was really sensible to become a singer instead of an actress, now he said every few minutes how awfully pleased he was about her voice. Perhaps with the constant repetition of how pleased he was, Herbert was trying to convince himself. To Viola her father was magnetic, she felt more alive. For her he could achieve anything and when he was there she felt that she could be worthy of his faith in her. As a child he had compelled her to float. As a girl to fly. Now all he had to say was 'Become an opera star'.

Music had never been more than a background for a play to Herbert Tree and it must be supposed that the complications of it bored him; he was easily bored and more especially by a talent which was not his own. But he loved Viola. She had been so sweet to him during all the years, he only wanted her sweetness not to change in the future. So he managed to look cheerful about music, remarking: 'I see now that singing is more of a *science*.'

Herbert was perhaps not as thrilled about her voice as Viola felt he was, but he continued to make plans for the young people. Perhaps it would be better to help the young man too, just in case of failure.

In an age which expected marriage settlements, Viola felt that she could not marry Alan until he had a good degree from Oxford, and a post in the Civil Service, and she had become a famous singer. Then everything would be before them. Herbert, who knew the pitfalls of the world, remained sceptical and kept his options for his child open. Perhaps Alan could adapt a play for His Majesty's. Viola wondered could Alan perhaps manage it— after his exam. If he didn't pass, she could not marry him, he must realise that. If he was merely to become secretary to her father, he might as well have done it four years ago. She found it difficult to explain to her father why they didn't marry. He couldn't understand how they could bear to be apart.

By the following week Herbert was sending telegrams about Viola going to Berlin to sing. Strauss was willing to hear her sing the page, or the Marschallin.

But Viola's visit to Strauss was not a success. She was bluntly told that she sang like an actress. For London, Strauss stated he wanted a voice which was ready. Hers was not only uncertain, it had not grown. He felt sorry for her disappointment but told her that his music was not easy. It was very complicated and she may have had the wrong impression from the Italians. The Italians never listened to his music with attention, they were too impatient. She was a young singer—it was not good that she should attempt parts beyond her range. His music was hard on voices, he did not spare them.

Madame Strauss admired Viola's hat and, having eaten some of Madame's excellent cream cakes, the aspiring opera singer left disconsolately. Herbert could use his influence in everything except in making Viola's voice better than it was.

The impression which Viola's letters about her singing career give is that everyone was playing up to Herbert for reasons of their own. It was suggested that she should appear for one night— as an understudy. That would be quite out of the question from her father's position and from hers. The whole point of her becoming an opera singer was to be something new, a diva of the first rank—not to be seen as an also-ran, an understudy! What was more without a salary! It must be thought that Viola's views of herself at this point in her career outstripped her talent.

As it happened her first appearance in London in her new role was not impressive. She went straight from All Souls Place to the Duke of Rutland's house where Society and the Stage were mingling to rehearse for a charity function, wearing a very tight skirted dress with wide revers, looking, said her father, like a tadpole.

Herbert was over-indulgent with Viola, he had given her leading parts in his productions, he had never criticised her and, having succeeded in putting her before the public as an actress, felt that he could do the same with her as a singer.

During the winter season of 1911 he had decided to do Offenbach's *Orpheus in the Underworld* as *Orpheus in the Underground*. Herbert had already tried Viola out in a scene from *Hansel and Gretel* as a curtain raiser. He was leaving no stone unturned. He had already cast the mistress of a man called O'Neil, who was a newspaperman in Paris, for the leading part of Eurydice. Viola arrived from Italy for the first night of *Orpheus* which had a moderate success, but as she put it had not the scurrilousness of a revue 'nor the beauty of the poetic plays my father put on'. It fell between two moods.

Orpheus in the Underground was not a success, and Herbert felt this was a good opportunity to achieve two results—by putting Viola in the lead he would revive interest in the play, and give her a sparkling debut. She came back from Italy, picked up the score and went off to Belvoir Castle for Christmas with the designs for her costumes. She studied the part in a week and took over from the American girl who was singing the role.

Viola rehearsed, feeling bereft without her father, who had dashed off to Russia to see Gordon Craig's production of *Hamlet*. He arrived back with a flourish to see the dress rehearsal. O'Neil understandably annoyed at having his mistress dismissed was watching from the back of the circle when Herbert joined him. When Viola finished her first song, the American snapped: 'I don't think much of your goddam daughter, Tree.'

Tree's reply was unruffled but typical: 'Mr. O'Neil, neither you as a lover—nor I as a father are unbiassed.'

O'Neil's mistress had been paid off and that was that. All that Viola remembered of the first night was her father calling out, 'bis, bis!' for the Bacchanalian song at the end of the first act in which she did succeed as a singer.

She was offered £200 a week to sing in the music halls when the run ended, an offer which, as a potential opera star, she refused. Bernard Shaw disapproved of her action and also of her turning the American girl out of her part. He had already written a warning to Viola. 'I know all about that wonderful perfected voice', and he related to her a parable: 'I knew a man once who pursued it until he was within six months of conquering the world with it. On the very brink of the realisation of his dream, the Truth stepped in with scythe and hour-glass; and lo! An old man lying dead in University College Hospital. . . . Viola how can you be so deaf? Don't you know there are no perfect voices and never will be. . . . ? The Italians, as a rule sing worse and teach infinitely worse than any other nation in the world. . . . To be lovely and slim and ten feet high is a whole bunch of qualities. . . . O irrational Viola, why don't you take steps to get over the fright by singing in public—were it only at a street corner? You must assert all your personal peculiarities as merits and qualities, and not intimidate yourself by being ashamed of them as defects.'

But Viola did not listen. She continued to employ two or three teachers and returned to Italy. Her father remained patient, loving and helpful. By the spring of 1912 she had decided to become engaged and to marry by the summer. She had not renounced her plans for being a great *diva*—marriage was to be an interval before returning to Italy and her great debut. In her attitude towards marriage she was before her time, it was not the be-all and end-all of her life. Her career was to come first. Perhaps she had reservations about marriage itself. She asked her fiancé if he were advanced enough in life to realise how great a thing they could make of their love—or how little? She had, for her age, been much buffeted by life. She might not know it by experience, but in her heart she realised how easily marriage can become cynical, snobbish, worldly, merely devoted to ambition and to outward show.

Was Viola thinking of her parents when she wrote this, and did she hesitate so long because of these feelings?

Once the engagement was announced Maud came into her own. She insisted on inviting everyone, because of Herbert's great position and the fact that it was a great event not only in Viola's life, but Herbert's. She went round looking at churches and places to hold splendid receptions. Herbert was less excited by the event.

He was going to see Alan that evening. He wanted to know Viola's feelings about her wedding. Did she want it to be large and fashionable or small and friendly? He realised, perhaps thinking of his long years with Maud, that marriage was a *solemn* thing. But ideas about how solemn things should be solemnised varied. What did she think?

Viola was carried along with Maud's wedding preparations. She asked Alan Parsons to find out whether her father was really poor and was concerned about how much she could spend on clothes. Viola, who had as grandiose ideas as her mother, was torn between Westminster Abbey and St. Paul's for the wedding, but Lady Diana Manners had suggested a compromise, St. Martin-in-the-Fields. Even Viola approved. She liked the idea of the 'populace cheering' in Trafalgar Square and passing His Majesty's Theatre on the way to the church.

She was married eleven months after the birth of Peter Reed, in July of 1912, and her own children were born in 1914 and 1915. Herbert's children and grandchildren were to be divided by only a short margin of time.

Peter was born on 9th August at Daisyfield. Five months later, on 11th December 1911, Miss Pinney went to the Registrar's Office with a man called Henry Marcus Allen and made a Statutory Declaration to the effect that on the birth certificates of her children, Carol Reed, Juliet Reed and Peter Reed, the mother's name should read 'Pinney', and that the father's name Herbert Reed and the words 'of independent means' should be omitted. Why this was done, why only three of her children's birth certificates were amended, and what legal reasons she had for carrying out this change remains a mystery, as does so much else about Miss Pinney.

Viola's wedding was a great social event. Three days before the marriage *The Times* devoted several inches to the wedding presents; the bridegroom gave a bright green enamelled laurel wreath crown to the bride and the bride gave the bridegroom— a gun. Sir Arthur Pinero presented the happy couple with a silver pheasant, presumably to herald a good shooting season. The class-consciousness of the age found even in theatre circles is reflected in the list of other wedding presents. 'The friends of the bride', at His Majesty's Theatre, weighed in with silver entrée dishes, silver candlesticks and a silver tray, while 'the staff' at the Theatre merely contributed dessert knives and forks. 'The servants at All Souls Place presented the bride with a silver bowl and ladle, and the servants at Mr. Parsons senior's vicarage, a silver cake basket.' It was an up-stairs down-stairs world, where duchesses gave mere amber necklaces and servants gave silver. The Prime Minister-to-be, Mr. Lloyd George, contributed a small enamel box, while the current Prime Minister, Mr. Asquith, concluded the list with an edition of Shakespeare's works, a gift surely superfluous to the requirements of a girl who had been acting and hearing Shakespeare all her young life.

More artistic tastes were reflected in the church decorations. The pillars of St. Martin's Church were garlanded with bay, while the chancel was adorned with honeysuckle, sweet peas and lilies. The page was Anthony Asquith, the Prime Minister's son, wearing a white satin Empire uniform. The bridesmaids included Lady Diana Manners and all the sisters of the bride and bridegroom, wearing white net dresses with coats of yellow chiffon and tulle caps. They were rewarded with amber necklaces which seem to have been much in evidence in the summer of 1912.

The tall, graceful, bride in her traditional Empire style dress bordered with orange-blossom, had a train of ruffled lace. The guest list was impressive, beginning as it did with the Prime Minister and Mrs. Asquith and sprouting into the strawberry leaves of various dukes and duchesses, then descending from marquises, earls and countesses, down to mere barons. The arts were not forgotten—Sir Edward Elgar, Sir Arthur Pinero, Sir Philip Burne-Jones, Sir Hubert Parry, Lady Gregory, the play-wright, Miss Marie Corelli—and many wives of actors who were themselves presumably playing to good houses at their matinées. Well down on the list came the bridegroom's mother, sandwiched between Miss Pauline Chase and Professor Gollancz. *The Times* Social Page knew that titles came first and mere mothers of bridegrooms were popped in where convenient.

On the way to the church Herbert not only passed His Majesty's, he got out of the carriage and dashed in to see that everything was going on as well as could be expected without him.

In Trafalgar Square the press of the crowds was so great that the traffic had to be stopped. Viola's wedding, like Herbert Tree's first nights, was a great public event. When the carriage stopped at the church door and as Herbert was about to hand Viola out of it he suddenly said: 'Do you *like* Alan, dear?' Was he suddenly voicing his own last minute feelings about marriage and the long years of struggle he had had with its difficulties?

The pageantry of weddings was one thing, but the reality of it was quite another. Marriage, as Herbert had confided to his note-book, was not a gift of God, but a visitation of Providence.

During the long years of his infidelities and his second family, he must have found the public image of fidelity difficult to uphold. Yet the tug of his youthful love for Maud, her intelligence, her loyalty and her help were all leading strings which bound him to his first family, though his second family was twice as large.

'Mother has been so sweet to me,' he once said to Viola. His daughter would be luckier in having a faithful husband, and she would make a faithful wife. He regretted losing her. Maud said that the day of Viola's wedding was a great day for Herbert, great with pride, but it was also great with pain. He felt he was losing so much of what he loved.

The reception was given at All Souls Place and the guests drifted from the studio attached to the Trees' house into that of Sir David Murray next door. Herbert was embarrassed that people had sent such costly gifts. He said to Maud: 'It seems so awful, we never give a party, but when we do, each guest has to give the wealth of Ind to come to it.'

He also regretted losing his daughter as part of his company at the theatre. 'The Twig' had left its parent branch. 'Viola would have made a great actress,' he said to Maud. She married in July and went back to Italy in September, but by October she had trouble with her throat. She was to make her debut at Genoa in *Salomé*.

The rest of the story was told in telegrams. On 24th October Herbert telegraphed anxiously about Viola's health. Four days later Maud telegraphed, perhaps the impresario would give Viola a fortnight's holiday. She must not hesitate, she must come to England immediately and see the best specialists in London about her throat. Money was no object where her dear Viola's health was concerned.

On 4th November Herbert telegraphed she must wire him immediately the result of her treatment. He would come to Genoa via Venice and Milan if the news was unsatisfactory. Three days later he wired again, that if it would be of the slightest use to her, he would fetch her from Genoa, if she wired him that night.

The impresario put a notice in the paper: 'Tonight *Salomé*. For this part the management have engaged Anice Baron in place of Madame Viola Tree, who could not be appreciated by our public because of the very grave illness of her throat.'

Viola telegraphed to her husband. It was useless. She was travelling home with her father. Would Alan tell her mother? Alan wired to his dearest Viola to come home to him, and to come quickly.

Her attempt to make a career on her own, and break away from His Majesty's had failed and so had her voice. She returned to her marriage and her family.

Chapter 15

Not Getting on with Shaw

In 1907 when Tree was in Dublin astonishing his public with his quirky performance of Paragot, Forbes-Robertson was appearing at the same time in the same city in Shaw's *Caesar and Cleopatra*. Tree paid the author a handsome tribute. 'It was the play of a great Irishman who, even in his own country, was acknowledged to be great today. He had come into his own. Whatever differences there might be as to Mr. Shaw's qualities as a dramatist there was one great quality which he had. He dared to tell the truth. The men who had the courage to tell the truth in their own times were the men who towered above the minor thinkers, whose ideas were not cribbed, cabined and confined by that basest of all virtues—tact.'

Herbert was always a great stickler for truth—so long as it did not come out. Tact he avoided by retreating behind his veil of vagueness. Bernard Shaw had no use for tact at all, and used truth —or his version of it—as a rapier to pierce the vital forces of his opponents.

Tree, in private, was not so complimentary about Mr. Shaw. He felt that G.B.S. destroyed everything, even himself in his plays. The theatre was for those who love the drama, who love the joy of life and the true presentation of history. It was only secondarily for those who fulfil their souls in footnotes.

The contrast between the two men was sharp. On one side Shaw, the ascetic intellectual, who was before his time and out of his time, the man who revelled in politics as the supreme game of life, but who shunned women and the elemental forces which they represented to him, and who rated love and life below political controversy. On the other side, Tree who wrote: 'I would rather play a man who died from love than from ambition.' He was *l'homme* more than *moyen sensuel*, exactly of his time, the lover of women, who saw politics as ludicrous and men and women as supremely fascinating.

Shaw, the barren, preferred to shun the Life Force and keep his sexual encounters strictly to the written page. Tree, the philoprogenitive, found the end product of a marriage or an affair to be families. Herbert remarked on what he called the sterilised passion of Bernard Shaw, who lacked nothing—except the essential. The earthiness and gusto of the real life force Shaw primly avoided. Yet by a curious irony the comedies of Shaw continue to spark audiences into life. Writing comedy, unlike acting it, is a timeless art.

Shaw and Tree were two clever, witty, intellectual men who should never have been allowed into the same theatre. Each of them underrated the other. If Shaw thought he had cleverly dissected Tree down to the bone, in many senses Tree deceived Shaw because he was a much more complicated man than he chose to make public. Tree noticed that Shaw had the capacity to take an entirely opposite point of view if he was agreed with and to sound equally impressive and sincere supporting his anti-thesis as he was in supporting his thesis. It is a trick of most political speakers to hold any view with passionate-seeming sincerity.

Even before the production of *Pygmalion*, Shaw and Tree had been sparring. Herbert had been annoyed that Shaw had written to *The Times* stating that the reason Herbert had been knighted was because he had fallen in with the Lord Chamberlain's views and refused to produce *Blanco Posnet*.

According to Shaw, Tree was also shocked by the irreverent passages about God: 'He's a sly one. He's a mean one. He lies low for you. He plays cat and mouse with you. He lets you run loose until He thinks you're shot of Him; and then, when you least expect it, He's got you.' Tree was agnostic, but whatever kind of God there was in whom Shaw believed only perhaps Shaw knew, thought Tree.

From Shaw's point of view, Tree had been frightened by the sentiments in *Blanco Posnet*, although the part would have given him a wonderful melodramatic role. What it did not give a theatrical manager was a whole evening's entertainment, for it was only a one-act play with a dozen characters and a complicated set. But in Shaw's polemic to *The Times*, that was forgotten, he was engaged in one of his favourite games, having a little fun, and advertising himself at the same time.

Having read and digested Shaw's letter Tree thought he should reply. He was not going to sit down while Shaw accused him of underhand methods of behaviour. It was not true. He, Tree, had been knighted for a *much* worse reason; the mere threat of a production of *Blanco Posnet* had caused the honour to be conferred upon him at once.

Tree decided not to send the letter. He was sure, he remarked, that people would know him sufficiently well not to be influenced by Shaw's suggestion.

If Tree had taken Shaw's publicity seeking seriously then one joker had trumped another. Finally, Herbert mildly remarked that Shaw wrote far too much to *The Times* and not enough *for* them.

Herbert could sometimes be touchy about himself, he knew that although humour was a delicate sense of proportion, a man's sense of humour generally stopped short at himself, and he admitted that it was difficult to kill the nerve of an aching tooth with ridicule. Shaw was to prove a constant toothache to Tree during the production of *Pygmalion*.

These two clever men treated one another like fools. These two artists felt the other was a philistine. These two supreme egoists reproached each other with egotism. Tree wrote that Shaw was bounded on the North, East, West and South by Shaw, it was a limiting factor. Shaw described Tree as never happier than when he stepped in front of the curtain and spoke in his own immensity to the audience, a monarch addressing his courtiers. What did Tree care for Hamlet—or Higgins? His real objective was to promote his amazing self.

Tree and Shaw were old sparring partners. Shaw had given Good Dog Tree a pat on the head for producing Ibsen's *An Enemy of the People*. But Tree had an ambivalent attitude towards Ibsen. He felt Shaw was over-enthusiastic. On the other hand Tree met a former censor in the street who remarked, to Herbert's sarcastic amusement, 'Ibsen is a dirty old blackguard.'

Shaw had amused himself at the expense of many of Herbert's productions—from *Fedora*, and *The Dancing Girl* to Dumas' *Mademoiselle de Belle Isle*. Tree's greatest success, Svengali, he had dismissed without a word of praise or criticism, but said his Falstaff should have been given to Mr. Lionel Brough. Shaw had given Tree a very modest credit for his Antony in *Julius Caesar*, but added that he had neither made the most of it, nor handled it with any pretence of mastery or certainty. But Shaw forgave Tree for many things—he was after all, the only manager in London to contribute to a drinking cup to mark Ibsen's seventieth birthday. On the whole Shaw's critical attitude towards Tree in public was that of cheerful contempt, lightened with occasional dabs of appreciation.

When writing privately to other actors, Shaw was more incisive. In 1903 he wrote to Forbes-Robertson: 'I incautiously witnessed Tree's *Richard II* the night before last; and the spectacle of our friend sitting on the ground telling sad stories of the death of kings, not to mention his subsequent appearance in Westminster Hall in the character of Doré's Christ leaving the Praetorium, has almost been too much for me.'

Most actors in London had turned Shaw's plays down. They had been refused as absurd and undramatic by Irving, Wyndham, Terriss, Alexander, Fanny Coleman and Ellen Terry herself. Tree was in good company. But having doffed his motley Paragot cap to Shaw in 1907 he was supposedly frightened off with *Blanco Posnet* in 1909.

And then came *Pygmalion*. It had been whispered about, recommended, turned down, and praised by Mrs. Patrick Campbell for whom Shaw had written it in 1912. The two years' delay in the London production was not only due to the inevitable theatrical uncertainties about the leading man, but to Mrs. Patrick Campbell's taxi crash outside the Albert Hall. The press had happily remarked that her injuries were not serious and she would soon be back at St. James's Theatre acting in *Bella Donna* with George Alexander. It was not true. She had by a mere hair's breadth missed being killed and had been severely cut, bruised and concussed. Frightened that she might lose her looks and incapable of any action, her doctor Sir Alfred Fripp advised six months in bed. It was at this moment that Shaw suddenly showed himself, like his character Blanco Posnet, capable of touching human kindness and sympathy. He called on her, cajoled her, bullied her, flattered her and led her back into life and, with a reading of *Pygmalion*, back into the theatre.

By the beginning of 1914 the play had already been produced in Vienna with Lilli Marberg and with Frau Tilla Durieux in Berlin. Mrs. Pat, who was to be the very first Eliza, was in fact the third actress to create the part.

Mrs. Pat had completely turned down the idea of Tree playing

Higgins, but by the end of 1913 she was in dire financial straits. She had not acted for months and she was deeply in debt. Shaw had helped her with her doctor's bills, but she needed some money and she needed work. Her creditors were pressing, her bank manager was no longer accommodating. It was then, much to Shaw's surprise, that she suggested Tree for Higgins. Any port in a storm—even His Majesty's Theatre. By December of 1913 she was becoming anxious and wrote to Shaw: 'You haven't told me of your interview with Tree. I was grateful to you for *minding* the "Stella Campbell"—how it betrays him—ugh!' Mrs. Pat was unconventional, but remained aware of her dignity; Tree, with his aristocratic background and sureness of his place in the world, had no dignity and needed none.

At the beginning Mrs. Pat, needing the money, was all feline, managing charm. She wrote to Shaw:

Oh goodness we're in for it—and let's be *very* clever—he's fixed and you can manage the lot of us—and then indeed you'll be a *great man*! He wants to be friendly and his admiration for you—and the play is ENORMOUS. I'll be as tame as a mouse.

Very few tiger cats can behave like mice, and Mrs. Pat's accident had not improved either her tractability or her temper. In the springtime of the productuion Mrs. Pat felt she would be able to manage Shaw, to her own advantage, against Tree. At the beginning of 1914 she wrote to Shaw that she would have to haggle with Tree, and she was sure he thought she was trying it on, and that turned her stomach. She was determined to be civil to Henry Dana, Tree's right-hand man, as that would be much more comfortable all round. She enclosed a note she proposed to send to Sir Herbert:

Dear Sir Herbert, You seemed very upset at my terms—£130 a week, full salary matinées, and $2\frac{1}{2}$% with eight weeks guarantee. The best I could do is to make it 2% after the first £700.

She sent her warm regards. Tree was used to actresses who seemed sweet and charming muffled in their veils and furs, but who speedily changed to jungle beasts when it came to contracts. His views on women were pleasantly cynical, but not detached like Shaw's. He believed that women often showed a sincerity of the moment; but he understood that they, like men, were attracted to money in different degrees. There were women, he decided, to whom the crackle of a bank-note will convey an almost sexual thrill. It is possible that he did not realise the full extent of Mrs. Pat's indebtedness. If it was not fashionable to parade one's sexual aberrations, it was also not *à la mode* to admit to poverty. Poverty was for the lower orders. Mrs. Pat was a great actress, and it was possibly only to Shaw that she was able to confess the extent of her penury.

So, very slowly, the preliminary skirmishes like shadow boxing took place. The real battles would only commence with the rehearsals of the play in February of 1914.

Shaw, perhaps misguidedly, had decided to direct the play. Unaccustomed to the strange disordered ways of His Majesty's Theatre, he plunged straight into choppy waters.

It could be said that two of the protagonists were ready for fights on all fronts long before the rehearsals began. Mrs. Pat, broke and touchy, was ready to overplay the great actress. Shaw had already formed his ideas about Herbert's acting capacities for which he had registered only lukewarm enthusiasm. Shaw hated amateurs in any field. He had always prided himself on his professionalism and was ready with an Irishman's fighting capacity to do battle with the arch 'amateur' Tree.

Tree, on the other hand, sailed into the fray also unaware of what lay before him, secure in the knowledge of being in his own theatre and knowing how to run it. Or at least knowing how he ran it himself.

Pygmalion was the very first of Shaw's big commercial successes in a commercial theatre. But he despised the commercial theatre. Most of the leading actors and actresses had refused to see that he had written splendid parts for them. According to Shaw they were like the old Italian opera singers confronted with Wagner, they had no idea of the chances he was offering them.

Shaw was an intellectual and proud of it. Tree, on the other hand, adopted the stance that intellect was a pose of the middle class. He realised he was above the general run of men. He once remarked that he could not help being exceptional. He was full of ideas but took these for granted and he could see the funny side of being out of the ordinary. He was amused when the commissionaire at his own theatre said to him: 'You may think I am out to flatter you, but a gentleman coming out of the pit said there was not more than a dozen actors in your line of business that could play the part better!'

Shaw, unlike Tree, was out to trumpet the fact that he was a genius, in case no one had noticed. This amused Tree. He had heard that when Shaw met Anatole France in Italy, Shaw went up to the Frenchman—presented his card and said: 'We are two of a craft—I am a genius.'

France replied that he was also a genius, but when one was a prostitute one called oneself a merchant of pleasure.

Tree considered himself a merchant of pleasure; the main point of the theatre was not to instruct but to amuse. Boredom was to be avoided at all costs—even the boredom of pernicketty playwrights. He reflected that Shaw was suffering from the debilitating effects of culture, and the enervating results of athletic pursuits like bicycling and swimming.

The battle commenced. Shaw walked into the theatre ready to direct and mould Tree and Mrs. Pat, to the strict formula of his playwright's imagination. Shaw knew what was the matter with Tree's productions. Tree treated all authors as nothing but a literary scaffolding on which to exhibit his own creations. Shakespeare or Shaw, authors were merely 'lame dogs to be helped over stiles' by the ingenuity and invention of Mr. Tree, the actor-producer. Tree, it must be admitted, never worked happily with authors. He had quarrelled with Henry Arthur Jones, he had upset Brieux by falsifying his message and Pinero had always refused to work with him. W. J. Locke had admittedly worked well with him, but then he was prepared to bend his characters to Tree's inventions.

So the comedy of rehearsal errors began. Shaw turned up primed and ready to run an efficient ship. Tree wandered in, seemed happy to see Shaw, as if he had invited him round from the Club. Pursued by a troop of hangers-on, Tree would wander off in the middle of a scene on some pressing business up in the Dome and then become extremely hurt that Shaw had carried on with his understudy. No one ever used Tree's understudy when he was in the theatre, even if up in the Dome, they waited until he chose to return. He insisted on Shaw going back to the place where the scene had been broken off.

Mrs. Pat was as unprofessional as Tree. She did not like playing downstage, which did not please Shaw, who liked his words to be heard. On one occasion, when rebuked that he as a producer had all his characters looking towards the audience, he said: 'But the people on the stage *know* the words, the audience don't.'

Tree always entered completely into his part. He was accustomed to become the person. This facility was lovingly remembered by his daughter Viola. She, and all his fellow actors in the theatre, appreciated what a wonderful thing it was to 'meet' him on the stage. He was always so unpredictable, always so adventurous, so unexpected. Whatever it was he always struck the right note to inspire. It might be that the mere artisans of the theatre never transform themselves into their parts; they may be able to reproduce the same expressions and gestures night after night, but this was not her father's way. He would change himself into the person he was playing. What the loving Viola did not mention was that this hit or miss acting was hard on his fellow actors. Sometimes he was brilliant and sometimes he merely walked through his part.

That type of behaviour was never going to do for Shaw, the committee man, who wanted everything perfectly oiled and running like clockwork.

Viola's rememberance of her father's Richard II, which Shaw so much despised, was full of emotion. It was the very best time she had ever spent in any play with him—he entered dressed in black, tired and distrait. He looked up—and caught sight of her—astonished to see her standing there. They were in reality saying goodbye—it was the ultimate moment of sadness for them both.

Caught in his mood, Viola fell on his neck sobbing. The stage, the audience and the play had disappeared for her and for him. Choked with emotion, he could not begin his speech, her tears troubled him—he could not see her eyes for the blinding tears which clouded them.

That sort of thing was never going to do for Shaw. *Being* the person, becoming the person, that was not what was required. What he wanted was an actor to mould, who was going to say his words clearly and with the right emphasis in the right places.

Stella wanted plenty of limelight on her face. Shaw brutally told her it made her look a dinner plate with two prunes on it, and then added a little Irish ointment—it was a beautifully modelled head, why not make the best of it?

Shaw himself described the chaos of the rehearsals. 'Tree was always attended in the theatre by a retinue of persons with no defined business there, who were yet on the salary list.'

There *was* one capable man who seemed to be able to get things done, and Shaw decided to treat him as the stage manager. He was happy to notice that his name was on the bill as actually *being* the stage manager. At His Majesty's Theatre one never knew. He remarked that Tree did not seem to know what an actor was, and remained unaware of theatre etiquette. One minute he would outrage someone's sensibilities and the next he would be kindly and friendly, utterly oblivious that he had usurped someone's functions. The theatre is a place of hierarchy, where underlings know their place and upperlings are determined to see they keep it. But Tree was amiable and modest, admitted Shaw. It was charming that he did not know his own place, 'which was the highest in the theatre, but it was exasperating in him not to know anyone else's'.

In spite of his Socialist principles, Shaw was very conscious of hierarchy, something of which Tree was totally unaware. Tree recognised this lack of a sense of social superiority in himself. He wrote cheerfully in one of his stories: 'his manner was the same to a Duchess as to a dairymaid—an idiosyncrasy which got him into trouble with both sections of the community'. At first angered by this quality in Tree, in the end Shaw gave up all expectation of being treated as otherwise than a friend who had happened to drop into the theatre. 'So finding myself as free to interfere in the proceedings as anyone else who dropped in would apparently have been, I interfered not only in my proper department, but in every other as well—and nobody gainsaid me.'

Tree floated in and out as he always did, but on one occasion even he was stung into reproof. 'I seem to have heard, or read somewhere that plays have actually been produced, and performances given in this theatre, under its present management before you came. According to you, that couldn't have happened.' Tree looked at Shaw. 'How do you account for it?'

'I can't account for it,' said Shaw, 'I suppose you put a notice in the papers that a performance will take place at half past eight, and take the money at the doors. Then you *have* to do the play somehow. There is no other way of accounting for it.'

Twice Shaw, like Henry Arthur Jones before him, walked out of the theatre. But unlike Henry Arthur Jones, he did not return with his solicitor, he came back at the urgent pleadings of Mrs. Pat to get them out of the ensuing mess. When he did get back to the theatre, Tree received him with the utmost cordiality and a general feeling that it was good of Shaw to spare the time to see how things were getting on. For Bernard Shaw it was like trying to give a knock out punch to an eiderdown.

Mrs. Pat was not behaving very well either. She was either prima donna-ish or else she listlessly walked through her part. In addition she was plotting to marry Mr. George Cornwallis-West and engaged with her own sentimental plans. But she was also writing letters to put her 'Joey' (Shaw) off the scent.

'Now I go upstairs to study to be a human Eliza for two hours. You are *wonderful* at rehearsal, and we'll all shed our blood for you.' she wrote untruthfully. 'George only stayed a moment . . .' she added, equally untruthfully. A few days later she wrote, 'It will be AWFUL if in the end I find even *Boucicault* easier to work with than you Joey!'

In another undated letter from 33 Kensington Square Mrs. Pat refers to her dresses, always a point of dispute with actresses. 'I drew them whilst my thoughts were distracted by the memory of your misery of our work today.' And added sharply: 'I thought them the sort of dresses *men* would have chosen.' Stella Campbell's letters also give a running commentary on the progress of the rehearsals. One minute she is assuring Shaw that he will pull them through, that she will help all she can. He must forgive her and she *will* have the chair—if it has a back to it.

The furniture, like the costumes, was a point of dispute. Mrs. Pat was constantly moving it back so that she could upstage the other actors and Shaw would have it moved forward. Finally he had it screwed down, 'except the grand piano', said Shaw, 'she can move that—if she likes!'

Having been tiresome at rehearsal Stella would then write a repentant letter from Kensington Square. Could Joey come round and see her? She was willing to go through her part, it would help her so *enormously*. She would have no pleasure unless she had been faithful to the part. She would try and take things lying down. As for Tree it was splendid of him to 'accept with gentle indifference letters that would have made a Frenchman "call you out"—why did he? because none of us can spare the time to take that side of you that *hurts*—seriously.' Joey was not sparing his actors.

It must be thought that, like Stella, Tree felt that all the words and dashes in Shaw's letters were 'wind and the buzzing of bees'.

When Tree and Shaw lunched together at the R.A.C. Shaw said to Tree: 'Have you noticed during the rehearsals that though you and I are no longer young, and have achieved all the success possible in our respective professions, we have been treating one another throughout as beginners?'

Tree reflected on the statement, it was quite true, they were beginners to one another. Herbert was not used to running in double harness, while Shaw—according to himself—was used to multiple harness, in politics and the theatre. He had been trained to foresee everything and consider everybody. It is to be suspected that though Shaw may have considered himself to be a good committee man, whether the rest of his committee would have agreed with this statement is a different matter.

Shaw remarked shrewdly that Tree never considered persons, or facts, he found uninteresting. It was impossible to lodge an uninteresting fact in his mind. Engage Tree's feelings and he was human, shrewd and tenacious. Shaw considered this tendency to blot out boredom a disability of Tree's when it came to acting. He never remembered passages in the play which had no bearing on his own part. But this had one shining advantage.

He never fell into that commonest fault of the actor, the betrayal to the audience that he knows what his interlocutor is going to say, and is waiting wearily for his cue instead of conversing with him. Tree always seemed to have heard the lines of the other performers for the first time, and even to be a little taken aback by them.

In the scene at the end of *Pygmalion* when Eliza throws Higgins's slippers in his face, Shaw had taken care to have a pair of very soft velvet slippers. He knew Stella Campbell, she was a Dead-eye Dick when it came to throwing things. Tree got the slippers right bang in his face. 'The effect was appalling,' said Shaw, 'He had totally forgotten there was any such incident in the play—it seemed to him that Mrs. Campbell, suddenly giving way to an impulse of diabolical wrath and hatred, had committed an unprovoked and brutal assault on him. The physical impact was nothing, but the wound to his feelings was terrible.'

Shaw described how Tree collapsed into the nearest chair and everyone had to rally round soothing him down, explaining that it was part of the play and even showing him the prompt book to prove it.

But if Tree's daughter is to be believed, it was probable that Tree had so imagined himself into the part of Higgins that he had become Higgins, and the wrath he felt was Higgins's wrath—this girl he had dragged out of the gutter, created, and made to speak and move beautifully, had assaulted him. It was diabolical! But Shaw chose to believe that it was Tree himself who was insulted. They were two men who found it difficult to understand one another; they lived on different planets.

Bernard Shaw was, in many ways, contemptuous of the actors he needed to launch his comedies into orbit, and Tree was only one of many actors who were unbusinesslike and muddled. People, said Shaw, might ask him how could a man like Tree run a huge theatre like His Majesty's for so long without being capable and wide-awake and yet forget everything that did not amuse or interest him? The reason Shaw gave was simple. 'Theatrical business is not like other business. A man may enter on the management of a theatre without business habits or knowledge and at the end of 40 years know less about business then when he began.'

People would be quite wrong to think it could not be done. But Shaw was also wrong, Tree was not interested in money, but that applies to many imaginative business tycoons who leave the account books to underlings. But when it came to his theatre, Tree was not unbusinesslike; both Viola and Constance Collier remarked that he would walk by, seemingly unaware of what was going on, and then send for people to remedy things he did not like.

Even Shaw had to admit that, unless Tree had been as amiable and kind as he indeed was, the irresponsibility and power of his position would have made a fiend of him.

Shaw and Tree finally agreed to disagree. Shaw should have been an actor, said Tree; and Tree, said Shaw, should have been an author. Instead of messing about with other people's plays, Tree should have written his own. Shaw admitted that Tree showed a very marked literary talent. 'Even as an amateur, his writing achieved a finish of style and sureness of execution that was not always evident in his acting, especially, when, as in the case of *Pygmalion*, he had to impersonate a sort of man he had never met.'

Originally Tree had wanted to play Doolittle, the dustman. He was probably right theatrically, for it is a marvellous acting part, and always achieves that most satisfying of tributes to the actor— exit rounds. But Shaw was a stickler for etiquette. It was impossible for Sir Herbert to play a minor role in his own theatre. He must play the lead, that was Tree's right and natural role.

Maud agreed with Shaw. How well she remembered the reading of *Pygmalion* in the Dome and her passionate eagerness that Herbert should accept it. He was undecided at the first reading whether to play Higgins or the dustman. But Maud insisted that while it was true that no one could possibly play the dustman as Herbert would have done, the part, although undeniably showy, was obvious. He must play the dominating Professor Higgins, that was the unexpected part for him. When it came to the plaudits of the audience on the first night Maud knew how right she had been.

When a play or an actor succeeds, most bystanders take the credit for having discovered the shining jewel. When it proves to be dross, everyone admits to having foreseen the failure. Shaw said: 'When Tree resigned himself to his natural task he set to work to make this disagreeable and incredible person (Higgins) more sympathetic in the character of a lover, for which I had left so little room that he was quite baffled until he hit on the happy thought of throwing flowers to Eliza in the very brief interval between the end of the play and the fall of the curtain.'

Shaw remarked that had Tree not been so ingenious so entirely well-intentioned, 'he would have driven me crazy. As it was—he made me feel like his grandfather. I should add that he never bore me the slightest malice for my air of making the best of a bad job.'

Shaw refused to come to the first night, remarking that he would come to the hundredth night, adding sharply that this was the equivalent of not coming at all.

The rehearsals were interrupted by Mrs. Pat taking a week-end off to get married, and then re-appearing radiant and lovely with a husband young enough to be her son whom she had filched from Winston Churchill's mother. In one way it was a triumphant proof of Mrs. Pat's continuing attractions. But in another, it was not a sensible move, George, though attractive, had no money and money was the one thing which they both needed.

The rehearsals resumed, and the battle re-commenced. Shaw was bombarding Mrs. Pat with last minute instructions. Although he had no intention of being at the first night, he was not letting his grip on the play or players slacken. Stella wrote back, 'You haven't hurt me at all. You have only bored me with your cease-less teasing and braggarting. I wanted *you* to produce the play, and Tree not to be sufficiently insulted by you as to throw it up—in this I have succeeded—though there are a few more days!!! For myself the last three months and more particularly the last few days have been full of anxiety.'

And then in an unaccustomed mood of resignation she wrote: 'I expect I can act as easily in one place as another, the time for choosing the more comfortable is over. I have told you before, many actresses would play the part better than I.'

Perhaps she felt this because Shaw had said that she could act the part—though she was too old for it. Then she had a flash of self-respect:

What I bring to it that is my own, you couldn't give nor take away. The accent will always trouble me a little I expect. I hope you will make heaps of money Joey and keep your gay belief that you and your play alone did it and that without you there would have been but failure and fools. Any more directions you have for me give me through Bell. [Stanley Bell, Tree's stage manager.]

Shaw had tired his actors out. There is a point when they can give no more and performance notes, exhortations, and blame, do more harm than good. The point of no return had been reached, for good or ill.

But Shaw continued to worry and growl like a terrier at a rabbit hole. Even on the day of the first performance he wrote to Stella a long letter headed FINAL ORDERS. It was full of ideas about pronunciation, how to speak certain lines, how to smile: 'Make that smile an inch wider and you may as well stand on the points of your toes and raise your arms gracefully above your head.'

He was not proposing to come to the first night but, on the other hand, he was still pursuing his quarry. 'The danger tonight will be the collapse of the play after the third act. I am sending a letter to Tree which will pull him together, if it does not kill him. But a good deal will depend on whether you are inspired at the last moment. You are not, like me, a great general. You leave everything to chance, whereas Napoleon and Caesar left nothing to chance except that last inch—that is in the hands of destiny.'

Tree's own final comment was that when a man comes to the last straw he usually puts it in his hair—if he has any left.

Shaw tried to 'damage' his performers into his mould until the very last second. 'Tree, must you be so treacly?' And to Stella: 'Good God, you are forty years too old for Eliza—sit still, and it is not so noticeable.'

Mrs. Pat remarked that to sit still with your hands folded in your lap for three-quarters of an hour, a glare of indignation in your eyeballs, while somebody else stands with his back to the fire and another sits in an armchair, 'is Joey's idea of perfect stage management'. For according to Stella, Shaw's passion for debate often cut across the rhythmical movements of his drama and harmed the natural sequence of emotion. It made his actors feel that their own imagination was but an interruption.

There was another sticking point.

The Lord Chamberlain, that bugbear of Edwardian playwrights, had passed the word 'bloody' which came out with such effect in the tea party scene. Yet for once Herbert had cold feet. Suppose the audience should feel insulted?

But as Stella Campbell wrote: 'Surely no first night has ever gone with more success, and with such joyousness. The "bloody" almost ruined the play; people laughed too much.'

The audience may have laughed too much, but members of the Theatrical Managers' Association were not amused and they were snapping at Tree's heels. Some two or three weeks after the first night of *Pygmalion* H. Blackmore, Secretary of the Association, wrote:

Dear Sir Herbert,
    If you have had time to notice the agenda for today's Council Meeting you will have seen that the 4th item deals with the low language used on the stage. A letter of protest from a member on the subject of the language used in your play was read to the meeting.
    I was instructed to write and acquaint you of this fact and to

point out that the Association, with a view to retaining the respect of the public for the theatre, would be much obliged if you could see your way to have the objectionable words deleted.

But Herbert still had the laughter of the audience ringing in his ears, which had quite effaced his original doubts. He instructed Henry Dana to reply to H. Blackmore:

Dear Sir,
    Sir Herbert Tree has asked me to acknowledge your letter to him of the 8th instant. He declines to accede to the suggestion contained therein, and he considers the tone of your letter to be wholly unjustifiable.

On May 15th the indefatigable secretary was still writing totally without humour,

Thank you for your letter of the 13th instant conveying Sir Herbert's instructions as to his reply to my letter to him on the subject of the words: 'Not bloody likely!'

He was sorry to say that there was no Council meeting for some weeks and would be glad to hear why Sir Herbert objected to his letter. Although he was conveying the wishes of the Council, the words were his own and he would be glad to convey the view of Sir Herbert to the next Council meeting; he was certain that the Council had not wished in any way to hurt the feelings of a gentleman who had been their President for so many years.

The objections subsided. The audience continued to laugh and much to Shaw's surprise, the play ran. Stella wrote to Shaw: 'Come soon—or you'll not recognise your play.'

This was perfectly true because when Shaw duly saw it, as he had promised, on the hundredth night, he was hardly elated at the extra curlicues of by-play added by Herbert and Stella to 'improve' on the original. But then authors are traditionally devoted to words, and actors inclined to feel that tripping over a log, or eating a bun, can get a better audience reaction than the most subtle of witty repartee.

But Stella added soothingly, and practically, 'I hope you make £40 ordinary nights and £80 Wed. and Sat.—then perhaps you can accept the mushy show with some sort of tolerance.' Not that Mrs. Pat was tolerant of Tree's performance—he was taking five minutes between each word and each bite of the apple in Act 4, 'I have facial paralysis from trying to express some sort of intelligent feeling, so now I hide my face until it is well again.'

On 17th June she wrote ecstatically, 'Queen Alexandra and the Empress of Russia enjoyed your play mightily—and clapped and nodded with joy.'

But by the end of the month the climate had changed. If all was not well in the company, while the play was running, from April till June, Mrs. Pat was equally not pleased when Tree—in his usual way—got bored with Higgins and was preparing to take a holiday. Stella wrote to Shaw on 28th June 1914: 'Will you see Tree or Alexander please at once?—and me? It is quite absurd that the notice should go up at the end of a £2,000 week.' Tree, much to Stella's fury, was preparing for his usual visit to Marienbad. A mere £2,000 week was not going to alter his plans.

On 28th June when Stella was writing passionately about the fate of *Pygmalion*, Francis Ferdinand was murdered at Sarajevo. Greater events than a comedy took the stage.

Chapter 16

1914:
The Return from Marienbad

The summer of 1914 found the whole Tree family abroad. Maud had taken one of her usual furnished houses, this time in France, La Maison du Canal at Pont de l'Arche on the Seine. Here the family were walking, laughing, fishing for trout, and lazing the long summery days away. Herbert was to join them on his way back from Marienbad.

His faithful chauffeur, Sam Wordingham, was driving him there in a new car and all was set for the usual restful time after the strenuous summer of Shaw and *Pygmalion*.

Wordingham described the trip in a letter: 'About the trip to Marienbad, or as far as we got.' Wordingham paints a very vivid picture of the confusion of those few days before the war broke out. It seems as if the chauffeur went to fetch a new car from France, and they motored to St. Quentin. Something went wrong with the car, and Sam worked all night on it. He got up early, swearing at the waiter, and with every 'damn' the waiter brought him another pacifying croissant. 'Sir Herbert came in', Sam reported, 'and said that I had better leave off, or we should have all the bread there was.'

The French, according to Sam, were very over-excited at the prospect of war, they were, they exclaimed much better prepared than in 1870. Sir Herbert remained unmoved and simply wired to Joseph Langton, his lawyer in London, to know if it was all right for him to carry on with his holiday. He was not to be put off by mere rumours. They were supposed to receive a reply from Langton at Longwy on the French/German border. All they saw were people drawing money out of the banks, peasant women taking things to market and gossiping outside the cafés. On the frontier they noticed that although the French had an armed guard twenty strong, the Germans had only one man. That seemed to promise well. They called at the Post Office—there was no telegram from Langton telling them to return and they decided to drive on to Luxembourg. In the hotel and the garage, all the talk was of war. 'But Sir Herbert said we were too civilised for war—it would never come. A political game he called it.'

But the Germans in the hotel took another view. They were more than ready, and would be in Paris in nine days. The English, they said contemptuously, would never join in. They had the suffragettes, and the Irish question, to keep *them* quiet.

Sir Herbert was not going to be put off from his three weeks restful recuperation in Marienbad. All this was mere gossip. The French were hysterical, and so were the Germans. They continued on their way, the car was running well and they had a good day's motoring to Frankfurt. Admittedly, there were lancers riding along the roads and guards on the bridges, but that meant nothing. They stopped for lunch. The waiter at the hotel had known Sir Herbert, for he had worked at the Carlton, next door to His Majesty's. But they were a long way from the Haymarket and the waiter, no longer subservient, was disposed to dispute with Sir Herbert. The waiter *knew* the Germans would go to war and they would win a splendid victory in two months.

The following day they reached Frankfurt. The idea, said Sam, was to start late. He had the car all greased, and fitted up. From the accounts of him, his exploits, and his own description of the trip, he comes over much as the cheerful Cockney chauffeur in *Man and Superman*. He knew all about engines and was no longer disposed to touch his forelock. He was the new man.

Tree's diaries are littered with stories and thoughts about motoring presumably with Wordingham. In 1904 they left London for Dover. Suddenly the brakes gave way. They seemed to be hurtling to immediate death between a steep drop on one side and some rocks on the other. There were two carts in the road— the car bumped into one and ricocheted against the other. Tree's car seemed to be in the last throes of the death rattle. The Cockney chauffeur remained perky. Tree fixed him with a steely eye and remarked that the car was done for. 'We were nearly killed.' The chauffeur still remained perky, he even winked. It was a good advertisement for the car, sturdy it was.

Tree had a reply ready that it was better to be five minutes too late and alive, than five minutes early—dead. Those who try to cover the ground too fast find the road covering them. But the chauffeur remained chirpy—the car had proved itself. A jolly good machine.

But in 1914, things were different. The time for motoring jokes was over. Sam was disturbed. Boys were delivering newspapers every half hour—*free*. With his Cockney common sense Sam felt there was something wrong about that. When he got to the garage the proprietor told him that the British Fleet had sailed for an unknown destination. 'The Germans must have had a presentiment—for that seemed to sober them up a bit', said Sam. He went round to try to warn Sir Herbert, but at ten o'clock he was still asleep. At eleven he still slept soundly, but finally Sam bearded him in his room.

'I told Sir Herbert the people were very excited—in fact worse than yesterday—and that the Russians had all gone home three days before. Lots of English had left the hotel.'

Sir Herbert was disposed to remain calm, but he supposed he must get up. Sam said that he thought they should go back. Tree, unruffled, replied that he wondered why. Finally, in response to Sam's urgent pleas, he had the idea of going round to see the British Consul and took a cab there. When Tree came back he announced, at last, much to Sam's relief, that they were going home. Shots had been exchanged with France.

At this point the truth seemed to have suddenly come home to Herbert. The unimaginable had happened. The whole world was crumbling about him. He looked at Sam, and then pointing to his breast said, 'I can't tell you—something seemed to break inside me when I heard it was war—wicked! wicked! wicked!'

Sam tried to coax him to eat, but he only shook his head and could not finish his coffee. They put the luggage on the car and started, as the British Consul had advised, to make for Holland or Belgium. For an hour the car ran well, but then according to Sam 'the car fell away'. They stopped for beer and a piece of bread and cheese to allow the engine to cool. 'We put in a gallon of lubricating oil and decided that we mut go slower or the car would let us down.' Sam said: 'I wished we had a good English car now, but we dared not go faster as the loss of oil varied.' They were running along the Rhine, but after the first three bridges they were pulled up by soldiers with fixed bayonets. Sir Herbert got out and started to walk over the bridge. The officer signalled to Sam and climbed on to the footboard, and two of his soldiers got into the back—with fixed bayonets. Sam expostulated in his British way that he was damned if he was going to drive that lot. But Sir Herbert beckoned him to go over the bridge and the officer on the footboard said: 'Don't swear!' Sam, always practical, asked if they were already at war and 'the officer said no, and he hoped we never should be, but the orders were that all cars were to be escorted over the bridges—so that they could not blow them up.'

They were now being stopped every ten miles for their passports. Sam kept them handy, for the soldiers sprang up with their guns at the ready. Later, on reflection, Sam said he *thought* they must have been loaded. It was a reasonable supposition.

On arriving at Cologne, Sam nearly ran over a child, and the crowd, waiting in the streets for the troops to go by, turned on the car, stoning it, but Sam drove on. While he and Sir Herbert were having tea the crowd attacked the car again, but only made a few dents in the panel, the careful Sam noted. The car was their means of escape and so long as the engine was intact, they were safe. It was impossible to go more than two miles an hour through the town as the streets were surging with people watching the troops go by. They put up at an hotel near the railway station. It was, according to Sam, the hotel Hoff or Koff—he had forgotten the name, but he remembered it was only a hundred yards from the station, which was just as well as it turned out. Sam's petrol was running low and, although the mounted police did not worry him, he was still able to push his way only slowly through the crowd; they booed and sang songs, but on the whole did not seem in an ugly mood. Sir Herbert, out in the town looking for an English newspaper, was strongly advised to go back to the hotel.

In the morning Sam was up early to get his car in trim, but the garage proprietor refused to understand English. Sam, not to be put out, fetched the hotel proprietor to translate. There was no petrol, the Government had banned the sale of it from ten o'clock the night before. The car was useless. He reported to Sir Herbert, and it was decided that a train was the only thing.

The car was abandoned to the care of the hotel proprietor. Herbert later said ruefully that the Kaiser owed him a new car. Their tickets were bought and their luggage stowed in the hotel omnibus. They boarded the train and then realised that their luggage had not been loaded. They dashed out of the station as the omnibus was starting back—complete with luggage. If the proprietor had appropriated the car, the staff were making an attempt to make off with the luggage.

But Sam and Sir Herbert weighed down with dressing-cases, coats and rugs managed, with the help of a soothing golden sovereign, to get themselves and their luggage all on to the train at last.

On the train itself there was international confusion. People making their way in different directions for different reasons. All were guessing which side was going to win and like spectators at a horse race were putting their money on the supposedly winning side.

Tree fell in with some French acquaintances, a man and his wife. 'I believe,' said Sam, 'She was some great artist in the theatre, as she said "Herbert Tree!"' as they boarded the train. She and her husband were making their way to Paris, much upset at the turn of events.

The world which they, and Tree, had known was splitting asunder. The French couple were making for Paris, and yet also on the same train Herbert met an Englishwoman whose daughters were married to German officers; she was returning to England to draw out her money, a good round sum according to Sam, and intended returning to Germany. She had lived there long enough to be totally convinced that the Germans were invincible.

The train was full to overflowing. People and luggage packed the corridors, there were Americans making for home, and French students singing cheerful songs, convinced that this time they were going to force the Germans back over their own frontiers.

At Brussels Sam nearly lost the dressing-cases again, and when they finally arrived at Ostend—the boat had sailed. They had to wait till eleven o'clock on the Saturday night for another and finally arrived to see the day breaking over the cliffs of Dover. They were home.

Sam's account of the return from Marienbad ended: 'Sir H. said that the time would come when the man who made the war would be the first in the firing line; London would be in flames and all the best and strongest gone. He meant that by killing all the robust and healthy, the nations of Europe would degenerate.

We saw an old man mowing corn, and he painted a picture from that as we rushed in the train across Belgium "One man to have the means to send so many as food for powder".'

Tree's world was slipping away, as he knew. The world of the international hotels, the swift trains from one capital to another, the obsequious porters ushering the international élite from Baden to Berlin, from Paris to Pau—it was all fading like morning mist into the pleasant past.

*

Constance Collier, unlike Herbert, did not realise what was happening. She was acting in Maeterlinck's anti-war play *Monna Vanna*.

'None of us had grasped the significance of the leading articles in the papers, or the whispers of war. It all seemed grossly exaggerated, and so the night of the declaration came as a complete surprise to most people. We did not realize what it meant. After the performance I went with several members of the company to the gates of Buckingham Palace in the hope that the King and Queen would come out on the balcony. It was the gayest scene, crowds round the Palace and boys riding about, cheering and shouting on the tops of taxi-cabs and everybody in the streets singing and buying little flags and sticking them all over themselves.'

She kept the little Union Jack which she had bought for a penny on that night outside the Palace. She walked back up the Mall and down the Haymarket arm in arm with three friends, cheering and singing.

'In the darkness, leaning against the railings, we came upon Herbert Tree. His face was ashen. He seemed stricken. His whole manner was a shock to me. It was my first realisation of the seriousness of it all. I never forgot the expression in his eyes. They were filled with the horror of the tragedy that was upon the world. He stopped me and said: "You won't be singing those songs long, my dear." Then he passed on without another word. He looked a broken man.'

The truth about the war dawned slowly on Constance. She saw the street lights dimming and the theatres closing and suddenly no one seemed to have any money. People came to the box office— perhaps business was going to look up?—but they merely changed a five pound note and were pleased to go away with silver and gold in their pockets. They were anxious to get rid of their paper money, they were not interested in seeing the play.

Unknown to Constance, and perhaps to Maud, there had always been another hidden side to Tree, a compound perhaps of his distant Russian and close German blood. His notebooks and diaries are a jumble of luncheon dates, jokes, quips and lines for plays, but interspersed amongst them are darker thoughts. He saw the beginning and the end of life as things of terror, the earth as a stricken star; for in life death was ever present.

Fragments of unpublished stories give sudden insights into the dark side of his nature. How was it possible to understand God? It was easy to feel exaltation when looking at the stars, or reading a great philosopher, or standing before a picture by a great painter. But who has not felt the loneliness and the despair of the meannesses surrounding man? Who has not sobbed on the breast of a loved one, lonely even when loved? Who has not been angry at injustice, or stood under the pillars of the pines, whose spreading branches sigh with the Soul of the World?

Like many people with Germanic blood he felt as he wrote, that his home was amongst the pine trees. It is hard to understand this strange pull towards pines which are gloomy, depressing trees lacking in life, for little grows under them. They oppress the landscape and, unlike other trees, never put on much spring green like a promise of renewal. But pine trees appealed to the hidden depths in Herbert's nature.

Another fragment of writing is from 'Death and the Maiden'. The scene, the borders of a pine forest in which sits the figure of Death at midnight. When Death speaks he takes on the form of the spirit of Cain cast forth to wander doomed through all time to expiate his sin. He passes through hovels, mansions, temples, soaring churches, through all the busy city no one can resist him— the cottager, the king, the bishop, the humble docker, the seaman, the factory hand, the clerk in the warehouse, or the bank. Each man looks on him and to him all men are the same. Kings are lumps of earth and lumps of earth kings. We are all totally unimportant. No longer people but merely a means of increase like seed thrown broadcast in the spring.

Perhaps in these strange overwritten thoughts lay the secret of Herbert's roving nature. He needed life and increase to shut out his black thoughts and subdue them. Having relieved his mind of darkness, Tree cheered himself up—pessimistic thoughts should be said cheerfully. Perhaps *au fond* he saw himself as a cheerful pessimist. He was always aware of the different strains in his blood, for he saw instinct as the inherited knowledge and the accumulated wisdom of our forefathers. He understood the Germans, and that is perhaps why from its very outset he recognized the War for the shattering tragedy it was to become. The German Emperor he thought had made God in his own image, but he was Emperor of the Shambles—the War was a madman's holiday. If only the Germans had been allowed to express themselves in music—and populate the world. Perhaps in time Germany would recover from her drunken stupor and people would come to regard war like cannibalism. He felt that Germany had come to flower in 1870. After that there had been nothing but a decline into the Kaiser's hireling philosophy. He saw mankind's poets becoming 'Prussified' and shrank from the glorification of war.

In one of his speeches he said: 'We must not merely fight for our own country, for England, but for the freedom of the world. The world is more important than the nation. Frontiers should be abolished. No longer should men and women be Serbians, English, Italians, French or Germans. Prayer should be common to every child. Racial differences are all superficial—we all suffer hunger and thirst, informed by the same passions.' It was all in Shylock and in Portia's quality of mercy speech. Shakespeare had said it all.

He broke off here but added that we were all blind seers in the dark, sowing joy and reaping sorrow. For happiness was, he felt, a kind of self-hypnotism. But it was a quality which he managed to achieve. He subdued his dark thoughts and got on with his life. In darkness there was only lack of achievement. Maud remarked that Herbert hated drab things, drab thoughts, drab days, drab intentions, or drab points of view. He needed light and colour.

Theatrical London was panic stricken for the first few days after the declaration of war, and light, colour and action were what was needed. Herbert kept his head. He immediately opened his theatre with the most patriotic play he had in his repertoire—*Drake*—and acted in it himself. *Drake*, a play by Louis Napoleon Parker, had first been produced in 1912. The very realistic scenery sets the tone of the play—ships with tattered sails, cabins of ships, the wooden walls of England, filled with fighting men, the cottage gardens of Devon, an ancient village church, with accompanying immemorial oaks. It was all a perfect setting for a play of patriotic feelings set in the lush countryside and amongst the fighting men defending it, with speeches to rouse the sentiments of a nation pushed into what it felt was a just war.

In opening with *Drake*, Tree gave employment to a great number of people, and both he and the author gave the profits to War Charities. It was the kind of gesture which Herbert knew how to make.

Having bridged the gap between war and peace with *Drake*, Tree's next production was an adaptation of Dickens' *David Copperfield* also by L. N. Parker. Like Bottom in *The Dream*, Herbert may have wanted to play all the parts in *Copperfield*, but he contented himself with only two, Peggotty and Micawber.

Sir Herbert Tree doubles the parts of Dan'l Peggotty and Wilkins Micawber and succeeds better with the latter character which is not only better suited to the actor's methods, but to begin with a distinct personality and not a mere type like Peggotty. There are many fine touches in Sir Herbert's rendering of the old fisherman—not when he hears of the flight of his niece with Steerforth, but when he is telling of his wanderings through Europe in quest of the erring one.

With Micawber Herbert was less restrained. Most of the papers praised Mr. Micawber making punch, unmasking the monster Uriah Heep, while making play with the office ruler on the knuckles of the sinuous tyrant, Mr. Micawber proposing a toast, clad in oilskins for his voyage to Australia.

Captious Critic of the *Sporting and Dramatic* did have reservations about this dazzling portrayal. At his best, Sir Herbert was splendid as Micawber, 'all the same I wish he could cure himself of the habit of being nearly always audible, even when he has no words to speak, by breathing heavily, or by emitting grunts, groans, and other noises from his throat; he often distracts attention from what the other actors are saying'. Sir Herbert's Micawber must have been a very difficult character to act against.

Again, like the sets of *Drake*, the scenery of *David Copperfield* was calculated to appeal as a nostalgic reminder of that ideal England which glimmered in the minds of men and women at war. There were eleven changes of scene, among them the dining-room of the Golden Cross, a cottage with a background of Canterbury Cathedral, 'rising against a distant sky of much serenity and grandeur'; a schoolroom; Peggotty's seaside shack; and a garden set filled with such profusion of flowering chestnuts, lilacs and the endless glow of out-of-season border flowers as would delight the heart of any seed salesman.

The pictures of the sets of *David Copperfield* give the impression more of a film than of theatre sets. One curious thing which strikes the mind when looking at the photographs of the production is that the younger actors—Owen Nares as David Copperfield, Evelyn Millard as Agnes, Basil Gill as Steerforth and Nigel Playfair as Mr. Dick seem to have much more natural and less exaggerated expressions than the older players. The 'Gerald du Maurier' school of playing down was gaining ground.

Tree himself was much in character and feeling the Mr. Micawber of the Dickens novel. Perhaps the foolish optimism of Micawber found more of an echo in his heart than the passive acceptance and simple goodness of Peggotty.

Having tired himself out playing both Micawber and Peggotty Herbert retired to take the waters. A newspaper report stated that it was not thought that he was at Harrogate. 'His precise whereabouts must not be divulged, but his absence from town nevertheless cannot be greatly prolonged as he is under promise to play his old part of Cardinal Wolsey soon, at His Majesty's.'

As a 'fill-in' at his beautiful theatre Tree had found a play by Edward Knoblock. This was *Marie Odile*, a sensitive study of innocence, with Marie Löhr playing a foundling girl brought up in a convent expressly to join the community of nuns when she is of the right age. From the costumes, it seems as if the play is supposed to have been set in the 1870 war which gave it a frail connexion with the current 1914 conflict. The nuns flee before the advancing troops, the girl is left behind. A corporal arrives, and the girl—rather curiously, even for an innocent—takes him for St. Michael. She spends a tender time with him and as a result conceives a child. When the nuns courageously come out of hiding and find her, she is turned out with her miracle baby by the ruthless Mother Superior.

It is to be supposed that middle-aged gentlemen who have lived a full rich life on the sexual front are greatly drawn to the idea of the frailty of innocence. The critics did not like the play. Some thought it dull, others that it would give offence to Roman Catholics. Tree, always apt to shrug off adverse criticism, remarked that it was impossible to serve art and criticism. The notices of *Marie Odile* had been, he said, written by tired men who hated the theatre, but the evening was said to have been saved by the sensitive acting of the beautiful Marie Löhr.

When Herbert revived *Henry VIII* with its marvellous costumes, sets and its wonderful pageantry, he was reviving it with America in mind.

He needed to make money in America, and at the same time was determined to carry on propaganda for the Allies. It may have been that the idea had been suggested to him as a form of 'war work' by Asquith, who was then Prime Minister. In spite of the dangers Herbert sailed for America in the winter of 1915—much to Maud's distress. In her book about him she quoted:

> Thou goest; to what distant place
> Will thou thy sunlight carry,
> I stay with chill and clouded face;
> Ah! how long wilt thou tarry
> Where'er thou goest the morn will be;
> Thou leavest night and gloom to me.

The poem, wrote Maud, was a favourite of Herbert's and it continued optimistically: 'Bid souls of eager men awake; Be kind and bright and tender.' In spite of their differences, at this moment of parting, he seemed to Maud to have always had all those qualities.

He sailed taking Iris with him, taking his kindness, his brightness and tenderness, taking also the glint of his enthusiasm, his eagerness, and above all his hopefulness, said loyal Maud.

No doubt, up in the house Daisyfield on Putney Hill, 'Mrs.' Reed née Pinney felt that Herbert was also taking the brightness from *her* life, and from the lives of her children, Robin, Guy and Carol Reed, and also from her two youngest, Peter and Juliet Reed, who were still only four and five years old. But she had one consolation: Claude Reed, her eldest boy, was in New York, and acting under what might be called his rightful name, 'Beerbohm', although his actual status seems a little ambiguous, for, when he met his father at the quayside on the arrival of the boat, Herbert said to Iris: 'Be kind to your cousin.'

Herbert had been making plans to go to New York for some time. His diary for the year 1915 was more chaotic than usual. He was jotting down things to do before the journey. He must send a cheque for the Frohman memorial. (Charles Frohman had been drowned in the *Lusitania* disaster in May of 1915, a fact which explained Maud's great nervousness about Herbert's American adventure.)

The list begins with his Will. He certainly had a great deal to make a Will about: one wife, one unofficial wife and nine children ranging in age from thirty to four years old. He must look at his private cheque book—how did that stand? The list continued with a jumble of ideas—what about the Russian Front and the League of Mercy? He must thank the American Ambassador for his help and Seager Hunt for the Gin. His mail and cables better go to the Plaza on Fifth Avenue.

The Red Lamp, an old favourite play, might make a good film. He must think about that.

The cinema seems to have loomed very largely in his mind at this time, for he wrote a very long list of possible subjects for it ranging from Shakespeare's *Richard II*, *Merchant of Venice*, *Othello* and *Macbeth*, to Sheridan's *School for Scandal*, and such old and new successes as *David Copperfield*, *Oliver Twist* and Tolstoy's *Resurrection*.

He reminded himself in his plans for New York that he needed a press agent, and asked himself the question if he himself produced the plays was it correct that he should have fees? What plays should be prepared during his absence? His Majesty's must be kept going—and profitable. He returned to the subject of his Will and asked himself another question: 'Is it possible to insure?' Insure what? Himself, his theatre, his scenery, his props, or his property? The diary leaves the question as a question and whether he ever did insure is also an unanswered query. He had the idea of being torpedoed in mind. Charles Frohman had disappeared into the holocaust of war. It could happen to him. He had always disliked the sea.

Under the heading 'Introductions' Tree put the names of his son by May Pinney, Claude, followed by his youngest daughter by Maud, Iris. Perhaps he felt that now he was getting on—he would be sixty-three on 17th December—it would be pleasant if in some way he could bring his large family together. But time and chance were against him and the best he could do was to introduce Claude to Iris as her cousin.

Tree arrived in New York on 24th November 1915. He met his son Claude whom he was proposing to engage in his company for a Shakespeare Festival in New York. William K. Vanderbilt, Clarence H. Mackay and Otto Kahn of the Metropolitan Opera, were reported as heading a group of men who had subscribed $50,000 for a three months' season of Shakespeare which was to be given by Sir Herbert at the New Amsterdam Theatre.

He spent three weeks socialising, going to the theatre, attending the opera and meeting old friends. His diary is full of luncheons and dinners with hostesses, and there are telephone numbers of various ladies, drives with ladies and dinners with ladies.

On 27th November he saw a play called *The Great Lover* at the Longacre Theatre, and decided to buy it. It was not an inappropriate play for Herbert to be attracted to, although when it was played later critics objected to the 'lover' running his lips up the arm of the heroine.

On 21st December, four days after his sixty-third birthday, he left for Los Angeles where he was to make a film of *Macbeth* with Constance Collier.

Herbert had thought and written about the new art of the cinema. He felt that it was only in its formative period, and had no traditions as yet. It was still an imitative rather than a creative art. But, as he said: 'New and vigorous impulses seem to me to be at work in it, and doubtless before long it will drop all slavish copying of the stage and strike out along fresh paths.'

But when Herbert set out for California, he felt that the stage could contribute to the cinema's progress and if his entering the new field was able to add 'even a very little to the momentum of its upward progress', he would be very happy indeed.

And so at the age of sixty-three he set out for Hollywood to try a new aspect of his art.

Chapter 17

California here I come!

Herbert and Iris travelled on the long-distance train to Hollywood by way of Chicago. Herbert liked Chicago. He said he found it seething with energy, its people warm-hearted and there was a barbaric pagan frankness in life there which he found pleasing. What was not pleasing was that he lost his wallet, but recorded later that it had been found.

They arrived at the Grand Canyon where he had stood on the summit with a puzzled smile on his face, wondering at the barren beauty of the dark shadows in the valleys and the torchlike peaks. He saw them as a background for the theatre of man's emotions, labours and progress. But in the scarred hollows there was a lack of life. He liked life, and turned with relief to the Indian camps huddled in the snow.

Officially Herbert appreciated scenery and the countryside. But privately the country and landscapes bored him. Iris felt that his spirit belonged to no land and wrote: 'He seemed like an exile from some country whose name he had forgotten, but whose beauty came back to him and left his eyes bewildered at gazing on things to which he had no kin.' It seemed to her that it was this aloofness which gave her father such a curious distinction. He once told her that he loved the gipsies and their music. But he held himself back from visiting them because he might become so fascinated by their life that he could never return to his own people.

It was perhaps the first time that Iris had been really alone with her father, away from his theatre. He told her of the things he had done, spoke of his love of pine woods, of Hungarian music and of his youth. While he spoke he seemed to Iris to be a different person, someone she had never known. It was the private, strange side of his character which he showed to few people—perhaps not even to Maud, except in the early days of their marriage, or even now, fully, to Iris.

Maud liked to shine in company; she was worldly, well-dressed and enjoyed the grandeur of her position. There was a side of Herbert which cared nothing for any of this, except as an audience for his beautiful theatre. Iris found her father shy, too sensitive to speak of the things which touched him the most deeply and this made it difficult for him completely to open his heart, or allow anyone—except one—to unlock its secrets.

Maybe it was this side of his character and of the secrets of his heart which he was able to confide to his dear friend May Pinney. In their long association stretching over twenty years, and a family of six children, there must have been some strong link which made her necessary to Herbert. Yet because of the complications of his forcedly double life, he had to close part of his soul to his legitimate family, and it could be that it was these two aspects of his life which made him an enigma to Iris.

But if Iris was puzzled by Herbert, Herbert was equally puzzled by Iris. He wondered why she, who was so cheerful, wrote such sad verse. Iris said that only happy people, like herself and the Greeks, could see the beauty of tragedy. Only dyspeptics wrote comedies.

Had Herbert thought about it, he might have looked into his own heart, and found there the two sides of his own character and seen them reflected in Iris.

*

They arrived at Los Angeles on 27th December 1915. Constance Collier had been in California for some time. She had crossed the Atlantic, as she said, with a lifebelt on, at the height of the submarine scare. There were plenty of alarmists on board who spent their time seeing phantom submarines, shadows in the depths of the ocean and scared the more timid travellers out of their wits. But nothing happened and she arrived quite safely in New York, spent one day with her husband, Julian L'Estrange and then set off for Hollywood and her new career in filming.

Constance was always one to enjoy a journey whether it was to meet a Kaiser, or see the Red Indians who came down to meet the train on the Santa Fé Railway, to sell her straw mats, beads and little wooden gods. She had already made two or three films in Hollywood when Herbert cabled her that he had an offer to do the picture, *Macbeth*.

Constance, ever enthusiastic, wrote glowing accounts of the soft warm Californian sunshine, the blue sea and descriptions of her idyllic bungalow where she lay, under the radiant stars, with the coyotes calling in the hills and the magnolias and the mimosa blooming in her garden.

She paints a clear picture of those early days of film making—waiting for the sun to shine. The film 'Gold Rush' was on, and several films were being made at the same time. Actors were acting love scenes, murders, and comedies, orchestras were playing, cameras clicking, guns were going off. The whole place was a frenzy of activity under the necessary sun. Everyone was made-up in their yellow make-up, ready and on the 'lot' at nine o'clock in the morning: they had to wait till the sun was well up in those days. There were beautiful girls, old men, raddled hags, grotesque costumes, wild animals, horses, cowboys and legitimate actors. Hundreds of people herded together in a jungle of total money-making confusion.

Hollywood was still a village and there remained many farms which had not been built over. The farmers regarded the mountebank film makers as disturbers of their peaceful way of life. Even opposite the Los Angeles railway station there was an ostrich farm where the curious birds stalked about, looking half-naked, according to Constance Collier.

After a while she began to find the restrictions of Hollywood claustrophobic. Even in its beginnings there was nothing to do but to make films, or talk about films. She longed for a London drizzle, but the sun never left off shining and the ocean was always calm. She became friendly with Charlie Chaplin, and they would talk about the London they knew—the Lambeth Road, the trams, the people and the places they remembered. She described Chaplin as a strange, morbid, romantic creature, who was quite unaware of the greatness that was in him. He loved England, yet the country of his birth had given him nothing and America had given everything. England had been full of bitterness, poverty and sorrow, yet in his soul he still longed to see the twisted streets and misty days, and hear Big Ben chiming over London.

Constance frequently had dinner with Chaplin, either on the verandah of her bungalow or in a cafeteria in Hollywood. They could not go to restaurants, or Chaplin might have been mobbed. He liked to remember and talk about the theatre in London, and told Constance how he used to sit in the gallery at His Majesty's whenever he could spare a shilling or two, for he would gladly miss a meal to see one of Sir Herbert's plays. Yet Chaplin was well on the way to becoming a king in Hollywood, for Constance had introduced him to Douglas Fairbanks and she was (as she said), 'the unconscious corner stone on which the United Artists Corporation was built'.

And now the king of His Majesty's, Sir Herbert Tree, was coming as a beginner to Hollywood. Constance's glowing account of magnolias, mimosa and sunshine had filled Herbert with equal enthusiasm. Once he read her encouraging letters, he could not wait to start for California and the sun and the blue sea. Constance had found a bungalow for Herbert and Iris with a tennis court, a garden full of flowers and advised them to bring summer clothes and bathing-dresses. She also found them splendid Japanese servants to cook and wait on them. All was prepared.

On the day Herbert arrived, so did the floods, which never subsided for two whole months. The tennis court was like a swimming pool. Water poured through the roof of the bungalow. Herbert and Iris had no warm clothes and the bungalow had no central heating. The chimneys, presumably built for show, were so wide that when they tried to light a fire the torrents of water, pouring down from the sky, put it out. Herbert was told that the floods had started *much* earlier than was expected. He *quite* understood. They were having 'the usual unusual weather', which always greeted him in every country.

*

Chaplin and Herbert became great friends. When interviewed about Chaplin later, Herbert said that he was a genius in the truest sense of the word, a natural comedian of subtle humour. 'Of the future of Mr. Chaplin, I can, of course only speak in conjectures but I shall be more than a little surprised if he had not a very brilliant future before him upon the legitimate stage, after his vogue in pictures is done.' Tree once said that he felt that Chaplin was, in a way, placed in a position where he could not exercise his talents to the fullest advantage. Splendid things could be expected of him when he felt at liberty to devote himself to a branch of the profession more worthy of his efforts. It is indeed interesting to speculate what might have happened if Chaplin had become a stage actor; perhaps his talents might have developed in a different way. Herbert ended, 'For the rest I find him a charming man, a very charming man.' But privately he echoed Constance's view of Chaplin, that he was a strange, complicated man, all attributes which he shared with Herbert. When writing in *The Times* about Chaplin Herbert said: 'Contrary to expectations, I found him to be a young man of a serious and sensitive disposition, who has artistic ambitions of a kind not suggested by his public records, and who in private life is thoughtful as well as versatile and entertaining.'

Once arrived in Hollywood, Tree became, as always, a glutton and a tyrant for work and threw all his energy into the new tasks in hand. But in the newspapers, Sir Herbert was recorded as revelling in the soft climate of California. He and his youngest daughter were staying at a picturesque bungalow staffed by Japanese domestics. It was flowers all the way in the gossip columns, not a mention of the word 'floods'.

The film *Macbeth* was being directed by John Emerson (husband of Anita Loos), but later it was taken over by the famous D. W. Griffith. Sir Herbert was reported as getting a 'fabulous' fee for his work in the picture, 'nearly as much as Charlie Chaplin'. But the charms 'on the set' were in total contrast to the charms of filming as depicted in the gossip columns. Herbert and Constance were worked hard indoors, and outdoors, in spite of the floods. They were often still at work at three or four o'clock in the morning, with camera men taking shots with flares through the eternal downpour. Sometimes they were so tired that they found it impossible to summon the energy to change out of their costumes. One morning, having sent away their chauffeur because they did not want to keep him waiting all night, Herbert and Constance, unable to find another car, walked along Sunset Boulevard—he in his Macbeth wig, beard and primitive Scottish dress, with his daughter's mackintosh keeping off the worst of the downpour, while Constance trudged beside him in flowing robes, crown and a borrowed overcoat over her head.

They were a long way from His Majesty's Theatre, with its flunkeys in their scarlet coats and white wigs, opening doors silently, while Sir Herbert's motor car was called to the stage door.

Iris, not a great lover of hard work herself, was amazed at her father's superhuman energy. In Los Angeles he would sometimes work for eighteen hours a day. She marvelled at his extraordinary power to ride over his fatigue, and then to find the strength to laugh and enjoy the hours that remained of the day.

Herbert had long arguments with the director and crew about the text of Shakespeare. He wanted the whole text, and nothing but the text. The camera man was obstinate, but decided to let Sir Herbert have his way. But he had found a way round the difficulty. He had invented a dummy machine and kept two cameras working at the same time. The dummy camera registered nothing, but kept Sir Herbert happy and when he had finished his speeches the real camera took over and recorded the picture. 'I could not act unless I *felt* the words', Tree had said. Although he may have felt a great deal, the camera never recorded those feelings. Later he found out the trick and took the fact that the cameraman had scored over him as a great joke.

He was loved by nearly everyone, especially the cowboys. But in the studios things were not so rosy. The picture industry had boomed and a good many dubious characters found themselves on the spot and able to take advantage of the boom. Constance noticed that few of them had the grace to show a great artist like Herbert the deference she felt was due to him. What did His Majesty's, or Sir Herbert mean to them? Occasionally she felt that they resented Herbert being there and would deliberately keep him waiting in the middle of a crowd, sometimes for five or six hours when he was already tired out. The new brash cinema was not to be impressed with visiting foreign actors. But Constance never saw him complain, and he would always be as laughing and as amusing as ever, however tired he may have felt.

Rumours of the difficulties had reached the *New York Times* which reported: 'Work of filming *Macbeth* got off to a bad start and as Sir Herbert's time was limited it was necessary, after things got moving, to make up for lost time. The distinguished star was hustled out of bed at daybreak and kept on the move till after sundown.'

The *Christian Science Monitor*, writing under the dateline Los Angeles at the beginning of January 1916, reported on his activities more soberly:

Sir Herbert Tree is now in this city rehearsing with an American company for a production of *Macbeth* to be released on the

Triangle Program. It is a tribute to the open mindedness and adaptability of Sir Herbert that although two motion picture versions of Tree productions have been made in England they were little more than film records of the stage plays. The American photoplay technique with its intimate and realistic telling of the story is almost unknown to the English photoplay makers except through American productions. Sir Herbert was entering a new and strange artistic world.

In spite of the hardships, Herbert took filming in his stride, as he always did anything which interested him. 'My first impression here was of the extraordinary vitality of this new industry. Its dynamics are stupendous. The easy certainty with which millions are spent in permanent improvements is most impressive and far-sighted. But my interest has naturally leaned to the artistic problems involved. To what extent could the plays of Shakespeare be placed upon the screen successfully and with due reverence to the spirit of the masterpieces, yet virtually without words?' And he added wryly, 'There is a popular fancy, you know, that the words of Shakespeare's plays are of importance!'

It was to be many long years before the music of Shakespeare's words were brought to the screen. In the state of the films at that time, before the talking picture was thought of, Tree was already wondering what the next stage of the film would be. The current technique seemed to him more a picture story, like Charles Lamb's Tales from Shakespeare. But he hoped that it might rouse the interest of the thousands of cinema-goers and give them a glimpse of Shakespeare, and influence them towards seeing 'the plays themselves for a taste of their ineffable glories'.

It was typical of Tree that when he came to write of his filming experiences for The Times he had forgotten all the hardships and the humiliations. All he remembered was the democratic camaraderie. Whatever Constance may have noticed, he only wrote that he had never met with any discourtesy and found the work of the pictures done in an atmosphere of happiness and high spirits 'which makes its monotony bearable'.

He had noticed, he said, an absence of system. It would have amused Shaw to read of Herbert, of all people, deploring a lack of system. 'Sometimes an artist will have to wait one, two, three weeks before he is called upon to take up his share of the work, then he will often work fifteen or sixteen hours a day. The latter was my experience with *Macbeth*.'

He described the departure for the mountains at midnight and arrival at a country inn, and then the actors would be up and dressed at seven o'clock next morning to ride out to catch the early sun, and meet the Witches on their selected Blasted Heath.

The mimic coronation of Macbeth at Scone took place about forty miles from Los Angeles at a place called Chatsworth. Thither the actors and hundreds of supers, together with the 'properties' of the occasion were conveyed in motor cars and motor buses. This scene was taken in brilliant sunlight while the arrival at the King's camp of Macbeth and Banquo after the victorious battle was photographed at two in the morning, the scene being lighted by huge electric lights. Through the ranks of the cheering soldiers surrounding their camp fires and through the flaring lights projected on their faces, Macbeth and Banquo galloped with the news of victory. This nocturnal scene was deeply impressive. The interior of the Witches' Cavern was enacted in a scene built in the studio. One scene was photographed no less than a dozen times; this ordeal was a somewhat trying one in the watches of the night.

But there were compensations. The floods had subsided, the healing sun had come out and Herbert began to appreciate California. He began to enjoy his bungalow with its acre of garden filled with bright flowers, and shaded by orange, lemon, grapefruit and eucalyptus trees. He was happy with his Japanese servants and enjoyed their cooking. The days might be hot but the nights were cool. When he was not wanted on the set, he was able to take drives along the coast to Santa Monica where at an excellent inn there was dancing to a ragtime band, and he was driven home through the night with the sweet smell of the orange and lemon groves drifting into the car.

D. W. Griffith and Lilian Gish went out of their way to try to make Herbert's life as pleasant and full of friends as possible. Constance Collier was always at hand, and Iris was always full of fun and even in the darkest of dawns always smiling and good humoured.

He rode in the Californian hills with Iris, but typically insisted on using the wooden property saddle which had been constructed for him for *Macbeth*, and as they rode Herbert opened a little of his mind to her. He enjoyed these riding excursions but there was one drawback, the horses which were trained by the cowboys occasionally performed 'all manner of unexpected gyrations'. He had become accustomed to the Mexican saddles and even to the horses standing up proudly on their hind-legs and beating the air with their hoofs. But once or twice he had unconsciously by a jerk of the reins given a horse a cue to 'die', and it had flung itself prone on the ground. Even the horses were actors in Hollywood.

He enjoyed motoring, the roads were good, and the fields on each side decorated with roses and flowering shrubs; sometimes he passed through these herbaceous borders for twenty or thirty miles. Herbert was seeing California in its innocent beginnings. He had even been driven from Los Angeles to Santa Barbara for a dinner party, over 210 miles there and back in one evening.

But at last the filming was finished and it was time to return to his natural home, the theatre, and the Shakespeare Festival in New York.

Constance Collier said that she would never forget Herbert's exit from Hollywood. The cowboys adored him and insisted on accompanying him to the station on their bucking horses, dressed in full regalia, with pistols. 'Sir Herbert was essentially a man of peace, and he hated guns. He was an indoor man. Some of us have indoor and some of us outdoor natures.' As the train was about to start the cowboys surrounded Herbert, making their horses rear with their hoofs over his head and then, in a final salute, fired their pistols into the air with one tremendous burst. Herbert was honoured, but he climbed into the train with the utmost speed. Constance, standing on the platform to wave him goodbye, remarked that his face had a look of supreme relief as the train drew out of the station.

Iris was staying behind with Constance Collier and they settled down happily together, Constance to work and Iris to ride in the country or sit in the sunlit garden writing a gloomy poem or two. Constance remarked that Iris had inherited many of her father's great gifts, if *only* she had inherited his energy. . . .

Herbert sat back in the train. Three or four days to New York and nothing to do but rest. He did not realise how exhausted he was by the filming of *Macbeth* until he was aboard the train. It was, he said, the most welcome rest he had ever experienced.

He arrived in New York on 7th March 1916 and immediately drove to the rehearsals of *Henry VIII*. There was not much time. The Shakespeare Festival was to open on March 14th. The three plays he was giving were *Henry VIII*, *The Merchant of Venice*, in which his son Claude was to appear as the Prince of Morocco, and *The Merry Wives of Windsor*.

Herbert enjoyed New York, where he said the earth seemed to spin more quickly round its axis. But the climate was vitalising and he felt renewed energy not only for the preparations for the Festival, but for newspaper interviews and speeches about the War. He felt that kind of impetus which 'afflicts those that cannot walk but needs must run'.

Herbert, and his backers, were all nervous as to how the jazzing, frenetic city would receive a diet of culture. They need not have worried. It was the tercentenary of Shakespeare's death, which gave the season an impetus and, as Herbert remarked, the incense of these celebrations 'blew our way'.

The production and Tree's portrayal of Wolsey were received with acclaim and the theatre was filled every night for the whole of the three month season. A tribute in the *New York Times* gave the flavour of Tree's reception in New York.

It is with sincere regret that we come to the final week of the production of *Henry VIII* with which Sir Herbert Tree has enriched and delighted the public. Not for many, many years has so soul-comforting and satisfying a dramatic offering been upon our stage.

It was, said the writer, a production of beauty and pictorial variety, but stress should not only be laid upon the stage pictures, the scenic architecture, the pageantry, the magnificence of costuming, the skill in grouping, the lavish, almost prodigal, use of every device known to modern stage-craft, these were all things which had been seen before in New York.

Emphasis should especially be laid upon the superb distinction of the impersonation of the wily, crafty, strong hearted Cardinal which Sir Herbert has given us. It is one of the finest impersonations which has ever graced and adorned our stage. The character lives and breathes. It is always in the picture, yet it stands out from the picture, clean cut, tangible, vivid, a creation vital, impressive, profoundly moving and sympathetic. There has seldom been presented an impersonation so free from self-consciousness. The personality of the actor so merged in that of the Cardinal that no one thinks of Herbert Tree, but only of the lofty spirit, of the dominating, commanding Cardinal.

Herbert had made the Cardinal the self-made man, the butcher's son who had made his way in the world, and the American public appreciated this reading. It was the kind of character they understood. Tree was living the character as he so often did and this time it had succeeded brilliantly with his New York audience.

There is no rant, no self-consciousness, no obvious effort to deliver a telling 'speech' about greatness, ambition, service of kings—there are displayed none of the usual devices of the actor. Wolsey speaks as if thinking aloud. His words come from his brooding mind, his introspective soul—words as if thought of now for the first time, convictions of the futility of all his daring plans, of the uselessness of his soaring hopes for greater glory and power . . . the final scene is most impressive. Only the greatest art, the highest poetry can make this impression. Only the great dramatic artist has the skill to interpret this poetry and make it a living vital thing. Herbert Tree has this marvellous skill of interpretation.

It had been worth the journeying to achieve this success in a land far from his own.

All the notices praised the production and his performance. 'Take your children—anyone over twelve-years-old can enjoy this play.' Right up to the last performance, *Henry VIII*, and Wolsey, were taking over £3,000 a week, an immense reward in the theatre at that date.

In between plays came the first private showing of the film *Macbeth*. By this time Constance Collier, who was to play Mistress Ford in *The Merry Wives*, had returned to New York. She was with Herbert when *Macbeth* was screened for the first time. It is, she said, a very sensitive moment when an actor sees himself for the first time on the screen. Constance was excited but nervous as they went to the little private theatre to see the film, a film which had cost them so much time and effort. The lights were lowered. Constance sat next to Herbert as the primitive machine began to click. The small room was filled with the most important people in the Motion Picture industry. They had paid very good money to bring this project to fruition. It was rumoured that Herbert had been paid £20,000. He appeared to be interested but not over excited. All the film moguls were waiting to hear the great Sir Herbert's verdict on the film, and on himself. Here in New York with solid success behind him he was highly regarded and his word was awaited breathlessly. The film clicked on. People spoke in excited whispers. Everyone seemed pleased with the result. Constance addressed a remark or two to Herbert but he did not reply. He was obviously absorbed and interested. She did not want to disturb him.

The finale flashed on to the screen. Sighs of admiration and delight were heard in the darkness, congratulations on the magnificence of the acting, the photography and the artistry with which this *Macbeth* had been brought to the screen. Everyone waited for Sir Herbert's final word.

The lights went up. Not a sound came from the great man. He was asleep. He had been working hard in the theatre and the room was hot.

His next success was as Shylock in *The Merchant of Venice*. He had always succeeded as Shylock. The *New York Herald* recorded that Sir Herbert came in like a lion with Henry VIII, and went out like a lamb with Falstaff.

Sir Herbert had ended his plays at the New Amsterdam Theatre in June of 1916, and simultaneously the film of *Macbeth* was seen publicly at the Rialto. The *New York Times* found the film a fine achievement. 'Both Sir Herbert and Miss Constance Collier were at the opening.' The critic found that he gave a picturesque performance. His acting in the theatre, said the *New York Times*, 'would prove a valuable resource should he take to acting in movies. . . . He rides up hill and down dale, vaults on to his horse, swings a broadsword, and generally weathers the merciless athletics of the cinema with a vigour and agility which laugh to scorn the Who's Who paragraph that would try to make us believe that he is in his sixties.'

But having given Herbert a pat on the back the *New York Times* came down on the side of the director. *Macbeth* had given the director chances after his own heart. Phantoms in the cave, the ghost of Banquo were more truly spectral than anything which the theatre could achieve. Only one thing upset the *New York Times*. The dagger could only be described as 'dinky'. Especially noteworthy were the scenes of darkness and storm, the black midnight quality of which pervaded the whole picture. Herbert and Constance had not suffered the floods in vain.

*

Herbert loved New York. He described it as an electric city. He wrote: 'On each successive visit to New York, I have been struck by its vital and energizing influences. One may be worn out, but one is never tired. The electric quality in the air is sometimes disconcerting to the new-comer. It has happened that on my being presented to a lady, a complete stranger, we have in shaking hands experienced a mutual electric shock which has caused us both to start back with an involuntary exclamation.'

Life in New York had no half tones, thought Herbert. There was a greater frankness in the life of the people. In fashionable hotels young couples sat hand in hand, feeling no awkwardness or shyness. Telegrams arrived in ungummed envelopes. Gardens, telegrams, manners, everything was open and frank. Life did not revolve round private entertaining; the life was the life of the restaurant and the great hotels. It was a life which seemed to suit Herbert since he wrote of it with such enthusiasm.

But the exhilarating climate of New York and its heady cheerful atmosphere had also had some effect on Herbert's private life. A small item in Herbert's diary noted that at 1.30 p.m. on 9th June in the year 1916 he was lunching with Miss Ridley.

*

Muriel Ridley was an English actress and dancer. It is not known why or when she went on the stage. Her press cuttings reveal that she was travelling in Europe from 1909 to 1911. She was born in May of 1883, being a year older than Viola, Herbert's eldest daughter. In 1916, when she met Herbert, she was thirty-two, a pretty accomplished actress who had made her first success as the Nun in Charles Cochran's *The Miracle*, at the Olympia Theatre. The creator of the part, Mlle Trouhanova, had flagged as the Nun. The Olympia Theatre was so vast that it needed a strong fit young woman to take on seven miles of running and walking at each performance. Muriel took over the Nun and made an immediate impact. She was described as 'the toast of the Town' and the most talked of young actress in London. She also acted in *The Pool* with H. B. Irving and, curiously enough, in a play with Claude Beerbohm.

Muriel Ridley went to America in 1914, where she toured the country until going to New York, and was introduced to Herbert by a German actress called Asta Fleming. This introduction presumably took place some time during his successful season at the New Amsterdam Theatre. Perhaps she had auditioned for him, although there is no record of this amongst Herbert's notes. Sometimes he wrote down his impressions of actresses he had seen. One he had condemned as 'too prim' and another as 'pretty but lacking in personality'.

Miss Ridley was presumably not prim, for when she lunched with him, on June 9th, she was already carrying his child. It must have been an awkward luncheon and yet in a way an achievement. To be a father for the tenth time at the age of nearly sixty-four was a tribute to the electric atmosphere of New York, and a success to add to all the others on film and on stage which Herbert had achieved.

Herbert, who had perhaps been over-exhilarated by the climate of New York, decided on a visit to White Sulphur Springs. His diary carefully recorded his weight which was 178½ lbs. on 18th June and by the 21st it was down to 172 lbs.

On July 3rd he went back to Los Angeles for a brief visit and then suddenly decided to return to England. He was homesick.

Maud and his family pleaded with him not to come back. The Zeppelins were attacking London and the submarine menace was as bad as ever. His contracts with American companies made it necessary that he could only come home very briefly. But he paid no attention. He left the United States on 26th August, read *The Great Lover* on the boat and by the beginning of September he was back in London and taking up the threads of his old familiar life. Maud was amazed at his courage. The bombs were falling on London, the U-boats lurked under the Atlantic and yet he came back to his family. Maud's admiration was unbounded, how could he who had even been afraid of someone touching him in the dark have summoned up so much bravery?

One evening, during Herbert's brief holiday, Maud had left him at All Souls Place. She and Iris had gone to the theatre to see

Henry Ainley in *Quinneys*. In the second act the bombing began.
Maud was distraught, she had left dear Herbert alone and in an air
raid. But five minutes later—there he was—in their box, having
rushed through the darkened streets of the West End to make sure
that his 'dear ones' were safe.

On 12th September he had a long talk with the Prime Minister,
and presumably they discussed the question of Herbert's propaganda in the United States. The tide of opinion was gradually
turning for the Allies in America and it might be a moment to
reinforce the change.

His social engagements show that he took up the threads of his
old life in London with eagerness, even if it were only for a few
weeks. He arrived back in New York on 1st October.

By 16th October he was already on an extended tour of American cities from Boston to Kansas City, St. Louis, Toronto and
Montreal in Canada. At the end of November, and over Christmas
of 1916, he was in Chicago. On December 18th he made a
patriotic speech to the Farmington Society at the Blackstone Hotel
where he was staying.

He also sent several telegrams from his hotel to New York.
They were telegrams of comfort and congratulation to Muriel
Ridley who had given birth in January 1917 to Paul Ridley-Tree,
Herbert's tenth child, and his sixth son.

Chapter 18

1917 — Still Radiant

Tree toured America and Canada from November 1916 to the end of March 1917, his closing performance being at His Majesty's Theatre, Montreal.

Wherever he went he made patriotic speeches to Women's Clubs, Press Clubs, to the Daughters of Chicago, to Fine Arts Clubs, Rotary Clubs, Dickens and Thackeray Clubs. He spoke in churches, in halls, in hotels and in theatres, and at Benefits for Wounded Soldiers; he made propaganda speeches at universities too. And all the while there were the gruelling performances at the theatre.

When Herbert had gone to America in 1915 he had not found the pro-Ally sentiment very strong. He had walked and spoken carefully. He was ever conscious of the anti-British sentiment amongst the Irish immigrant population, and spoke gently and with great feeling for the Irish people. He was also aware that little had been done by way of propaganda by the British. The German system of propaganda he observed had been perfectly conducted through the press and through pamphlets. Literature pointing out that Great Britain had made the war for trade purposes, that the British Navy was a menace to the Freedom of The Seas was put into his hands at every hotel he visited.

He found that there was one force which had more potent appeal than any other when addressing American audiences—that force was humour. Whether in the pulpit, or the theatre, American audiences were quick as lightning to respond to its touch. He found the American people innocent and childlike—they wanted to be informed, they wanted to be understood and they wanted to be praised. But the praise must be sincere.

He thought that if the British had 'spared some of their great men to visit America at the beginning of the war' understanding might have been reached much sooner. He had spoken to a diplomat who had given his opinion on propaganda in America. 'What we have to do is not to tell them what they *ought* to do—not to tell them what is right—but to make them *like* us. We do not', he added, 'love a woman for her virtue but because she is pretty.' The last sentiment was bound to strike an echo in Herbert's heart.

Herbert felt that had Wilson made his declaration even six months earlier he could have caused a civil war. 'By appearing to be holding back, he allowed the people to push him on . . . the spirit of the people had to be prepared, the proletariat had to be hypnotised.'

He believed that the result was as much due to the press of New York as to the President. New York, being a cultured and cosmopolitan city, had always been pro-Ally, but the Middle West and the Far West were too far away from the battlefields to sympathise with the suffering, or to understand the causes of the war. 'They were not unnaturally guided by motives of local self-interest rather than by world patriotism, while a very large element was undoubtedly opposed to Great Britain owing to the ever-open sore of the Irish question. Illogical as it may sound, there were many who, in their German-Irish sentiments would have substituted the 'Watch on the Liffey' for the 'Wearing of the Green'. He ended by writing, 'I cannot help thinking that with the settlement of the Irish question would vanish the last dregs of bitterness in the cup of Anglo-American relations.' Sixty years on little has changed on the Anglo-Irish front.

Speaking later he said that when he first landed in the United States during the war he felt that he was skating on the thin ice of neutrality, but soon he felt the feeling subtly changing. By 1917 everything was transformed and Sir Herbert's patriotic speeches were received with enthusiasm in every city. When he opened in New York with his old success *Colonel Newcome*, a newspaper report recorded his success and also drew attention to his sterling work for the Allies in America.

England has every reason to be grateful to Sir Herbert Tree for the unofficial but none the less valuable aid he has rendered as ambassador in the cause of the Allies. He was on the stump with speeches full of patriotic fervour and benefit performances in aid of the British Red Cross and Allied Funds—as we were reminded on the first night of *Colonel Newcome*, when the eminent actor in the first act ingeniously interpolated a toast to the British Navy

—which could not be traced to Thackeray, while the thunders of applause with which it was greeted inspired Tree to add, 'And let us not forget our friends across the Seas!' The salvoes of applause which have broken out at every performance testify to Tree's knowledge of the public and their enthusiasm.

The fact, too that Tree has been forced to make a speech at almost every performance during the last month at the New Amsterdam Theater in addition to innumerable outside engagements is proof of his intellectual and oratorical activities.

At a meeting of the Junior Patriots of America at the Hippodrome and at the Metropolitan Opera House for a benefit in aid of the mutilated soldiers, when, in his military attire, Tree finished a fine peroration with the simple but sincere words: 'Colonel Newcome begs respectfully to salute the Star Spangled Banner!' Sir Herbert brought those vast audiences to their feet.

He had the same success everywhere. He was planning to produce *Drake* in New York and used one of the speeches from that play to reinforce his propaganda.

We have opened the gates of the sea—we have given you the keys of the world. From this day forward the merchant can rove whither he will, and no man shall say him nay. Our labor is done —yours is to begin. Men pass away, but people abide. See that you hold fast the heritage we leave you—yet teach your children its value; that never in the coming centuries their hearts may fail them, or their hands grow weak! Hitherto we have been too much afraid—henceforth we will fear only God!

'And then', added Tree, 'the multitude assembled in the presence of Queen Elizabeth and Drake, sang this hymn and the audience joined in:

> 'Let God arise, and then His foes
> Will turn themselves to flight;
> His enemies then will run abroad,
> And scatter out of sight.'

He ended, 'May this spirit grow among you every day, as it has inspired the French and British people, and united as we are, there can be no doubt our strength will prevail over the enemy.'

Herbert had dreaded and been shattered by the idea of the war, but now that he was caught up in it, he intended to do his best to help to end it. But by the spring of 1917 Herbert decided to go home. Perhaps he was, at long last, feeling the fatigue due to his long exertions of the last two or three years. His diary records that he visited a doctor. This was unusual. Numerous visits to dentists are recorded over the years. Herbert had very good teeth and was obviously determined to keep them that way. But his health had always been good and his annual visits to Marienbad helped him to 'unswitch' which he had always found the salvation of the nervous system. But now he was sixty-four and had been overworking ever since the war had started. Perhaps it was time to go home and take things a little easier.

But wartime regulations made things difficult for travelling actors, however eminent.

He sent two telegrams: one to his wife, saying that he was distressed to be detained. He was making speeches daily. The play *The Great Lover* by three Americans was excellent, *Blind Eyes* by Laurence Housman more difficult. He sent his love to all.

The other telegram was sent via his lawyer Langton, who lived at Albany in Piccadilly and was in his confidence. He thanked him heartily and asked him to tell May how *deeply* distressed he was at being detained. He was still hoping to cross. In the middle of all his wartime frustrations, he remembered to send his son, Claude, a message of good luck for a new play. His loving thoughts were with them all. It might be thought that his message to May Pinney was more loving and caring than the quickly scribbled telegram to his wife. He could not telegraph to May direct but she was in his thoughts.

He had opened in *Colonel Newcome* on 10th April 1917 and on the 29th he met Muriel Ridley (who is called Mrs. Ridley in his journal) at the St. Regis Hotel for dinner. He was making future arrangements for the maintenance of her son. Everything must be settled in an honourable manner. He was also somewhat concerned about his trunks. When he went to America he had taken with him the correspondence of thirty-five years. There were several trunks full. He had sorted and destroyed them. It had taken him many weeks of labour. It was a labour which the biographer can only regret.

He noted too that he had left interesting letters in New York in a black trunk, as well as duplicates of all his speeches and Maud's and Viola's letters for 1916 and 1917. One trunk of his books had been left at the Plaza. It was odd that a man who purported never to read had trunks full of books.

But military regulations or non-military regulations, Herbert was determined to get home and eventually he achieved his object, travelling on a circuitous route by way of Spain. From Madrid to London, he became a King's Messenger, taking on a real life romantic role. He arrived at Calais and waged another battle against the Army, Navy and Civilian authorities who wanted to ship him home via Le Havre to Southampton. Dover was the place in England where Herbert wished to arrive and it was there that he landed.

Maud was staying with the Asquiths at The Wharf, Sutton Courtney and on the Whit Sunday she heard of his arrival. She welcomed him with a loving and grateful heart. They were by the river in the loveliest house at the loveliest season of the year.

For once Herbert seemed to delight in the countryside. Buttercups, birds, the river, the hawthorn hedges in the moonlight, everything seemed to give him delight.

He kept the whole party amused being, as Maud said, 'the life and soul of the talking'.

He also seemed to have a new delight in his own home, All Souls Place. He had previously called it an unattractive triangular house, now it seemed to please him. He stood on the stairs and, looking round at everything, suddenly said that it struck him as full of charm.

Herbert was in cheerful optimistic mood and why not? He was making a great deal of money out of his theatre which was playing to capacity with the record breaking *Chu Chin Chow*. This had been written as a kind of pantomime by Oscar Asche, who had acted for some time in Tree's company. Asche showed his script to Freddie Norton who agreed to write the music. It was turned down by several managers, in the usual way of smash hits, and finally, after a very good lunch at the Carlton Grill, Oscar Asche managed to persuade Henry Dana to have it read.

So one day in the afternoon some time after their Carlton Grill luncheon, there were assembled Henry Dana, Joseph Langton, Percy Anderson, Lily Brayton and for some reason—possibly financial—the Prince of Monaco. The songs were played and sung, the play was read, the models of the scenes and the designs of the costumes were displayed.

Dana and Langton were convinced and said with one voice: 'We'll do it here at His Majesty's but Tree must come into it.' They cabled Herbert at once that they were putting £3,000 of his money into the project, Lily Brayton put up an equal amount. Oscar merely had half his author's royalties, for he had sold the other half to his wife for a modest £500 at a time when he was 'temporarily embarrassed'. This was something he was bitterly to regret.

Many years after the event, when he was long divorced from the beautiful Miss Brayton, his resentment crackles from the pages of his autobiography. 'I asked Lil to lend me £500.' Lil replied, 'On what security?' Oscar was a gambler and Lil was not. 'I have no security but I will sell you one-half of my royalties in *Chu Chin Chow* for £500.' Lil quickly wrote out a cheque and received Oscar's agreement in exchange. To Miss Brayton, husbands were husbands, but deals were deals.

The first night of *Chu Chin Chow* was on 31st August 1916 and it was to run until July of 1921. Everyone concerned with it, even Asche with his half-share of author's royalties, made a fortune. And so did Tree, although he did not totally approve of the show, in spite of its rich returns. Yet it was exactly what the tired war-weary soldiers and the equally war-weary public wanted, and in seventeen weeks took more than £50,000. It was the biggest financial success that Tree and His Majesty's had ever had.

The early summer of Tree's return from America found him financially stable, and full of plans. He was going to produce *The Great Lover*, he had made preliminary notes for his book of memoirs, and he was happy to plunge once more into the life of the London he loved. He was constantly at the Garrick Club meeting old friends. Much to Maud's surprise he seemed to accept every invitation. He and Maud lunched with the Charles Wyndhams and Maud remembered how they dined with Sir Charles and Lady Henry, and T. P. O'Connor. Herbert and T.P. kept Carlton House Terrace ringing with their wit and sheer fun, and then they all sat in the June twilight, as the darkness of the garden gradually closed around them. Every day and every hour of Herbert's time was full of gaiety, of projects and of eager hopes for the future.

He went with Maud to see George Alexander in *The Aristocrat*. Alexander was very ill on that night, but insisted on going on. He must go on he said: 'because Herbert is coming'.

In July, Herbert went down to Constance Collier's cottage on the coast at Kent. She had bought it some years before when the Government were selling off coastguard's cottages. It was, she admitted, very tiny with two bedrooms, a sitting-room and a kitchen. But outside there was an old sea wall and a view over the sea to the Goodwin sands. In summer, the little garden guarded a few wind-blown roses, hollyhocks and sunflowers. It cost Constance £12 a year, was furnished simply with kitchen furniture, and Constance's mother had made the chintz curtains and chair covers. But in spite of its primitive simplicity—water had to be drawn from the well—Constance was always lending it to her friends. Herbert adored the cottage more than anyone else. He would buy large stocks of cold food from Fortnums and go down there by himself, working long quiet days with only the sound of the sea for company. In the evening Herbert's chauffeur would drive him back to London in time for 'curtain up'.

The cottage also proudly boasted an accompanying maid, a village lady, who was, Constance said, 'a born boss, the only person who could dominate Herbert. She made him draw water from the well, boil the kettle for his tea, and ordered him about like a handy-man. He loved it.' As he spent his time giving orders, it was a change for him to obey and he humoured Constance's village lady.

So in June of 1917 he went down to 7 Epple Bay, Birchington. Constance was still in America and he did not bother to ask permission, he knew that she was happy for him to use the cottage whenever he liked. It was very old and, apart from the well, there were other disadvantages. The steep winding staircase had a hand-rail which Constance had always meant to have renewed, for 'it suddenly stopped at the most unexpected place, and you found yourself holding on to nothing'.

Herbert put out his hand, held on to nothing and fell down the twisty stairs. He called out for help and the village lady found him at the foot of the stairs, trying to help himself up by the banisters. 'I think I've broken my leg', he said.

She helped him into the tiny sitting-room. The fall had also broken the heel of his shoe. While she was telephoning the doctor, he tried to get up from the sofa, and fell again.

When the doctor came he found that Herbert had ruptured a tendon above the knee-cap. The following day his car came down from London and he was taken to Sir Alfred Fripp's nursing home in Henrietta Street, Covent Garden. On 18th June he was seen by Sir Alfred, who decided to operate on the knee. As it was a minor operation Herbert was given nothing but gas and oxygen and was able to take his usual intense interest in the preparations for the operation. As he went to sleep he murmured, 'I shall see you again!'

The operation was a complete success. He was soon in his usual buoyant mood, reading *The Great Lover* over and over again, and pleased because he already knew it by heart: 'No need to study it at all when it comes to rehearsals.' He wrote to Viola sending her £10 'to pay little debts'. When his surgeon took out the stitches, the wound was clean and healed. Tree told Fripp that he proposed to get up, go out and preside at a dinner of the O.P. Club. Fripp said he was neither getting up nor going out. Tree said he was not taking orders. But the surgeon replied that they had changed roles.

It was becoming very difficult to keep Herbert quiet. But he liked the visits of his friends and colleagues, the messages, the parcels and enquiries about his health. He was overjoyed and surprised that everyone was so concerned about him. He had always been a modest man and quite unaware, as Shaw remarked, of his own position either in, or out of, the theatre. So he rejoiced at so many people coming to see him, the flowers and baskets of fruit that arrived, the love letters and the petting everyone gave him.

Oscar Asche went to see him. He sat with Maud near Tree's bedside. Asche found him as witty and ebullient as ever. He rejoiced with Asche at their joint success. The money was rolling in. 'Keep *Chu Chin Chow* going, Asche, as long as it will. If your dear wife will put up more money to re-dress or alter it, as you may think best, I will provide an equal sum.' Herbert added without regret, 'I have never had a Chu Chin Chow myself.' Then he laughed. 'Someone asked me at the Garrick the other night my opinion of the piece—I said I considered it more navel than millinery.'

Later when Asche was keeping him company at Henrietta Street he suddenly said: 'Asche—you can have my theatre for £90,000.' Asche, less prudent than Lil, his wife, said he did not happen to have a sum like that handy. Tree took an optimistic view. 'You can easily raise it on the name of His Majesty's Theatre and *Chu Chin Chow*.' Asche said that it was easier to find another theatre for the piece than another *Chu Chin Chow* for His Majesty's. No more was said about the sale of the theatre. But Tree had already been considering selling it when he was in the United States, as his note-books prove. Perhaps he was thinking that he would like to retire, write a little and only act in pieces which amused him. He was sixty-four and the responsibility of his beautiful theatre was beginning to seem a heavy load. There were more amusing things to do in life than worrying about finance. He might revive *Pygmalion*. Just before his fall he'd met Shaw and they had dis-cussed it. Shaw recalled that, as usual, 'he made me feel like his grandfather—he was incredibly young and sanguine, and made me feel hopelessly old and grumpy. He was discussing a revival of *Pygmalion* as if it promised to be a renewal of the most delightful experience of our lives.' Shaw remembered their bitter rows with wry humour. Tree had forgotten them.

Shaw may not have seen it, but Max had noticed a gradual change in Herbert. He felt that in the last years of his life he had grown to care less for acting. 'His versatility had ranged over so vast a number of diverse interpretations. What new thing was there for him to do?' He could not mark time, but Max was very conscious of Herbert's impatience with his work. When they met at Max's mother's house, after Herbert's return from America in 1917, Herbert was splendidly well and as animated as ever. But in all the river of his witty talk, he never once mentioned acting.

There could be other things which he could do. Plans, projects and visits were keeping Herbert moderately quiet in his bed which was a pleasure, and a relief to Sir Alfred. For Alfred Fripp was not only Herbert's surgeon, he was also a personal friend, and would often drop in for a second 'non-professional' visit in the evening after dinner. Maud, sitting at Herbert's bedside remembered, with bitter-sweet remembrance, the laughter and hilarity of those evenings with Herbert and Sir Alfred.

On 2nd July, some two weeks after the operation, Herbert was sitting up in bed. He had eaten his dinner and was peeling a peach for his dessert. He asked his pretty nurse: 'Will you open the window?'

When she turned round, his head fell forward. He was dead. That rest, which Sir Alfred had insisted upon and which is now considered unnecessary, even dangerous after some operations, had caused a blood clot to form which had killed him. Perhaps

Herbert was right—he should have got up and gone to preside at the O.P. Club dinner.

He left behind him a fund of kindness, and a legacy of laughter. As Max wrote, 'I shall always miss him . . . and I am always wishing him back again. . . . When I saw him early next morning, he lay surrounded already with the flowers he had been fondest of. His face was both familiar and strange. Death, that preserves only what is essential, had taken away whatever it is that is peculiar to the face of an actor. Extreme strength of character and purpose was all that remained and outstood now. But at the corners of the lips there was an almost whimsical, an entirely happy smile. And I felt that Herbert, though he was no longer breathing, was somehow still "radiant".'

Constance could not believe that Herbert was gone. 'His Majesty's was no more, like a light that was extinguished. He had been kind and generous to me for many years, and had given me my great chances on the stage. . . . We were true comrades and he told me his troubles and joys and was utterly uncomplicated and simple in all the years I knew him.'

Maud mourned. She felt that she had never had a sorrow until the sorrow of Herbert's death. Only his leaving her made her acquainted with grief.

'Mrs.' Reed must have mourned and with greater anxiety than Maud. Two of her boys were grown now, but she had four children under twelve.

'Mrs.' Ridley, with Herbert's son Paul, left so suddenly unprovided for, must have mourned even more bitterly.

Maud may have felt that her life was over, but the next twenty years brought great richnesses to her. She lived to act on in the twenties and thirties, right into the age of Korda when she became an excellent character actress. She lived to be enriched by seeing her children and grandchildren depending on her and looking to her for the help, comfort and succour of a family life full of laughter.

Constance achieved great fame in Hollywood, but sadly when she came to write her autobiography the photograph of her 'family' consisted of two hairy dogs, a parrot and a Siamese cat. Although at the moment of Herbert's death Maud may have felt bereft, he had left her the legacy of a loving family.

Herbert was cremated and even the funeral procession to

Golders Green crematorium turned into a great production number, for the orchestral accompaniment to the cortège in 1917 was the bursting of bombs and the crack of anti-aircraft guns across the sky. A daylight air raid added the final drama to Herbert's funeral. It could have been taken from his own production of *Macbeth* with its flashes of blinding lightning, rocks falling and oak trees being split asunder.

In spite of the war, columns of space recorded Sir Herbert's achievements: his acting, his productions and the building of his theatre. Everywhere it was felt that his going was the end of an era, a glittering era when the theatre seemed to be at the peak of its social success and achievement.

When the *oraisons funèbres*, the critical appraisals were over, the laurels laid aside, the funeral flowers faded, then came the Will.

This may have come as a draught of cold water to the family. When all the legal verbiage was cut away, Herbert's 'faithful friend of many years', May Pinney, inherited half his estate 'for her own use absolutely'. She also had £1,000 for her immediate needs. Maud and her daughters had inherited the other half—but on trust. Herbert was having a care to Maud's future.

The Will must have been made some time in 1911 before Viola's marriage for it speaks of Alan Parsons as his son-in-law 'to be' and appoints him a trustee. Joseph David Langton, who had been the confidant of May and Herbert, was recommended as manager of any business to do with the theatre.

The little mouse in her corner on Putney Hill had inherited half the cheese. But it was rough justice. Maud had fame and a profession which she was to follow right up to the day of her death. May had only her six children. She needed her part share in the £105,000 which the lease of the theatre fetched.

Eulogies and tributes poured in from the rich, the famous, the distinguished, from friends and from colleagues. There were no dissenting words.

Perhaps the best and simplest of all tributes came from Alfred Trebell, Herbert's dresser at the theatre 'I feel as though I had lost my own father, and I know I shall never again have so good and kind a master.'

Ten days after Herbert's death, the Bishop of Birmingham preached a sermon at his memorial service. Before the distinguished congregation, or perhaps audience would be the better word, the

Bishop found comfort, consolation, and something typical in the fact that the last words which Herbert had uttered were: 'Will you open the window?'

'May we not confidently believe that, as Sir Herbert felt the first freshness of the atmosphere of Paradise—things before only vaguely conceived of—became by him understood, and in very truth a fuller life began.' Unlike the Bishop, anyone in possession of the facts would find it difficult to imagine a fuller life. A different life perhaps.

The Bishop confided to his worldly congregation his view of Herbert. They were in church today, all of them, friends of the great artist and the loyal comrade who had been so suddenly taken from them. 'In very truth I doubt whether Sir Herbert ever realised in this earthly life how fond men were of him. He had a kind of absent-mindedness, which some people thought to be almost aloofness and which held them back at times from the kind of companionship which is the outward expression of affection, but his death has unloosed shy tongues and now they tell of how much their owners cared for Herbert Tree.'

Herbert put it much better.

'It is difficult to be thoroughly popular until one is quite dead.'

Select Bibliography
and Index

Select Bibliography

The Beerbohm and Tree families
Notebooks and Diaries of Herbert Beerbohm Tree.
Contemporary letters to and from Herbert Tree.
Contemporary cuttings, newspaper accounts and souvenir productions of Tree's productions with introductions to the plays, many by Tree himself.
Tree's acting versions of *The Tempest* and *Henry VIII*.
Herbert Beerbohm Tree, *Nothing Matters*, Cassell, 1917.
———— *Thoughts and Afterthoughts*, Cassell, 1913.
———— *The imaginative Faculty*, E. Mathews & J. Lane, 1893.
———— *Henry VIII and his Court*, Cassell, 1910.
Herbert Beerbohm Tree—Some memories of him and his art, edited by Max Beerbohm but containing writings by Maud, Viola and Iris Tree, Hutchinson, *c.* 1920.
Max Beerbohm, *Around Theatres*, Rupert Hart-Davis, 1953.
Viola Tree, *Castles in the Air*, Hogarth Press, 1926.

James Agate, *Those were the Nights* (an anthology of criticism 1880–1906), Hutchinson, 1947.
Oscar Asche by Himself, Hurst & Blackett, *c.* 1920.
E. F. Benson, *Final Edition*, Longmans, 1940.
Sir Frank Benson, *My Memoirs*, Ernest Benn, 1930.
Lady Benson, *Mainly Players*, Thornton Butterworth, 1926.
Margaret Blunden, *The Countess of Warwick*, Cassell, 1967.
Eugène Brieux, *Théâtre Complet*, Librairie Stock, 1928.
Mrs. Patrick Campbell, *My Life and Some Letters*, Hutchinson, 1922.
Hall Caine, *The Eternal City*, Heinemann, 1901.
David Cecil, *Max*, Constable, 1963.
Constance Collier, *Harlequinade: The Story of My Life*, Foreword by Noël Coward, John Lane, 1929.
St. John Ervine, *The Theatre in My Time*, Rich & Cowan, 1933.
Elizabeth Fagan, *From the Wings*, Collins, 1922.
Sydney Farebrother, *Through an Old Stage Door*, Frederick Muller, 1939.
Daphne Fielding, *The Rainbow Picnic: A Portrait of Iris Tree*, Eyre Methuen, 1974.

Sir Johnston Forbes-Robertson, *A Player under Three Reigns*, Little, Brown, 1925.

Harry Furniss, *My Bohemian Days*, Hurst & Blackett, 1919.

Kate Terry Gielgud, *An Autobiography*, Max Reinhardt, 1953.

Jimmy Glover, *Hims, Ancient Modern*, T. Fisher Unwin, 1926.

—— *His Book*, Methuen, 1912.

S. Baring Gould, *The Tragedy of the Caesars*, 2 vols. Methuen, 1892.

Joe Graham, *An Old Stock Actor's Memories*, John Murray, 1930.

Richard Grant White, *Studies in Shakespeare*, Sampson Low, 1885.

Harry J. Greenwall, *The Strange Life of Willy Clarkson*, John Long, 1936.

Charles Hawtrey, *The Truth at Last*, with introduction by W. Somerset Maugham, Thornton Butterworth, 1924.

H. G. Hibbert, *Fifty Years of a Londoner's Life*, Grant Richards, 1916.

—— *A Playgoer's Memories*, Grant Richards, 1920.

Vyvyan Holland, *Son of Oscar Wilde*, Rupert Hart-Davis, 1954.

Laurence Housman, *Blind Eyes*, Sidgwick & Jackson, n.d.

Henrik Ibsen, *Pillars of Society and Other Plays*, Dent, 1906.

Henry James, *The Aspern Papers*, Macmillan, 1888.

Henry Arthur Jones, *Life and Letters*, Gollancz, 1930.

—— *The Tempter*, Macmillan, 1898.

—— *Carnac Sahib*, Macmillan, 1899.

—— *The Dancing Girl*, Samuel French, 1907.

Dame Madge Kendal by Herself, John Murray, 1933.

Gertrude Kingston, *Curtsey while you're Thinking*, Williams & Norgate, 1937.

Rudyard Kipling, *Life's Handicap* (Short Stories including 'The Man Who Was'), Macmillan, 1937.

—— *Verse inclusive Edition 1885–1926*, Hodder & Stoughton, 1927.

Mary M. Lago, and Karl Beckson, *Max Beerbohm and William Rothenstein: Their Friendship and Letters 1893–1945*, John Murray, 1975.

Anita Leslie, *Edwardians in Love*, Hutchinson, 1972.

W. J. Locke, *The Beloved Vagabond*, Queensway Press, 1936.

E. V. Lucas, *The Colvins and their Friends*, Methuen, 1928.

Kenneth McClellan, *Whatever Happened to Shakespeare*, Vision Press, 1978.

John Merrylees, *Carlsbad and its Environs* (with a medical treatise on its waters by B. London, M.D., Resident Physician at Carlsbad), Sampson Low, 1886.

Luther Munday, *A Chronicle of Friendship*, T. Werner Laurie, 1912.

Owen Nares, *Myself and Some Others*, Duckworth, 1925.

Julia Neilson, *This for Remembrance*, Hurst & Blackett, 1940.

Alfred Noyes, *Two Worlds for Memory*, Sheed & Ward, 1953.

Gilbert Parker, *The Seats of the Mighty*, Methuen, 1896.

Louis N. Parker, *Drake, A Pageant Play*, Bodley Head, 1912.
—— *Joseph and His Brethren*, Bodley Head, 1913.
Hesketh Pearson, *Beerbohm Tree, His Life and Laughter*, Methuen, 1956.
—— *Bernard Shaw, His Life and Personality*, Collins, 1942.
—— *The Last Actor Managers*, Methuen, 1950.
Stephen Phillips, *Herod*, John Lane, 1901.
—— *Nero*, Macmillan, 1906.
—— *Ulysses*, John Lane, 1902.
W. McQueen Pope, *Carriages at Eleven*, Hutchinson, 1947.
—— *Haymarket, Theatre of Perfection*, W. H. Allen, 1948.
Beatrix Potter, *Journal*, Translated from code writing by Leslie Linder, Frederick Warne, 1966.
J. B. Priestley, *The Edwardians*, Heinemann, 1970.
Graham Robertson, *Time Was*, Hamish Hamilton, 1931.
William Rothenstein, *Men and Memories*, 3 vols. Faber & Faber, 1931–39.
Mrs. Clement Scott, *Old Days in Bohemian London*, Hutchinson, 1919.
Bernard Shaw, *Complete Plays*, Constable, 1931.
—— *Music in London, 1891–1894*, Constable, 1931.
—— *Our Theatres in the Nineties*, 3 vols., Constable, 1932.
Bernard Shaw and Mrs. Patrick Campbell, Correspondence edited by Alan Dent, Gollancz, 1952.
Herbert Swears, *When All's Said and Done*, Geoffrey Bles, 1937.
James Baker Tillotson, *Pictures from Bohemia*, Religious Tract Soc., 1895.
J. C. Trewin, *The Edwardian Theatre*, Basil Blackwell, 1976.
Barbara Tuchman, *The Proud Tower*, Hamish Hamilton, 1966.
Irene Vanbrugh, *To Tell my Story*, Hutchinson, 1948.
H. M. Walbrook, *A Playgoer's Wanderings*, Leonard Parsons, n.d.

Index

Biographical Note

Madeleine Bingham has written a number of theatrical biographies, including *Henry Irving and the Victorian Theatre*, *Masks and Façades* (on Sir John Vanbrugh), and *Sheridan: The Track of a Comet*. She has also written a biography of Mary Queen of Scots and *Scotland under Mary Stuart*, and is the author of two autobiographical works, *Peers and Plebs* and *Cheapest in the End*. She is married to the writer John Bingham, and has two children, Simon and Charlotte.